Love Can, In Fact, Be Calculated

ZOEY CHARIF

I dedicate this book to you,
my gentle readers.

Love is a brave and beautiful
endeavor, and it is my honor to
be a part of your journey.

-Zoey

xo

Table of Contents

Preface

I was twenty years old, committed, and as happy as I could be. Steve and I weren't talking about getting married yet, and sure, we had our issues like any couple.

But I *loved* this man.

He was sound asleep next to me on an ordinary Tuesday night. As I watched him sleep, something deep inside me—a voice I had never heard before, a voice I hope I never hear again—told me to check the messages on his computer.

Once I heard it, I couldn't get it out of my head. It grew louder and stronger by the moment, soon becoming the only thing I could hear. Finally, I decided to sneak into the other room where his computer was charging. I hoped he couldn't hear me; I didn't want to get caught snooping.

But my gut yelled at me to keep going.

First, I opened his emails. *Nothing suspicious here.* I almost gave up, but that little nagging voice kept at it: *Don't forget the MSN messages!*

And what do you know? A woman named Christie appeared in his conversations. She seemed friendly. *Too friendly.* Especially last Friday at 7:36 p.m., when she said, "Come over. Can't wait to see you."

No. It can't be. I stayed there for a few seconds, frozen, just staring at those words. *It must mean something else.* I scrolled through the messages, looking for anything to clear up this situation, but the conversation only got worse. I kept squinting at the screen—*was I really reading this?* I read and reread the chat in utter shock. I had to step away from the computer to think.

But...why would Steve do this? *I thought he loved me...*

Somehow, I managed to pull myself together. I had questions, and I needed answers *now*. I walked into the bedroom, woke Steve up, and asked, "Who is Christie?"

The initial sign of guilt was clear—he couldn't look me in the eyes. Instead, he laughed nervously and asked, "Why, what did she say?" That was all I needed to hear.

Steve was cheating on me.

"You need to leave. Right fucking *now*."

I still remember him walking out the door with his box that night. He stopped in front of me, teary-eyed, and said, "Can I just have a hug, Zoey?" As he walked toward me, I gathered every ounce of strength and pushed him away. At that moment...I broke.

For the first time in my life, I experienced a deep sorrow my heart hadn't felt before. The door closed behind him, and I realized our relationship was over.

That's it. It's done.

That fateful night marked the beginning of my quest for answers about love and heartbreak. In fact, it became an obsession; I *needed* to know everything about the workings of the heart. *Why do we love? Why do we hurt? And why do we hurt the ones we love?* Over the course of my search for concrete answers, I came across many theories, many concepts, and many psychological studies, but none of them really resonated with me.

Lo and behold, one day I discovered a phrase that truly struck me! It said: "You can only fall in love with someone who's a good match." A statement that was simultaneously so simple yet so profound.

It really got me thinking.

Match. Match? How could I figure out if someone was a *good* match for me? Had I not been a good match for Steve? Is that why he betrayed me?

And so my theory started to take shape. The first iteration went something like this: You will only pursue a relationship with a partner who meets or exceeds your standards, especially in the areas that matter most to you.

At this stage, my newly formed interpretation of love and relationships was far from perfect. It was still too vague and abstract. I wanted it to be clear, practical, and, more importantly, measurable. *But how can you even measure relationship standards?*

Through trial and error, I finally got it! I created a calculation to define relationship standards and measure how well they are being met. I call it the Love Formula.

In the course of all my subsequent relationships, I kept this little calculation handy. I applied it to some of my truly amazing partnerships that were filled with laughter, deep bonds, mutual respect, and genuine love. But oftentimes, good times were closely followed by bad ones. One after the other, I experienced breakups, rejections, and betrayals, leading to heartbreaks. All the while, I continued to learn about the relevance of the Love Formula, refining and redefining it continuously.

Fast forward to the future. I was thirty-two years old when I experienced my first real-life crisis. Having endured years of failed long-term relationships, short-term relationships, and *shit*uationships, I'd finally reached my breaking point.

I questioned my worth and value as a partner. "Am I even a catch?" Those ugly words haunted my thoughts for days on end. They were closely followed by similar thoughts about my supposed flaws: *Maybe if I had done more, if I WAS more, I'd be in the relationship of my dreams.*

My pity party quickly turned into anger and resentment. I hated love. But mostly, I hated how much we, as a society, took love for granted. No one seemed genuine or committed in their emotions or actions.

Why is it so hard to make relationships work these days? Are all the good ones dead or taken? Is the notion of "happily ever after" even a fucking thing?

No matter where I looked, everyone else around me seemed as outraged as I was. That's when I realized I needed to be proactive and solidify this theory to help not only me but also others make wise relationship decisions and share it with anyone who cares to listen.

This book contains every lesson I learned whether it came from successful relationships or total failures. It has evolved into the current version through rigorous analysis and refinement.

The Love Formula has been a game changer for many, including myself. I've seen people, *real people* with everyday struggles, use this method to turn their love lives around. Thanks to this calculation, they've formed meaningful connections, moving away from shallow and short-lived interactions. And the best part? These aren't fleeting romances; they're the kind of love stories that last.

And now it's my pleasure to share my discovery with you: *Love can, in fact, be calculated.*

Introduction

Hollywood's repeated portrayals of "happily ever after" and "love at first sight" are magical, fantastical, and utterly divorced from the harsh complexities of real life. We think we've found "The One" when we see big romantic gestures and our hearts skip a beat. We're taught to endure pain and hardship, thinking that true love is worth any sacrifice, just like in the movies.

But think about it—how many times have you actually seen someone live out that perfect fairy-tale finale? What these fictional stories don't tell you is that sometimes, it just doesn't work out as planned. As the wise members of our society say, "Shit happens."

Yet, despite the ups and downs, successful partnerships *do* come with a lot of perks and benefits. Having someone reliable in our life often leads to better health and a deeper sense of fulfillment. So *how can we make this happen?* More specifically, *how can we make sure that the person we choose as our partner is truly compatible with us?* This shift from fairy-tale aspirations to practical relationship building is where the journey of the Love Formula begins.

What if I told you there is a quantifiable process that can help you understand your relationship standards and effectively assess the long-term potential of your partnerships? What if this method could reveal deeper insights about yourself than ever before?

My approach is straightforward. The Love Formula is a blueprint for a successful relationship, helping you make sensible choices as you search for your perfect partner. Along the way, you'll find the answers to the following questions:

- What are my standards?
- How well do I meet my own standards?
- Is my partner meeting or exceeding my standards or falling short of them?

In this book, I've transformed abstract ideas about love and compatibility into a clear, measurable framework, making it a user-friendly resource for those seeking clarity in their relationships. Consider it a versatile toolbox that can offer you ways to assess and quantify your relationship standards, placing lesser emphasis on emotions alone. It'll help you understand the reasons behind your decisions and why you may have been stuck in a cycle of less-than-ideal situations when it came to love and companionship.

The Love Formula can be customized to evaluate your current situation or applied to past relationships you're struggling to move on from. Whether you're experiencing the thrill of a new romance, working through a forty-year marriage, or focusing on self-improvement, you will find this book useful.

This inclusive approach transcends all boundaries of gender, sexual orientation, ethnicity, and socioeconomic background. As you browse these pages, you'll encounter diverse stories—some drawn from my personal experiences and other incredible ones shared by friends and family.

You may be thinking, "How do I know if this calculation applies to my context?" This method is for you if you are:

- **Single**: Use it to identify the partner you truly desire and build self-confidence.
- **Part of an on-and-off relationship**: Discover if it's salvageable and how to improve it, letting go of toxic patterns along the way.
- **Part of a couple**: Deepen your connection, minimize the impact of difficult conversations, and ensure a healthy, lasting relationship.
- **A therapist, counselor, or coach**: Use it to teach clients a new method of self-reflection, relationship assessment, and making informed, healthy choices.

This book is made of six parts: Part I explores the challenges of modern love, complete with a solid academic foundation that combines evolutionary psychology with social theories.

In Part II, you'll learn how to apply the Love Formula to your own situation using mathematical calculations, with real-life case studies as your guide. Part III examines relationship dynamics, where you learn about good and bad case scenarios.

Part IV explores Personality Types, helping you to better understand your approach to love and relationships and how to make them healthier. Part V tackles relationship imbalances, providing insight into distorted dynamics that are often rooted in insecurities. Finally, in Part VI, you'll learn how the Love Formula can help you build lasting self-confidence and attract a fulfilling relationship that aligns with who you are.

Rest assured that this theory is supported by survey responses from 300 individuals across the United States. The data has unequivocally validated the merit of this theory, demonstrating that the longevity of relationships can be both predicted and measured.

As you venture further into this book, I urge you to firmly keep one principle in mind: What you learn from these pages is meant to be put into action. Don't let this become just another "shelf-help" book that gathers dust. I encourage you to apply these principles in your everyday life and shed the insecurities holding you back from stable love.

At the same time, please remember that while the Love Formula is grounded in data, interviews, and expert insights, it's still evolving. Academic researchers interested in digging deeper into this topic or therapists seeking practical applications are most welcome to use the concepts and theories presented in this work. Like any theory, ongoing research is vital—and wholeheartedly encouraged—for gaining a comprehensive understanding of these complex ideas.

So without further ado, let's dive into the "heart" of the matter!

Chapter 1

The Love Formula

Many believe that love and relationships are guided by the heart rather than the mind. We speak of things "tugging at our heartstrings" rather than "tickling our brain cells." And we're often encouraged to "follow our heart," but screw the brain, right?

It's time to cut the *BS.*

There is a common tendency among us humans to romanticize the heart's decisions, but in reality, dismissing rational thinking can leave you vulnerable. Instead, let's emphasize reason and intellect. Your brain, the forgotten hero, is now your compass.

The Love Formula isn't designed to overlook feelings, but rather to help you pause and reflect before making impulsive decisions driven by love or lust. By taking a more thoughtful approach, you can identify the qualities you seek in a partner and evaluate how well someone aligns with these preferences. Here's a quick overview of how it works:

- **Pick your "Top 5 Values"**: Start by determining the Values that are most important to you in life.

- **Calculate your "Self Score"**: Give yourself a numerical rating for each of these Values. This is your *Self Score.*

- **Calculate your "Partner Values Score"**: Next, assess how well your partner meets these Values and give them a total *Partner Values Score.*

- **Pick your "Top 5 Traits"**: Traits are inherent characteristics or physical qualities that attract you to someone.

- **Calculate your "Partner Traits Score"**: Evaluate your partner based on these Traits and give them a total *Partner Traits Score*.

- **Calculate the total "Partner Score"**: Add the Partner Values Score and Partner Traits Score for an overall partner assessment, called the *Partner Score*.

- **Compare your Scores**: Compare your Self Score with the Partner Score.

In the following chapters, you will learn how to generate and, more importantly, understand the implications of these numbers.

The Significance of Scores

To understand why Scores are important, let's talk about human nature. Naturally, you form judgments and make assessments about people you meet. Your mind is forming opinions about everyone in your social environment, and it's equally (if not more) judgy when it comes to choosing a partner.

Think about what's really important to you. How often are you checking if your partner ticks these boxes? Whether conscious or not, you rate how well they measure up to your standards, and you give them a Score. Funny enough, you're not just scoring them—you're also sizing up how well *you* match your own standards, in the process scoring yourself too!

Then your mind does a mental calculation to compare your Self Score against your Partner Score and determines whether it's a match. Imagine this process as a comparison chart—you create two columns, one for you and one for your partner. What's more, this method categorizes, quantifies, and evaluates Scores *based on your perception,* creating a deeply personalized approach.

My research suggests that relationship success and longevity are most likely achieved when your calculations result in both a <u>high</u> Self Score and a <u>high</u> Partner Score. The closer your Scores, the greater your compatibility and the healthier your relationship.

In fact, toxic relationships often stem from a negative assessment of either one or both people having low Scores. Makes sense, right? It means your standards aren't being met.

Here are some key statistics regarding the validity of the Love Formula, using <u>73% as the average Self Score</u> based on our survey answers:

- Individuals <u>currently in a relationship</u> showed a high Self Score and high Partner Score, with a 4.6% difference *in favor of the Partner Score.* This is the closest mathematical match observed in our survey group.

- Individuals <u>on a "break"</u> had an average Self Score and a low Partner Score, with a 5.7% difference *in favor of the Self Score.* This close match could indicate why they are not officially broken up, as there seems to be a lot of alignment at play still.

- Individuals who <u>initiated a breakup</u> reported a high Self Score, and a low Partner Score, with a 24.1% difference *in favor of the Self Score.* This is the biggest mathematical mismatch observed in our survey group.

- Individuals who were <u>broken up with</u> indicated a relatively low Self Score and a much lower Partner Score with a 16.3% difference *in favor the Self Score.* This group had the lowest Self Score rating.

- Individuals who experienced <u>a mutual breakup</u> had a relatively low Self Score and a much lower Partner Score with a +10.1% difference *in favor of the Self Score.*

It's important to remember that both Self Scores and Partner Scores are inherently subjective. While a significant mismatch often appears in the case of those who are no longer together, remember that an initial misalignment doesn't have to be permanent. The relationship is still redeemable with self-love and love for a partner. The key to a healthy relationship is ensuring that you view both yourself and your partner in a positive light, but *it always starts with you*. When you cultivate strong self-love, you develop clear standards and understand that compromise is a natural part of any relationship. This foundation allows you to be both strong and humble, working together toward mutual goals and reciprocated affection. By prioritizing your own well-being, you create a solid base for a fulfilling and enduring partnership. These subjective dynamics are all quantified by the Self Score and Partner Score.

Before we delve into the mechanics of these calculations, let's first explore some evolutionary psychology and social theories to better understand the instinctive human drive to seek love and how the Love Formula aligns with these principles.

Part I

Nature, Nurture, and the Love Formula

Ah, yes—the timeless drama that is love. For thousands of years, we've met, paired up, and started families. Rinse and repeat. As we try to make sense of this convoluted maze of partnership and fulfillment, it's clear that love has never been easy. I'd even argue that it's become increasingly challenging over time.

A Pew Research study revealed a 29% increase in single individuals aged 25–54 from 1990 to 2020. In 2019, another Pew Research study surveyed 4,860 US adults, mostly women, and half of them thought that dating had become more challenging. Moreover, two-thirds of those who were actively dating weren't happy with their love lives, and a significant 75% of the study participants had trouble finding compatible partners.

Why are the results so grim? It seems like everyone, experts or not, has their own theory. Well, I've also evidently jumped on the theory bandwagon. But before I begin, it's important we cover the basic concept of "nature vs. nurture."

Though dating seems like a new-age trend, it's actually driven by millennia-old forces. When academics dig into human behavior, they keep bumping into this big question: What influences us more, genetics or environment?

This question explores whether we're mostly governed by instincts and built-in responses (nature). Or if our decisions are mostly based on how we were raised, our life experiences, and the society around us (nurture). Even the brightest minds in the field can't pick a side; they agree both aspects shape who we are.

The Love Formula acknowledges and applies both sides of the debate. It takes a page from nature, recognizing that deep down, our brains are programmed to look for a "strong mate." But it doesn't stop there and also accounts for nurture. The way we crunch the numbers in the Love Formula is deeply linked to our personal history, our upbringing, and our surroundings. All this stuff really matters because it molds what we consider important and look for in others, shaping how we size up and score possible connections.

Let's begin with an analysis of nature's influence on us.

Chapter 2

Innate Patterns in Human Connection

Evolutionary psychology speaks to the nature side of the debate, showing us how human evolution affects our partner choices. Just like other animals, we have a built-in urge to survive, and in order to grow as a species, our brains are wired to seek a strong mate.

You might be surprised by this "fact" because it sounds so primitive. Well, evolutionary psychologists have really dug deep into studying our brains. And what they found is that the main parts of our brain haven't changed much for thousands of years. It turns out evolution is a painfully slow process. Just think—it took almost six million years for humans to descend from our primate ancestors. That's a huge interval, so you can't really expect to see big brain changes overnight. It also makes you realize—we haven't evolved much.

The Love Formula acknowledges that we're still running on the same brain wiring as our ancient ancestors and that not much has changed up there. Also, remember Charles Darwin's ideas about how we pick our partners? They're still pretty spot on.

Darwin's theory pointed to how the best traits get passed down the line in the animal kingdom. He believed that the survival of a species depends on qualities such as speed, strength, or the ability to blend in. His reasoning was simple: If you're good at staying alive, your kids probably will be too. So those top-notch genes tend to stick around in the gene pool.

As for humans, Darwin understood them the same way. Traditionally, guys were known for being strong, good hunters and protectors. They'd handle things like scaring off wild animals and making fires. Women, on the other hand, were recognized for their role in childbirth. These roles made sure we kept going as a species.

But today, humans find a suitable partner in more complex ways than before. We have developed a pretty extensive checklist that extends far beyond that of our primate ancestors (if they even had any notion of a "checklist"). The benefits we seek in a partner aren't straightforward; we're looking deeper. We question how well they match up with our beliefs and way of life. We also consider factors such as smarts, success, and ambition. It's a combination of things that adds up to someone being a strong mate in today's world.

And yet when we pick who we want to be with, we're using the same concepts pitched by Darwin—the same theories that applied to our "primitive" ancestors. Whether we realize it or not, we're always sizing up potential partners, thinking about what they bring to the table. We become drawn to people who have something special—maybe it's their style, sociability, or just something else that catches our eye. Choosing partners based on their benefits is just part of our wiring.

On the flip side, we also want to *be seen* as a strong mate. Presenting ourselves as valuable to potential partners is part of a mechanism called "mate choice." Dr. Timothy Richard Halliday believes that how we behave boosts our chances of winning over a desired partner. Mate choice theorists believe we demonstrate our value ("peacocking," if you will) in hopes that we appear as the strongest contenders in a sea full of options.

Evolutionary principles have been dismissed as a thing of the past, but they're still relevant today. Since we are all hardwired the same way, these concepts can be applied to everyone, including the LGBTQ+ community or folks who don't plan on having kids. Think of these evolutionary instincts like those body parts we don't really use anymore, like the appendix or tailbone: They might not play a big role now, but they're still part of us.

In 1995, Dr. David Waynforth and Dr. Robin Dunbar, two big names in evolutionary psychology, added more to what we know about picking partners. They found that the people we're usually drawn to mirror our self-image. It's pretty straightforward: We tend to go for partners who act and think like us. Let's say you think of yourself as a bit of an adventurer or someone who's always up for a laugh. Chances are that you'll be attracted to someone who's got that same adventurous, fun-loving spirit.

Another study in 2003 by researchers Peter Buston and Stephen Emlen backs this up. They found that in choosing partners, we often go for the "likes attract" approach, meaning we're drawn to people who have qualities similar to ours. You might have seen this theory play out in real life as well. People who think highly of themselves usually expect a lot from their partners. They're looking for someone who meets their own level of "greatness." In other words, their standards are determined by what they have to offer.

The Love Formula is right at the intersection of all these theories! It's all about picking the qualities and characteristics you value most and seeing how well your partner measures up. It's like your brain is constantly figuring out if they have what it takes for a strong, lasting relationship (and good genes to pass on).

As we wrap up the nature aspect of the Love Formula, it's clear that there's more to the story. Nature might lay the foundation, but it's only one part of the equation. Now we'll turn our attention to nurture. In the upcoming chapter, we'll learn how our environment, upbringing, and life experiences shape our approach to relationships.

Chapter 3

How Our Environment Shapes Us

It's time now to plunge into the world of nurture, as seen through the lens of social psychology. Nurture relates to the way our experiences shape us, especially during our growing years. Sure, the Love Formula is rooted in our instincts to find a strong mate, but nurture is a big player too because it influences the criteria we choose.

So *how* do we choose these criteria? They come from a mix of upbringing, personal experiences, and societal norms. All these elements come together to shape what you're looking for in a partner and also what you find attractive. Everything from your childhood memories to your dating history plays a part in shaping your Top 5 Traits, especially your Top 5 Values.

Social psychologists have long been studying how our life experiences influence us. There's a ton of information in this field, but one thing's clear: Our minds develop in response to the world around us. T. F. Hodge hits the nail on the head when he says, "What surrounds us is what is within us." In other words, we attract what we are.

Minds are formed during our early years, where our nurturing starts right at home. We learn how to love by observing our parents or caregivers. This forms our baseline for what's "normal" in relationships. As we grow, we're already forming ideas about love and what we find attractive, often mirroring what we've seen at home. Without even realizing it, we start drafting our own list of top Values and Traits. That's why we often end up picking partners who remind us of our parents or the way we were brought up.

But it's not always that straightforward. If you had tough times with your parents, you might find yourself trying to avoid certain patterns. As we grow and meet new people, our view of love changes and evolves. We're constantly redefining what love means and tweaking our Values and preferred Traits as we get older.

This leads us to the social exchange theory, developed by sociologist George Homans in 1958. He says that relationships are like a cost-benefit analysis, centered on what each person puts in and gets out and whether it's a fair trade.

In the same year, Ivan Nye distilled this theory further and outlined twelve key points. Here are the two most relevant ones:

- All things equal, we tend to connect with, date, or even marry people who share our values and beliefs. On the flip side, we often steer clear of those who consistently have opposing views.

- All things equal, we're more inclined to build relationships and marry people who are similar to us in terms of skills, achievements, and social status. Finding someone who matches up with us in the grand scheme of things is a top priority.

Nye's interpretation suggests that people aim for relationships that offer the biggest benefits, the best long-term outcomes, and the least drawbacks. Other things like immediate rewards, societal approval, and feelings of security also play a big role in our partner choices.

The principles of the social exchange theory strongly align with the Love Formula. It suggests that we naturally pick partners who mirror our own qualities, abilities, and social standing. Relationships have a bit of a give-and-take dynamic. At the same time, it's not about keeping tabs but more about connecting with someone who views life the way we do. And by the way, all this doesn't mean feelings aren't important. These discussions are simple reminders that when it comes to relationship dynamics, there's more to consider than just feelings.

After exploring how *nature* and *nurture* influence our love choices, let's step into a different arena: the world of modern love problems. This next chapter throws us into the reality of today's dating scene, where fast-paced lifestyles and technology have changed the game.

Chapter 4

Why Love Isn't Adding up Today

Nowadays it's common to encounter "love blockers." They are barriers in the way of intimacy, connection, and partnership.

Below are four major relationship barriers and how the Love Formula acts as a tool to overcome them:

1. **Commitment Phobia**

2. **Gender Roles**

3. **Media's Impact**

4. **New Dating Trends**

Love Blocker #1: Commitment Phobia

Romance, as we know it today, spans just a blip in human history. We used to be tied down by strict traditions and limited partner choices; we didn't have the plethora of options we have today. Think about it, it wasn't too long ago that arranged marriages were normal or that we were required to choose a partner from a tiny social group. Yes, we were restricted, but things *were* easier and more straightforward. Our great-grandparents and their great-grandparents didn't have the dilemma of "missing out" on other potential matches; having even a single choice was a luxury!

The shifts in our dating culture are due in part to our increasing access to the world outside. As time went on and technology improved, society changed in big ways. With every big invention designed to facilitate human connectivity, such as the car, the plane, and even the telephone, the dating pool grew wider. Little by little, we became pickier with our partner choices, making it harder to commit and stay the course.

And now with dating apps and so many choices at our fingertips, it's impossible not to get caught in a dangerous loop of *Is there someone better out there?* or *What if I can find someone who's just a bit taller, funnier, or more attractive?*

While the benefits of wider access to the dating pool are clear, the drawback is that we've developed a constant need to keep looking for that "perfect" partner. This "fear of missing out" or FOMO can make it really tough to invest in a current relationship, leading to dissatisfaction and making it hard to form deep, meaningful connections. It can turn what could be a great relationship into an endless quest for a unicorn. It poses a kind of an existential question: Are we searching for real love or the idea of perfect love?

The Love Formula teaches you how to pick a partner when faced with so many options. You'll learn to pinpoint your fundamental Values, preferred Traits, and what you really want in a partner. More importantly, it'll help you clearly see what's truly important in a relationship and whether your potential partner is worth investing in.

Love Blocker #2: Gender Roles

What are the benefits that women and men offer each other? The answer to this question is constantly evolving.

Historically, marriage was formed as a way to create a stable community and ensure clear family lines. Anthropologists believe that as human societies moved from nomadic lifestyles to settled farming communities, they needed more structured social systems. A crucial part of this structure was formalized relationships between men and women.

In the past, societal norms dictated that women were mainly responsible for domestic chores and childcare, while men were expected to be the main providers and defenders. The Industrial Revolution further solidified these gender roles, with men working outside the home as primary earners and women managing the household. Men were seen as the strong, logical, and providers, while women were viewed as the nurturing and morally guiding forces. These roles shaped how people behaved and thought within their marriages, a pattern that persisted into the nineteenth and twentieth centuries.

In the twenty-first century, everything has changed. Traditional duties have shifted dramatically, and gender roles are now more fluid and less defined than ever. The concept of love has evolved into something freer and more unpredictable. As Western society welcomes LGBTQ+ identities and lifestyles, the once clear-cut roles associated with men and women have become more complex.

This new wave of embracing individual identities is unquestionably a step in the right direction, but it also adds layers of confusion to dating. In the past, strict gender roles might have stifled personal expression, but there was a certain comfort in following a well-established script. The challenge now is making sense of love and dating in a world where these old guidelines no longer apply.

Nowadays, there isn't just one set recipe or blueprint for relationships. Each person comes with their own script, shaped by their unique views and how they choose to define their role in a relationship. This is evident in the growing number of stay-at-home dads and female executives.

The opportunity for women to pursue independence and career growth is fantastic, but it's important to recognize that not everyone seeks the same path. Similarly, while some men prefer to take on the traditional "breadwinner" role, others may adopt a less assertive approach. In fact, the whole spectrum from chivalry to misogyny has become more blurred. While there are obvious instances of misogyny, others might not be so easily identified.

The Love Formula is unique due to its focus on individuality, freeing us from any preset "boxes" about what we should look for in our relationships. It will empower you to define and choose what really matters to you, regardless of what society says. The Love Formula guides singles and couples to put pen to paper and jot down what's important to them. This is a crucial step to determining what they expect and prefer in terms of roles, responsibilities, and the general dynamics of their relationship. Encouraging clear communication helps partners truly grasp each other's needs, especially in this ever-evolving dating landscape.

Love Blocker #3: Media's Impact

Thanks to social media, we're constantly bombarded with happy-go-lucky couples who don't seem to have a care in the world. Your friends' social media performances can have a detrimental effect on your love life—which is why it's important today, more than ever, to pay close attention to how your social media feed shapes your view of relationships.

Social media often showcases idealized body shapes, immaculate features, and exaggerated versions of romance. Everything and everyone appears flawless, resulting in unrealistic relationship expectations and skewed perceptions of what a healthy and fulfilling relationship truly looks like.

Our social media feeds are filled with picture-perfect lives and relationships, causing feelings of inadequacy. As we lose ourselves in this endless scroll, we unknowingly move away from the real world and enter a realm of fantasy. The more we consume, the more our views of love and relationships become distorted.

Research shows that media influence can also be a source of self-doubt, *but is that surprising*? This happens because the media creates an environment where comparison is the norm, and we humans have a natural inclination to compare and contrast.

The social comparison theory, introduced by Leon Festinger in 1954, suggests that we often measure our own worth by how we stack up against others. When our social media feeds are flooded with images of flawless celebrities and influencers, it's tough not to feel inadequate. And this culture of comparison impacts both men and women.

Usually, we don't even realize how much our preferences are being shaped by the media. That's where the Love Formula can step in and bring you back to Earth. Taking the time to identify your Values and Trait preferences can be very revealing; it will help you determine whether your relationship choices are truly healthy and realistic.

In short, the Love Formula will push you to create relationships based on realness, paving the way for deeper, more rewarding connections.

Love Blocker #4: New Dating Trends

"U up?," "Sup?," or "Hey, cutie." Welcome to our dating era, where we have replaced traditional ways of romance with swipes, emoji, brief texts, and a ton of abbreviated expressions. This new way of flirting can be fun and exciting, but it also introduces new hurdles, making the search for meaningful and lasting connections more difficult and, frankly, confusing. New terms such as "ghosting," "fading," and even "roaching" have popped up in our vocabulary, normalizing behaviors that used to be considered poor dating etiquette.

Online dating has undoubtedly reshaped our approach to choosing partners, with a heavy emphasis on physical attributes and surface-level qualities such as career, education, and hobbies. Where's the depth? Referencing FOMO again, there's this prevailing thought that a better match is just a swipe away, leading to a culture where people are often viewed as replaceable objects rather than as individuals with emotional and spiritual depth. The search for deep, authentic connections tends to be overshadowed by the endless pursuit of an "ideal" partner, perfection being the endgame.

Put simply, online dating has deprived us of the fundamental concept of human connection. We miss out on seeing each other in person, catching each other's scent, reading body language, or sharing displays of emotion. How can we really connect when there is such dehumanization?

In this context, the Love Formula is a robust tool for facing today's dating scene. It motivates you to really hone in on what's important in a relationship, encouraging a shift from shallow criteria to qualities that foster long-term bonds. It offers a counterbalance to the superficial swipe culture, championing a more authentic and enduring approach to finding love in the digital world.

Based on what we've discussed so far, it's clear that our romantic lives are shaped by an intricate blend of our instincts and life experiences and the current dating climate. The love blockers we've examined—ranging from FOMO to changing gender roles and media effects—all play a part in hindering intimacy. By recognizing and understanding these barriers, we're in a stronger position to tackle them. In the coming chapters, you will learn how to apply the Love Formula to overcome the Love Blockers.

Part II
How It Works

What really makes the perfect partner? It's a question that constantly echoes in our thoughts as we sift through the sea of possible connections out there. Our checklist boils down to two fundamental aspects: *Values* and *Traits*.

Values are the bedrock of our lifestyle choices and ethical principles, such as a commitment to honesty, a strong work ethic, or the importance of family. Traits, on the other hand, are a blend of physical qualities and innate characteristics, such as humor or intellectual curiosity.

For the Love Formula to be effective, incorporating both elements is essential. Each of us has a distinct blend of preferences that align with our deepest desires. "Everyone is unique"—an overused cliché, but it's true.

For some, the priority might be how well the partner aligns with their core Values; for others, chemistry and attraction are key. This complex mix of ingredients highlights how truly unique we all are and why the Love Formula emphasizes individuality. Every person is one-of-a-kind, and so are the combinations of Values and Traits they seek in others.

Going forward, this book will guide you in pinpointing which Values and Traits are most important to you. This journey of self-discovery will reveal what truly matters to you in love and closeness. You'll gain a sharper ability to gauge the compatibility of a potential partner or assess the compatibility of your current one, making your search for the right match more effective.

Chapter 5

Values & Traits— Key Components of the Love Formula

Most people have identified their must-haves and deal breakers, but how often do we put pen to paper and actually assess these benchmarks? What makes the Love Formula unique is that it classifies these criteria into two distinct categories: Values and Traits.

Values are key in determining how well two people will mesh in a relationship. If partners share similar fundamental beliefs, they're less likely to face lifestyle conflicts. Meanwhile, Traits take center stage in determining the degree of physical and emotional attraction.

We'll start with Values and how they impact your pursuit of a fulfilling relationship. As you start to think about your checklist, keep in mind that this is a deeply personal process, and you have to trust yourself and your assessments.

Values

Values are shaped by the choices we make, the beliefs we cherish, and the behaviors we come to respect both in ourselves and others. They're the products of nurture, evolving and growing as we journey through life and interact with and learn from the world around us.

Values are more than just preferences for a certain lifestyle; they act as personal compasses, guiding us to friends and partners whose core beliefs resonate with ours. They play a crucial role in shaping our relationships, leading us to connect with people who share our key life priorities. For example, if valuing family is high on your list, you're more likely to connect with others who also cherish family ties. Essentially, your Values not only determine your social circle but also deepen the quality of your relationships.

However, Values aren't set in stone; they evolve as you do. No one sticks to the exact same set of beliefs and lifestyle choices throughout their life. Your Values change and adapt as you go through different relationships, travel, face traumas, make discoveries, and incur losses.

As far as Values are concerned, you might find yourself adopting new ones, tweaking old ones, and even completely transforming them at various life stages. What was crucial in your high school years, like being popular, might not even make the cut in your priorities as an adult.

The Love Formula embraces the wisdom of "to each their own." Whether your focus is on climbing the career ladder, putting family first, living a life of adventure, personal development, creativity, or spirituality, or finding a balance among these, the choice is uniquely yours. Your Values are a mirror of the lifestyle you aspire to have.

The Love Formula will prompt you to pinpoint your Top 5 Values. This is the moment to truly reflect, dig deep, and ponder on these questions:

- What lifestyle choices do I truly admire?

- What qualities do I respect in myself and in others?

- What kind of person am I aiming to become?

After considering your answers, you'll be asked to not only identify your Values but to rank them in order of importance. For example, you may rank *family* above *career* or *social status* above *education*.

The next task is to assign Scores to them. This involves rating yourself, which is called a Self Values Score. If you see yourself as strong in a particular Value, you'll award yourself a high Values

Score in that category. If you recognize an area for improvement in a specific Value, you will assign a lower Values Score in that category. These individual Self Value Scores add up to your total Self Score.

What's notable is that your Self Score acts as a mirror of your self-esteem. Put simply, it is a direct indicator of how "successful" you think you are in life.

After you've established a clear benchmark with a set of Values and your Self Score, the next step is to gauge how closely your partner matches them through the Partner Values Score.

If you give them a high Partner Values Score, it shows that you deeply appreciate your partner and hold them in high regard in the aspects that are meaningful to you. If their Values Score is close to yours, this suggests matching lifestyles and core beliefs.

On the flip side, if you assign a low Partner Values Score, it indicates a lower level of trust or confidence in them as a suitable partner. It suggests that you don't see them as a viable match for you and that they're not quite meeting your expectations.

At this point, you might be asking yourself how to figure out what your partner thinks about you. Well, you can't, and that's not something the Love Formula is designed to do. It's not a mind-reading tool. The Partner Scores you assign are based on *your* view of them, not theirs of you.

Here are some Values you might identify with; feel free to rephrase them in a way that resonates more closely with your personal preferences:

Education	*Self-Discipline*	*Social Status*
Wealth	*Domesticity*	*Self-Care*
Religion	*Cleanliness*	*Health*
Spirituality	*Parenting*	*Consciousness*
Materialism	*Family*	*Self-Growth*
Image	*Manners*	*Honesty*
Fashion Sense	*Communication*	*Dependability*
Career/Occupation	*Patience*	*Reliability*
Work Ethic		

For a deeper understanding of this category, we'll explore a real-life example of Values and how they might change over time.

> ## Evolving Values: A Case Study
>
> In her energetic early twenties, Anna thrived on excitement. Her Top 5 Values revolved around social gatherings, marked by a love for lively nightlife filled with fun, drinks, and the thrill of making new connections. It was during this phase that she met Jamal, a sociable and well-known figure in the party scene, who seemed to perfectly match her lifestyle. Drawn to each other, they quickly started dating, sharing numerous nights of partying, dancing, and the inevitable next-day hangovers.
>
> However, as years passed, Anna's enthusiasm for this lifestyle began to wane. She noticed negative shifts in her emotional and physical well-being, which she linked to her constant partying. She found herself longing for quieter nights at home, cooking and relaxing on the couch, and earlier bedtimes.
>
> As much as Anna wanted to share this new phase with Jamal, it became clear that he wasn't ready to leave his party life behind. His unchanged behavior led Anna to a realization—their relationship was no longer fulfilling. Her evolving Values and needs were no longer in sync with Jamal's. Recognizing that her priorities had shifted and Jamal wasn't meeting her new standards, she decided to end their relationship, seeking a partner who shared her desire for a more tranquil and healthier lifestyle.

With me so far? Good! Now let's move on to Traits.

Traits

A Trait you're drawn to is like a natural spark or a special feature in someone that just pulls you in. For example, if you always find yourself drawn to people with a standout sense of humor, that's a Trait you're into. This kind of attraction works from deep within our subconscious and is driven by instincts we can't always explain.

Ever felt that undeniable pull toward someone right when you see them? Maybe it's the air of mystery around the tall, dark stranger across the room or the irresistible charm of someone who always knows just what to say.

Just like Values, the Traits that grab your attention evolve throughout your life. Do you remember a time you had a change of heart about a type of food or music? Maybe there's a kind of person you didn't like at first, but then they gradually grew on you? That's your brain getting comfortable with it, starting to accept and even like it.

Now when it comes to the Love Formula, Traits are a whole different ball game from Values. *You don't give yourself a Score here.*

Why not?

Let's think about the saying "opposites attract." With Traits, it's not always about finding someone exactly like you, as it is with Values. Sure, you want compatibility, but comparing Traits is a bit more nuanced. Often, the Traits that attract us are the ones we don't have.

Think of yin and yang, where opposites complement each other. Maybe you lean toward someone more logical because you're more emotional, or you're drawn to an extrovert to balance your introvert tendencies. Since opposites often attract, you shouldn't rate your partner based on your own Traits.

But here's the twist: Values are usually all positive and good for you, while Traits can be a mixed bag—they can be positive, neutral, or even not-so-great.

Picking a Trait isn't about what you think you should want; it's about what naturally draws you in, that unexplainable pull to someone who has a certain quality. Even if logically they seem like a good match, the real question is whether you've always been drawn to such Traits. Always falling for the "bad boy" or "bad girl"? That's your Trait preference until you learn to shift it—something we'll explore later.

So what can you do to better understand the Traits that attract you? The first step is understanding your patterns. By scrutinizing your recurring attractions, you can pinpoint your Trait preferences. Recognizing unhealthy attractions is the first step toward change.

Here's a kicker—it's entirely possible to find a disconnect between your Values and the Traits you're attracted to. What if stability is important to you, but you keep getting drawn to unpredictable types? Or what if you care about dependability, but you keep falling for people who aren't dependable?

The real work starts with recognizing what drives these attractions and where they stem from. Once you grasp this, you can begin to alter these ingrained inclinations, both the ones you're aware of and those lurking beneath the surface.

The goal is to transform these automatic responses into conscious decisions that align with your true wants and needs. This means breaking free from harmful relationship patterns and making changes that lead to better outcomes. It's about breaking cycles.

Let's look at some Trait examples. Remember, even if they seem harmless, some Traits can be sneaky and not show their true colors until you know exactly what to look for.

Positive/Neutral Traits

Outgoing	*Clever*	*Sexual*
Extroverted	*Spontaneous*	*Comfortable*
Alpha	*Generous*	*Self-Aware*
Leader	*Thoughtful*	*Logical*
Shy	*Ambitious*	*Deep Thinker*
Introverted	*Intuitive*	*Good Listener*
Beta	*Perceptive*	*Handsome*
Easygoing	*Passionate*	*Pretty*
Intelligent	*Open-Minded*	*Strong*
Sharp	*Curious*	*Loyal*
Witty	*Free-Spirited*	

Destructive Traits

Over-giving	*Selfish*	*Irresponsible*
Indulgent	*Bad Boy/Girl*	*Neglectful*
Subservient	*Fuck Boy/Girl*	*Inflexible*
Controlling	*Drama King/Queen*	*Overly Flirty*
Stubborn	*Toxic*	*Cruel*
Unpredictable	*Narcissistic*	*Judgmental*
Moody	*Aggressive*	*Liar*
Aloof	*Self-Victimizer*	*Overcritical*

To gain more clarity on this topic, we'll explore another real-life example.

Toxic Traits: A Case Study

Bella grew up in a home where her father was emotionally distant and interacted minimally with her and her mother. He often worked long, physically taxing hours and turned to heavy drinking when he got home. Soon his alcohol problem led him to become anxious, detached, and temperamental. Bella's mom spent years trying to please him by cooking, cleaning, and showing him love, while patiently enduring his poor behavior—but to no avail. Bella's father remained indifferent.

As Bella entered adulthood and began dating, she found herself repeatedly drawn to men who mirrored her father's traits: emotionally distant, moody, prone to drinking, and lacking in affection. Each time Bella entered such a relationship, it left her heartbroken. Despite knowing the potential consequences, she felt powerless to resist the pattern.

Her early experiences had set a precedent, leading her to pursue men who were emotionally harmful, even though she yearned for a kind, emotionally present, and stable partner.

Can you see the disconnect between Bella's Values and Traits? While she yearned for a partner who valued family and personal growth, her ingrained Trait preferences, shaped by her upbringing, created a barrier for her.

Now that we understand how our Values and Traits can play out, sometimes in ways we don't expect—just like in Bella's case—it's time to roll up our sleeves and get into the nitty-gritty details. Up next we're diving into the actual steps of putting the Love Formula into action. The next chapter shows how to turn what you've learned so far into a plan you can really use, a way to ensure you're making choices that truly fit with who you are and what you want. Let's jump to the how-to part, where you start making real moves toward finding and keeping those deep, meaningful connections we're all after.

Chapter 6

Implementing the Love Formula

All right, it's go-time! We're about to start applying this game-changing Love Formula to our romantic lives. Gone are the days when we leave things to chance. Let's get down to it, step by step.

- Step 1: Self-Evaluation

- Step 2: Partner Values Evaluation

- Step 3: Partner Traits Evaluation

- Step 4: Prioritize Values and Traits

- Step 5: Determine Total Partner Score

- Step 6: Analysis

Time to put the steps into action!

Step 1: Self-Evaluation

Using Table 1 (sample) as a guide, identify your Values and calculate your Self Score.

Column 1 (Values): Jot down your Top 5 Values in order of how important they are to you. (Just a tip: If you feel like five isn't enough, go ahead and add more. Maybe you have seven or ten key Values. Customize this list until it perfectly reflects your priorities.)

Column 2 (Importance): Assign a percentage to indicate how important each Value is to you.

Important Note: The Love Formula's research followed a methodology where the importance of each Value was assumed equal (20% each). *But* you can adjust percentages according to what feels right for you. Maybe you want to assign equal weightage to each Value (20% each) in your Top 5 Values, or perhaps you have three Values at 30% each and two others at 5% each. Just make sure all percentages add up to 100%. Alternatively, choosing a split like 30%, 25%, 20%, 15%, and 10% can really help you prioritize. Plus, it lets you track how your Values evolve over time for better insight.

Column 3 (Self-Evaluation): Give yourself a Score for each Value based on Column 2. For example, if you rated the importance of a particular Value at 35% and you believe you're nearly perfect in that area, maybe you score yourself at 34 out of 35. If you're quite good but not perfect, perhaps a 30 would be appropriate. The crucial part here is to be honest in this self-assessment.

Table 1 (sample): *Self Score (Values only)*

Values	Importance (%)	Self-Evaluation
Family	20	19
Finances	20	16
Political Ideology	20	20
Communication/ Manners	20	18
Dependability	20	17
Self Score	= 100	**= 90** **Your Self Score is 90%**

Table 1: *Self Score (Values only)*

Values	Importance (%)	Self-Evaluation
Self Score	= 100	**= ___**

Your Values evaluation in Table 1 is your total Self Score, and *this is very important*. Remember, your Self Score will solely reflect your Values Score. But when it's time to evaluate a partner, you'll be looking at both Values and Traits to get a fuller picture.

Step 2: Partner Values Evaluation

Using the sample as a guide, complete Table 2 by filling in the Top 5 Values that you used in Table 1, including the weight assigned to each [Importance (%)]. Next, for each Value, rate your partner using the right column. This is your evaluation of your Partner Values Score, reflecting the degree to which you believe they align with your core beliefs and lifestyle choices.

Table 2 (sample): *Partner Values Score*

Values	Importance (%)	Partner Evaluation
Family	20	18
Finances	20	17
Political Ideology	20	17
Communication/ Manners	20	14
Dependability	20	18
Partner Values Score	= 100	**= 84**

Table 2: *Partner Values Score*

Values	Importance (%)	Partner Evaluation
Partner Values Score	= 100	= ____ **Partner Values Score**

Step 3: Partner Traits Evaluation

Moving on, fill out Table 3 to determine your Trait preferences and Partner Traits Score. This step is key to understanding what kind of characteristics really pull you in. Remember, you're not rating yourself here; you're just focusing on Traits in others. First, in Column 1, list your Top 5 Traits in order of importance. Next, in Column 2, assign each Trait a weight to show how important it is to you. Last, in Column 3, it's your turn to evaluate how well your partner lines up with these Traits that you find attractive.

Table 3 (sample): *Partner Traits Score*

Traits	Importance (%)	Partner Evaluation
Humor	20	18
Physique	20	17
Kindness	20	15
Leadership	20	20
Sexuality/Sensuality	20	17
Partner Traits Score	= 100	**= 87**

Table 3: *Partner Traits Score*

Traits	Importance (%)	Partner Evaluation
Partner Traits Score	= 100	= ________

Step 4: Values and Traits Priority Allocation

Next up, decide what holds more weight for you: Values or Traits? In Table 4, you'll allocate priority between Values (your core lifestyle choices and beliefs) and Traits (the physical and personality features that attract you; see the table below as an example). If you feel Values are more critical in shaping a relationship, then give them a higher weightage. But if you think Traits are key, then tilt the scale in their favor.

Table 4 (sample): *Priority Allocation*

Values	45
Traits	55
Total	**= 100**

Table 4: *Priority Allocation*

Values	
Traits	
Total	**= 100**

Step 5: Total Partner Score

It's time to do some math. Don't worry; it won't be graded...but it will impact your love life, so you may want to pay close attention. To evaluate your Partner Score, you'll want to use the following calculations:

Partner Values = (Partner Values Score) ÷ 100 x (Values Priority Allocation) = X

Partner Traits = (Partner Traits Score) ÷ 100 x (Traits Priority Allocation) = Y

Partner Score = X + Y

Here's a sample calculation for you:

Partner Values = 84 ÷ 100 x 45 = **37.80**

Partner Traits = 87 ÷ 100 x 55 = **47.85**

These calculations are shown below as an example; use the second table for your own calculations for the Partner Score.

Table 5 (sample): *Partner Score*

Partner Values	37.80
Partner Traits	47.85
Partner Score	**=86 (rounded from 85.65)**

Table 5: *Partner Score*

Partner Values Score	
Partner Traits Score	
Partner Score	**= _______**

Step 6: Analysis

Now it's time to analyze your results by comparing your Self Score with your Partner Score.

Your Self Score is indicated in Step 1, Table 1, and is the same as your Values Score. Your Partner Score is the final calculation in Step 5, Table 5. To calculate the difference, see the example in Table 6 (sample). *The closer this number is to 0, the better the match!*

Table 6 (sample): *Love Formula Score*

Self Score	90%
Partner Score	86%
Love Formula Score **(Self Score minus Partner Score)**	**= +4%**

Table 6: *Love Formula Score*

Self Score	_______%
Partner Score	_______%
Love Formula Score **(Self Score minus Partner Score)**	**= _______%**

This quantifiable figure offers a unique gauge of how compatible you two are. A small difference, say between 0% and 2%, points to an extremely close match.

As you keep applying the Love Formula in your interactions and personal growth, you might notice your Scores getting closer, particularly if there's a solid match in the making.

A positive result means you see yourself in a somewhat similar or significantly better light compared to your partner. On the flip side, a negative result suggests you view yourself as less positive than your partner. This gap between Scores is a predictor of how things might go between you two. It might seem a bit strange at first, but it's a crucial aspect to consider. But don't worry; as you continue with the Love Formula, this will start to make more sense.

It's important to remember that the Love Formula isn't a foolproof predictor of your relationship's future. Relationships are subjective, and your partner might see things differently. What you're really figuring out here is how well you believe that you and your partner match up.

Now we'll dive into some hypothetical scenarios of couples who've used the Love Formula. These examples will give you a better sense of how the Love Formula plays out in real life and the benefits it might bring.

Chapter 7

Rita and Garrett's Like at First Sight

Now that we've laid down the essential principles of the Love Formula, let's look at a real-life scenario to see it in action. Meet our first couple, Rita and Garrett.

Those closest to Rita often described her as a charming, witty, and intelligent woman. However, these lovable qualities weren't always obvious to everyone; she had a tendency to be real only with those she was close to. To the public, she often came across as reserved, introverted, and sometimes stuck up.

Rita was the epitome of a "high achiever." With her unwavering commitment to education, she was only a year away from finishing her doctorate. That said, she was also lonely. She often daydreamed about meeting a special someone she could share a life with.

One day, while Rita was waiting for her coffee, she crossed paths with Garrett and felt an immediate spark. Normally, Rita found it hard to start conversations with people she didn't know, but with Garrett, it was different. There was an undeniable pull that made chatting with him feel natural and effortless. Garrett kicked off their conversation with a casual question about her backpack, which led to Rita telling him that she was a student. Garrett, in turn, revealed that he had a similar backpack that he used for mountain biking escapades.

Garrett's extroverted nature was obvious from the get-go—he was outgoing and full of energy. The way he effortlessly initiated a conversation with Rita showcased his knack for connecting with people, something that instantly intrigued Rita. Feeling comfortable in his presence, she readily accepted his offer to join him for a coffee.

Rita was impressed by Garrett's blend of confidence and humility. He had a way of being funny without going over the top, and he was a great conversationalist. He shared more details about his life—he was a third-year computer science student and worked full-time at Chipotle. Their chat became even more enjoyable when they realized they were both fond of the works of the author and speaker Tony Robbins.

Clearly, the chemistry between Rita and Garrett was both magnetic and reciprocal. From the initial wait for their coffees to the final sips at the end of their impromptu two-hour date, they discovered a wealth of common ground. As their time together drew to a close, they exchanged numbers, with Garrett assuring her he would call.

Sounds promising, right? Let's see how Rita and Garrett assessed each other using the Love Formula. We'll start with Rita.

Rita

Rita pinpointed Top 5 Values, which included *education* (30%), *image* (25%), *personal development* (20%), *social skills* (15%), and *financial choices* (10%). Here's how she determined her Self Score:

1. **Education**: Rita's current pursuit of a doctorate degree demonstrated her commitment to her goals. She displayed relentless persistence and dedication in her educational endeavors, taking immense pride in her accomplishments, which included graduating magna cum laude from university. She was a total badass, and everyone knew it. She rated herself 27/30 in this category.

2. **Image**: Rita placed a lot of importance on her appearance and the way she came across to others. Growing up, she was deeply focused on her image, always looking for ways to enhance it. Hours spent watching MTV and E! led her to idolize Kim Kardashian, her epitome of the ideal woman. She put immense pressure on herself to "look" a certain way, but in her eyes, she fell short. She ended up rating herself 15/25.

3. **Personal Development**: Rita understood the significance of self-development and how it shapes one's quality of life. She believed that everyone should engage in a personal growth journey, whether through reading, setting goals, or embracing new experiences. Rita engaged in daily self-improvement practices and always looked for fresh ways to become better. She rated herself 19/20 here.

4. **Social Likability**: Rita was quite reserved. Social anxiety made it difficult for her to open up to people, and she always wished she could get over her social blocks. But she knew that once she overcame her shyness, she was a likable individual with good social graces. Still, for this category, she rated herself a 6/15.

5. **Financial Choices**: When she met Garrett, Rita was in the midst of her doctoral studies and wasn't earning much. Despite living comfortably in her dorm and taking great pride in her academic achievements, she harbored feelings of insecurity about her financial situation. She often found herself longing for the financial independence that her friends and family seemed to have. For this, she rated herself a 5/10.

Here's what Rita's Self Score looked like:

Table 1: *Rita's Self Score*

Values	Importance (%)	Self-Evaluation
Education	30	27
Image	25	15
Personal Development	20	19
Social Likability	15	6
Financial Choices	10	5
Self Score	**= 100**	**= 72**

Her overall Self Score was 72% (Table 1). Earlier, we saw that Rita clearly felt chemistry after her first encounter with Garrett, so let's recap their interaction and see how she evaluated him according to her Top 5 Values:

1. **Education**: Garrett was a third-year computer science student. To her, that was certainly worth something! But he seemed to be falling a *little* short. No offense to him, of course! This wasn't to discredit his efforts; being an undergrad nearing graduation is commendable. But Rita, deep into her doctoral program, couldn't help but feel that Garrett didn't match up to her own academic journey. She rated Garrett 20/30 in this category.

2. **Image**: Rita was very excited about this specific Value. Garrett had a sense of style, dressed impeccably, and had a knack for standing out, like someone straight out of the "Entourage" series. As they talked, she often found herself imagining what it would be like to be seen with him. She was so taken by his charm that she wanted to yell, "Look who I've got!" For this, she rated him an impressive 23/25.

3. **Personal Development**: Rita found Garrett's knowledge of Tony Robbins intriguing, which meant that he had some grasp of personal growth and the kind of life philosophy Tony advocates. She appreciated this aspect of him. However, as they spent more time together, she noticed that he really didn't partake in actual self-development practices, such as meditation, goal setting, or seeking out new experiences. As a result, Rita decided to give Garrett a somewhat lower Score in self-development, rating him 14/20 in this area.

4. **Social Likability**: Garrett was a confident talker. It was rare that someone could make Rita feel at ease the way Garrett did—it was very clear he had a natural charisma

that could make anyone feel at home with him. She rated him 13/15.

5. **Financial Choices**: Rita could see that Garrett was financially responsible. Even though working at Chipotle might not be seen as a major career move, his commitment to the job showed discipline. His dedication to paying off his student loans clearly demonstrated his determination and sense of fiscal responsibility. She knew he still had a long way to go, but he had potential. She rated him 5/10.

Table 2: *Rita's Partner Values Score for Garrett*

Values	Importance (%)	Partner Evaluation
Education	30	20
Image	25	23
Personal Development	20	14
Social Likability	15	13
Financial Choices	10	5
Partner Values Score	= 100	**= 75**

While Rita scored herself at 72% in terms of Values, she gave Garrett a slightly higher rating of 75% (Table 2). Scores this close point to a potentially great match! However, as we've seen, Values aren't the only thing that matters. In the workings of the Love Formula, the rating for Traits is just as crucial and plays a key role in fostering a harmonious relationship. Let's see how Rita rated Garrett for her Top 5 Traits, which included *humor (30%), good physique (25%), kindness (20%), extroversion (15%), and age (10%)*.

1. **Humor**: Garrett's sarcastic and dry wit completely captivated Rita. Her fondness for his effortless sense of humor was evident as she had a big smile on her face the

entire time they were together. Rita gave Garrett a rating of 27/30 in this category.

2. **Physique**: Garrett did not have Rita's ideal physique. She had a thing for tall and skinny guys, someone like Ryan Phillippe rather than Mark Wahlberg. Garrett, although a heartthrob for sure, had a wider frame—not Rita's cup of tea. Otherwise, he was easy on the eyes. She rated him a 20/25.

3. **Kindness**: Garrett came across as genuinely kind-hearted. During their date, his compliments about her smile and laugh were simple yet uplifting, adding to Rita's already buoyant mood. But what really clinched it for Garrett was his story of rescuing stray animals. That was a real deal-sealer! He shared how he had once found an ill and abandoned dog, nursed it back to health, and named it Buzz. This dog had been a part of Garrett's life for over five years, which deeply impressed Rita. She rated him 17/20 in this area.

4. **Extroversion**: Garrett had a way of making everyone feel at ease. When he asked Rita out for coffee, he didn't just stop there—he chatted up everyone in line, from the people waiting for their orders to the folks making the coffee. He wasn't just being friendly; he had a genuine warmth that made you want to talk to him. Rita couldn't help but admire how he navigated the crowd with ease, giving him a solid 13/15.

5. **Age**: Rita had a rule about the age gap in relationships—nothing more than five years. Garrett being four years her junior might have been a talking point for some, but for Rita, it was perfectly within her comfort zone. She rated him 9/10.

Table 3 shows how Rita filled out the Traits Evaluation for Garrett:

Table 3: *Rita's Partner Traits Score for Garrett*

Traits	Importance (%)	Partner Evaluation
Humor	30	27
Good Physique	25	20
Kindness	20	17
Extroversion	15	13
Age	10	9
Partner Traits Score	= 100	**= 86**

If Rita was looking for apples, Garrett had the whole orchard. He scored a whopping 86% for Traits, which was really impressive! While she acknowledged the importance of attraction in a relationship, Rita placed a slightly higher premium on shared Values, as seen in Table 4 below.

Table 4: *Rita's Priority Allocation*

Values	60
Traits	40
Total	**= 100**

Rita's Love Formula calculations for Garrett's Partner Score looked like this:

Partner Values = (75) ÷ 100 x 60 **= 45**
Partner Traits = (86) ÷ 100 x 40 **= 34.4**

She used these calculations to fill out Table 5:

Table 5: *Rita's Partner Score for Garrett*

Partner Values Score	45.0
Partner Traits Score	34.4
Partner Score	**= 79** (rounded from 79.4)

Table 6: *Rita's Love Formula Score*

Rita (Self Score)	= 76%
Garrett (Partner Score)	= 79%
Love Formula Score	**= -3%**

The Love Formula evaluation looked promising (Table 6). Rita felt confident in her connection with Garrett and was excited to go on more dates with him. Now let's move on to Garrett's Love Formula calculations.

Garrett

We all know someone who seems to have an endless circle of acquaintances, effortlessly mingling and making connections wherever they go. Garrett was exactly that kind of person. He had a knack for making everyone around him smile with his quick wit and playful antics. Yet, when the situation called for it, he could switch gears in an instant, dedicating himself to his work with a level of seriousness and commitment that was equally impressive. This blend of lightheartedness and competence made him a unique and appreciated presence in any setting.

He spent plenty of time thinking about what was important in life, and that included matters of the heart. Upon his initial interaction with Rita, his interest was undeniable. Unsurprisingly, he decided to use the Love Formula to see whether or not she aligned with his Values and Traits.

These were his Top 5 Values: *financial stability (30%), social status (25%), knowledge/wisdom (20%), self-care (15%), and family (10%).* Here's how he determined the ratings:

1. **Financial Stability**: Garrett was grateful to his family for covering his college costs, something he didn't take lightly. To make his own way, he'd been working at Chipotle, saving as much as he could. *His big money-saving trick?* Living at home! It might not be everyone's ideal situation, but it was working for him, and he had managed to save up $20,000 so far, with an eye on buying his own place in the next couple of years. He was pretty proud of how far he had come, so he gave himself a solid 25/30.

2. **Social Status**: Garrett came from simple beginnings without the luxury of wealth being handed to him. This reality sparked a fire in him to climb the ladder to success and break into the elite circle. His mom always nudged him toward mingling with the "affluent" crowd, hoping it would pave his way forward. Despite his general air of confidence, Garrett found himself battling feelings of insecurity in the company of high society, feeling like an outsider. Reflecting on this aspect of his life, he scored himself at 15/25.

3. **Knowledge/Wisdom**: Starting college was a turning point for Garrett, expanding his horizons far beyond the confines of his small hometown. While he never considered himself particularly philosophical or wise, he made it a point to live authentically, steering clear of the superficial. His goal was always self-improvement, to evolve into the best version of himself. Yet, he couldn't shake the feeling that he was still far from where he wanted to be. Reflecting on this, he rated his progress a 12/20.

4. **Self-Care**: Garrett knew that making connections with influential people required not just showing up but also presenting himself in the best possible light. That's why

he took his lifestyle and appearance so seriously. He stuck to a diet of organic, fresh foods, avoiding additives and unhealthy fats. Every weekend, you'd find him mountain biking; besides, he never skipped his regular workouts. His grooming was on point, his clothes always sharp, and he made sure to shower and shave every day. He believed that these habits didn't just make him look good—they boosted his confidence too. On this front, he felt pretty accomplished, scoring himself at 14/15.

5. **Family**: Garrett was deeply aware of the significant support his family had provided him, which placed them at the core of his heart. Valuing the close-knit nature of his family unit, he firmly believed in the profound joy derived from maintaining strong familial ties. Despite the occasional clashes and turbulent relationship with his younger brother, where disagreements were not uncommon, Garrett held a deep fondness for him and always treated him with kindness. His bond with his parents was even stronger, marked by deep affection and a solid connection. Reflecting on these relationships, Garrett rated his commitment to family unity and love at 8/10.

Table 1: *Garrett's Self Score*

Values	Importance (%)	Self-Evaluation
Financial Stability	30	25
Social Status	25	15
Knowledge/Wisdom	20	12
Self-Care	15	14
Family	10	8
Self Score	**= 100**	**= 74**

His total Self Score was 74%. Here's how he evaluated Rita:

1. **Financial Stability**: Garrett was initially impressed to learn that Rita was working toward a doctorate, but he quickly concluded that she must be buried in debt. Given her age and level of study, student loans seemed inevitable to him. As they spent more time together, he discovered she shared a campus apartment with a roommate. What really struck him was her apparent lack of urgency to move out or tackle her debt before completing her education. Financial security was a top priority for Garrett, one he felt she didn't share. Based on this, he felt compelled to give her a low Score of 10/30.

2. **Social Status**: Garrett genuinely respected Rita's pursuit of her doctorate, seeing it as a significant achievement that mirrored his own aspirations for success. He recognized not just the academic prestige of such a pursuit but also its potential to elevate her social standing. Also, when Rita told him that she hailed from a well-to-do family involved in community events and politics, Garrett's admiration only deepened. Impressed by her background and ambition, he rated her highly, giving her a Score of 23/25 in this category.

3. **Knowledge/Wisdom**: Garrett deeply appreciated Rita's outlook on life, recognizing it as a reflection of the profound knowledge and wisdom she'd acquired through extensive travel and advanced education. Her wealth of experience and adventure had seasoned her with a level of wisdom that surpassed her age, a trait Garrett found extraordinary. This remarkable depth and understanding led him to give her a high Score of 17/20.

4. **Self-Care**: Garrett noticed that Rita was a little disheveled; her hair was a bit of a mess and the stain on her shirt didn't go unnoticed. He thought she looked like she had just rolled out of bed and into the line. Although he acknowledged internally that his focus on her appearance might be considered shallow, the value he placed on personal

grooming and self-care influenced his impression. With this in mind, he assigned her a Score of 7/15.

5. **Family**: Garrett felt a surge of inspiration when Rita shared her dream of starting a family. Her values mirrored his own, with both of them cherishing their close family ties and aspiring to extend this warmth to their future households. Rita, with her three sisters and their shared vision of having children and building large, supportive families, struck him as profoundly family oriented. In his eyes, she was among the most dedicated to the family he'd ever encountered, and this rarity earned her a perfect Score of 10/10 in his book.

Table 2: *Garrett's Partner Values Score for Rita*

Conscious Values	Importance (%)	Partner Evaluation
Financial Stability	30	10
Social Status	25	23
Knowledge/Wisdom	20	17
Self-Care	15	7
Family	10	10
Partner Values Score	= 100	**= 67**

Her Values Scores fell a bit short, according to Garrett's calculations, at just 67%. However, let's see how Garrett assessed Rita in his Top 5 Traits. They included *good energy (30%), open-mindedness (25%), strong presence (20%), witty/clever (15%),* and *kind (10%).*

1. **Good Energy**: Although Garrett was an extrovert, there were only a few people he truly felt comfortable with. He considered himself an intuitive individual and trusted his gut. When it came to Rita, it was like they were kindred spirits. He immediately sensed good energy from her, which put him at ease. He gave her a 28/30 in this area.

2. **Open-Mindedness**: Garrett found himself wholly immersed in his conversation with Rita, discovering an array of impressive facets of her life. Her extensive travels and fluency in three languages stood out, showcasing her worldly experience. Rita's adventurous spirit, evidenced by her willingness to try any food and embark on new journeys at a moment's notice, left a significant mark on him. Reflecting on these qualities, he gave her a high Score of 22/25.

3. **Strong Presence**: Garrett was drawn to women who radiate confidence and can command a room with their presence, finding leadership qualities and charisma incredibly appealing. Rita, however, initially seemed shy and reserved, not quite fitting this mold until she began to open up. Recognizing her potential to grow into the kind of assertive presence he admired, he acknowledged this budding quality and gave her a score of 10/20, hopeful for her continued development.

4. **Witty/Clever**: Initially reserved, Rita quickly revealed herself to be incredibly sharp-witted, matching Garrett's dark, dry, and sarcastic humor with ease. Her quick comebacks were a delightful surprise, clearly showcasing her intellect. Garrett was thoroughly impressed by her ability to engage in witty banter, keeping the conversation lively and entertaining. She had a unique way of keeping him amused and alert. Reflecting on this dynamism, he gave her a high score of 13/15.

5. **Kindness**: From their first meeting, Garrett was struck by Rita's extraordinary kindness. It shone through in the way she engaged with the coffee shop staff and extended to her interactions with everyone around her. Rita's behavior radiated warmth and thoughtfulness, making those in her presence feel welcomed and valued. To Garrett, this trait was fundamental in highlighting Rita as a person who truly prioritizes the well-being of others. Impressed by her genuine compassion, he awarded her a perfect Score of 10/10.

Table 3: *Garrett's Partner Traits Score for Rita*

Traits	Importance (%)	Evaluation
Good Energy	30	28
Open-Minded	25	22
Strong Presence	20	10
Witty/Clever	15	13
Kindness	10	10
Partner Traits Score	= 100	**= 83**

An 83% for Traits! *Not bad!* Table 4 illustrates Garrett's approach to evaluating potential partners, striking a balance between Values and Traits. Unlike Rita, who might lean more toward one over the other, Garrett views both aspects as being of equal importance. For him, the essence of a person's character (Values) and their personal attributes or qualities (Traits) held equal weight in his consideration, making his preference an even split: fifty-fifty.

Table 4: *Garrett's Priority Allocation*

Values	50
Traits	50
Total	**= 100**

His calculation for his Partner Score looked like this:
Partner Values = (67) ÷ 100 x (50) **= 34**
Partner Traits = (83) ÷ 100 x (50) **= 41.5**

Table 5: *Garrett's Partner Score for Rita*

Partner Values Score	34.0
Partner Traits Score	41.5
Partner Score	**= 76** (rounded from 75.5)

Table 6: *Garrett's Love Formula Score*

Garrett (Self Score)	= 74%
Rita (Partner Score)	= 76%
Love Formula Score	**= -2%**

Garrett saw Rita as a true gem. The undeniable chemistry between them fueled his optimism for what lay ahead (results in Table 6). The standout aspect of their Love Formula results was how each discovered in the other a partner who excelled in certain areas—enough to be admirable yet still relatable. This realization gave them a shared excitement and a sense of incredible luck; they felt fortunate to have found someone who struck such a perfect balance.

Garrett and Rita indeed appear to have hit the jackpot with their Love Formula results. They both regard each other highly in terms of Values and Traits, laying a promising groundwork for a deeper connection. The future of their relationship now hinges on their willingness to put in the work—through communicating openly, maintaining equilibrium, and fortifying their bond. While the Love Formula has pointed them in the right direction, their continuous effort to nurture their relationship is key to its longevity and growth.

Let's take a look at another couple and how the Love Formula can give very clear clues pointing to compatibility—or a lack thereof.

Chapter 8

Tiffany and John Swipe Right

Meet Tiffany and John. Unlike Rita and Garrett, these two crossed paths through an online dating app. After the initial interaction of liking each other's posts and photos, they moved on to messaging, where the real getting-to-know process began. As they delved deeper into each other's digital profiles, it became increasingly clear that their online personas seemed to be in perfect harmony.

Tiffany's profile was a vibrant showcase of her adventures, from summiting peaks through cuddling with her dog to dressing to the nines for an evening out. On the other hand, John's profile featured his daring jet ski escapades, a laid-back beach day with friends (abs on full display), and moments where he was all dressed up, capturing his adventurous spirit and flair for style.

Following their initial spark, John took the next step and asked Tiffany out for lunch, an invitation she quickly accepted.

Tiffany

Tiffany, curious and hopeful, turned to the Love Formula to see if it could predict the success of her upcoming date with John. Her Top 5 Values included *dependability/reliability, health consciousness, philanthropy, career,* and *street smarts*. She assigned an equal importance to each Value, giving them all a 20% weight. Here's how Tiffany assessed herself:

1. **Dependability/Reliability**: Tiffany placed a high value on dependability, viewing it as essential for a lasting relationship. This Value represented a commitment to support one's partner in every circumstance—good or bad, in health and sickness. Confident in her capacity to be

a steadfast and supportive partner, Tiffany scored herself at 18/20 on dependability.

2. **Career**: Fresh out of college, Tiffany had embarked on an internship at NASA, a milestone that filled her with optimism for what lay ahead. Even with the nagging uncertainties about landing a full-time role there, she couldn't help but feel proud of her achievements. Reflecting on her progress and the promise of her future, she awarded herself a 19/20.

3. **Health Consciousness**: During her high school years, Tiffany battled an eating disorder, a struggle that carried over into her college life. It was then that she decided to seek therapy, a choice that set her on the road to recovery. With the guidance of her therapist, who introduced her to a health coach, Tiffany gained control over her eating habits. She found a healthy balance between nutritious eating and consistent exercise, maintaining a strong and fit physique. Reflecting on her journey to wellness, Tiffany scored herself at 18/20.

4. **Philanthropy**: Tiffany held passionate views on the perilous path humanity was treading, especially concerning climate change. An activist at heart, she was deeply committed to finding solutions to combat the root causes of escalating natural disasters, believing firmly in the collective duty to safeguard the planet for both present and future generations. Yet, after starting her career, her time for activism was significantly limited. The gap between her ideals and her ability to actively participate in environmental causes weighed heavily on her, leading her to assign herself a score of 9/20 in this area.

5. **Street Smarts**: Tiffany was a firm believer in the necessity of street smarts. Given the ease with which people can be deceived or exploited in today's world, she felt it was crucial to be aware and cautious. She prided herself on her ability to discern when someone might be attempting to take advantage of her, never turning a blind eye to potential

dangers. Confident in her alertness to and savviness in handling such situations, Tiffany gave herself a high score of 19/20.

Here's how Tiffany laid out her assessments:

Table 1: *Tiffany's Self Score*

Values	Importance (%)	Self-Evaluation
Dependability/Reliability	20	18
Career	20	19
Health Consciousness	20	18
Philanthropy	20	9
Street Smarts	20	19
Self Score	**= 100**	**= 83**

Overall, Tiffany scored 83%. Based on her initial impressions from their exchanges on the dating app, his online profile, and their first in-person meeting, here's how Tiffany evaluated John:

1. **Dependability/Reliability**: Tiffany naturally leaned toward trusting others, giving them the benefit of the doubt and holding them in high esteem until proven otherwise. She approached new interactions with an open heart, assuming good intentions and integrity, unless someone proved unworthy of her trust. However, John had stumbled early on in their acquaintance. Despite them making plans for Taco Tuesday, he had canceled mere hours before they were supposed to meet, leaving Tiffany disappointed. Though frustrated, she was ready to give him a second chance, hoping he'd redeem himself at their next arranged meeting. Reflecting on this, Tiffany cautiously rated him a 10/20 in this category.

2. **Career**: John held a significant position as a partner at a reputable accounting firm, a role he had maintained for

five years with plans for continued advancement within the company. Tiffany couldn't help but admire his leadership status, ambition, and dedication to his career. His drive for progress in life further compounded her respect for him. Impressed by his professional achievements and forward-moving mindset, Tiffany rated him highly, giving him an 18/20.

3. **Health Consciousness**: John was a devout gym enthusiast, hitting the gym twice a day: once in the morning and again after work. He was meticulous about his diet and always conscious of his physical appearance. There was a time when he might have taken his gym commitment to the extreme, experimenting with various steroids to enhance his muscular build and achieve that "manly" look. Tiffany didn't exactly condone the use of steroids, but this didn't prevent her from valuing his extensive understanding of physical fitness and body awareness. With this in mind, she scored him a 16/20.

4. **Philanthropy**: John appeared to be largely unaware of significant global concerns. When Tiffany brought up Greta Thunberg, a figurehead in climate activism, John seemed clueless and showed little interest in learning more. The topic of the climate crisis seemed to halt the flow of their discussion, as John preferred to stay disengaged from such issues. This left Tiffany feeling disheartened, yet she couldn't help but wonder if there was a chance his interest in these issues might be sparked in the future. Reflecting on her disappointment yet holding onto a sliver of hope, she scored him a 4/20.

5. **Street Smarts**: John struck Tiffany as exceptionally street-wise. Their conversations showcased his vast experience in dealing with diverse personalities and skillfully navigating through challenging situations with ease. He was anything but naive; his keen intelligence was evident, and Tiffany found a sense of comfort, security, and protection in his company.

Impressed by his savvy approach to life and the assurance he offered, she awarded him an 18/20 in this area.

Table 2: *Tiffany's Partner Values Score for John*

Values	Importance (%)	Partner Evaluation
Dependability/Reliability	20	10
Career	20	18
Health Consciousness	20	16
Philanthropy	20	4
Street Smarts	20	18
Partner Values Score	= 100	**= 66**

Tiffany assessed herself at 83% and John at 66% in terms of Values alignment (Table 2). Next, she turned her attention to evaluating how John matched up with the Traits she typically looks for in a partner. She outlined her Top 5 Traits, assigning equal importance of 20% to each: *ambitious/driven, intelligent/sharp, alpha/dominant, good physique,* and *emotionally unavailable.* Here's how she scored John:

1. **Ambitious/Driven**: Tiffany was naturally attracted to men who exhibited a strong sense of purpose, individuals who knew exactly what they wanted and were unwavering in their pursuit of it. John fit this description to a T. He had well-defined goals and consistently applied his efforts and energy toward achieving them. Impressed by this trait, Tiffany rated him an 18/20.

2. **Intelligent/Sharp**: John had the credentials, but did that make him a true intellectual in Tiffany's eyes? For her, there was a distinct line between being well-educated and being genuinely intelligent. Intelligence, as she saw it, meant having the capacity for critical thinking, a willingness to learn, and the ability to apply knowledge to form well-reasoned views and conclusions about the world. While

she valued education highly, Tiffany was also aware that being educated doesn't automatically equate to being intelligent. In her opinion, John fell short in this domain. His interest seemed confined to finance, and any attempt to diverge into other topics hit a wall, as he contributed little to nothing outside his comfort zone. This one-dimensional focus led Tiffany to give him a Score of 10/20 in this area.

3. **Alpha/Dominant**: Tiffany was aware that being attracted to leadership qualities and the confidence to take the reins could be a double-edged quality, especially considering her track record with alpha males. Nonetheless, she found herself gravitating toward these types again and again. John, with his unmistakable alpha presence—evident in his posture, tone, and actions—exemplified the kind of man who wasn't just in the room but commanded it. Impressed by his natural leadership, Tiffany rated him highly with a 19/20, acknowledging her enduring attraction to those who lead with assurance.

4. **Physique**: Tiffany's eyes always lingered a bit longer on men who prioritized their physical fitness. John, standing taller than her with a physique that struck the right balance between subtly muscular and fit, caught her attention— effortlessly. Whether he was dressed in a sharp suit and tie or more casually attired with his shirt off, John carried himself with a poise and grace that was downright captivating. His flawless posture and the smooth, confident way he moved had Tiffany thoroughly charmed. Acknowledging this magnetic physical allure, she awarded him an 18/20.

5. **Emotionally Unavailable**: Beyond her inclination toward dominant men, Tiffany found herself inexplicably attracted to those who were emotionally distant. She pondered over this attraction: Was it the challenge they posed, like a tricky puzzle? The sort of challenge that, despite its frustrations, felt incredibly rewarding once solved? The exact allure

remained a mystery, yet the attraction was undeniable. John, fitting snugly into this emotionally unavailable archetype, captivated her for reasons she couldn't fully articulate. Thus, she rated him an 18/20, acknowledging the strong pull she felt toward this complex type.

Table 3: *Tiffany's Partner Traits Score for John*

Traits	Importance (%)	Partner Evaluation
Ambitious/Driven	20	18
Intelligent/Sharp	20	10
Alpha Male/Dominant	20	19
Physique	20	18
Emotionally Unavailable	20	18
Partner Traits Score	= 100	**= 83**

Tiffany gave John an impressive Score of 83% on Traits (Table 3). But when it came down to her perspective on love and relationships, was she more inclined toward Traits or Values? While Tiffany aimed for a practical approach in matters of the heart, her emotions frequently tipped the scales, drawing her more intensely toward Traits. Consequently, she found herself valuing Traits much more.

Table 4: *Tiffany's Priority Allocation*

Values	**20**
Traits	**80**
Total	**= 100**

Her calculation for her Partner Score looked like this:
Partner Values = (66) ÷ 100 x (20) **= 13.2**
Partner Traits = (83) ÷ 100 x (80) **= 66.4**

Table 5: *Tiffany's Partner Score for John*

Partner Values Score	13.2
Partner Traits Score	66.4
Partner Score	**= 80** (rounded from 79.6)

Table 6: *Tiffany's Love Formula Score*

Tiffany (Self Score)	= 81%
John (Partner Score)	= 80%
Love Formula Score	**= +1%**

With a mere 1% difference between their Scores (Table 6), Tiffany saw it as a sign of compatibility! She was optimistic about their future together and decided to keep seeing John, looking forward to what their next dates might bring. Let's explore how John viewed their budding relationship.

John

John's Top 5 Values were *image, health consciousness, social skills, political ideology,* and *education,* each Value weighted at 20%. Here's how he assessed himself in these areas:

1. **Image**: John carried himself with confidence and a keen awareness of his appearance, thriving on the attention he garnered when stepping out in style. Something about slipping into a fine suit made him feel not just seen but respected— like a true professional with presence. In his eyes, this not only elevated his status but also amplified his appeal, granting him a sense of importance, allure, and self-assurance. Reflecting on how his image impacted his confidence and how others perceived him, he awarded himself a 19/20.

2. **Health Consciousness**: John was a staunch vegan, convinced that a focus on health was essential for everyone. His daily

routine included making smoothies thrice and practicing intermittent fasting to stay trim. Aware of the need to counterbalance his previous steroid use, he took his dietary and exercise regimen seriously. Given his commitment to maintaining his health, albeit with an acknowledgment of past choices, he assigned himself an 18/20 in this category.

3. **Social Skills**: John had always been acutely aware of the importance of social skills in both his personal and professional life. Growing up, he had witnessed firsthand the power of charm and charisma in winning people over and forging strong connections. In his professional sphere, John's adeptness at networking and fostering positive relationships played a pivotal role in his success. Outside of work, John's social prowess served him equally well. Overall, John rated himself 18/20 for social skills.

4. **Political Ideology**: John was a die-hard Republican, sticking to his guns when it came to beliefs about wealth and hard work. He saw liberals as the ones promoting laziness and dependency, which he thought was dragging America down. Those so-called handouts? Totally liberal agenda in his book. He felt dead-on about his political ideology, though he wished he had more time to keep up with everything happening on the political scene. Still, he gave himself an 18/20.

5. **Education**: John firmly believed in the adage that education equals power. To him, investing in education was not just about gaining knowledge; it was about elevating oneself to a position of respect and influence in society. He held great admiration for individuals who dedicated themselves to their academic pursuits. As a proud graduate of Stanford University, John saw his educational background as a testament to his hard work and determination. Reflecting on the value of education in shaping his life and opportunities, he gave himself a rating of 19/20.

Here's how John laid out his assessments:

Table 1: *John's Self Score*

Values	Importance (%)	Self-Evaluation
Image	20	19
Health Consciousness	20	18
Social Skills	20	18
Political Ideology	20	18
Education	20	19
Self Score	**= 100**	**= 92**

Overall, John assigned himself a solid 92%. Then he turned the same lens on Tiffany to assess her against the same Values:

1. **Image**: When he first met Tiffany, she had that "girl-next-door" charm that instantly caught his eye. Before her, the women who usually showed interest in him had a certain look, the Nicole Kidman type. Sure, they were easy on the eyes, but it was their warmth and approachability that really drew him in. Tiffany was different, though—in a refreshing way. He rated his connection with her a solid 19/20.

2. **Health Consciousness**: John really admired how Tiffany had managed to beat her eating disorder, but he still worried about her eating patterns. Sure, she had a health coach, but John felt uneasy about the advice being given to her. He wondered why she hadn't been swayed toward veganism yet. To him, going vegan was the clear choice for clean eating. He rated her progress in this area a 16/20, hoping for more improvement.

3. **Social Skills**: Tiffany was a total firecracker! Her laugh was contagious, and she always had a joke up her sleeve, making even the servers crack up. She radiated confidence and charisma, drawing people in like a magnet. Her conversations had this way of leaving a mark, so much so that even the manager had come over to their table just

to say hi and thank her. Yet, this vibrant personality didn't fully match the sweet, girl-next-door type John usually fell for. Still, he rated her a solid 19/20.

4. **Political Ideology**: John and Tiffany never really dove into political discussions, but John could tell Tiffany leaned liberal. With her enthusiasm for Al Gore, she found a way to weave climate change into nearly every chat. Tiffany made her points in a way that was persuasive and logical yet never pushy, showcasing her well-rounded understanding of political matters. Even though John respected her political savviness, he wasn't much for delving into liberal ideologies himself. So he ended up rating Tiffany a 6/20 on that front.

5. **Education**: Tiffany was both smart and well-educated, something that really stood out to John, especially with an internship at NASA under her belt. He had immense respect for her academic achievements and career aspirations. Her impressive background almost made him overlook her pretty intense political views. In light of all her accomplishments and ambitions, John felt she deserved a perfect score, so he gave her 20/20.

Table 2: *John's Partner Values Score for Tiffany*

Values	Importance (%)	Partner Evaluation
Image	20	19
Health Consciousness	20	16
Social Skills	20	19
Political Ideology	20	6
Education	20	20
Partner Values Score	= 100	**= 80**

Let's break down Tiffany's qualities based on John's Top 5 Traits, each accounting for 20% of the total Score. They included *physical appearance, spontaneousness/open-mindedness, forgiveness, mild-*

mannered and *emotional independence.* Here's how he rated her and his reasoning:

1. **Physical Appearance**: Just like in the category of overall image, Tiffany stood out in terms of body shape, height, and general appearance. John was particularly taken by the natural, unassuming beauty she possessed. Because she aligned so closely with what he looked for physically, he felt she deserved a near-perfect Score, so he awarded her a 19/20.

2. **Spontaneous/Open-minded**: John found Tiffany to be on the serious and inflexible side. From their initial interaction, it was clear to him that letting loose and going with the flow wasn't her strong suit. He anticipated that being with her might mean sticking to a tight script guided by firm rules and expectations, with little room for spontaneity. Reflecting on this, he rated her a 9/20.

3. **Forgiving**: John preferred women who were forgiving and allowed him the space to be himself, to act on his whims. This had previously led to conflicts in his relationships. Was he aware that his expectations might be seen as unreasonable or unfair? Absolutely. But changing his ways wasn't something he was prepared for. He gravitated toward partners who wouldn't push him into certain roles or make him feel guilty for prioritizing his needs. In considering a relationship with Tiffany, he sensed that he'd likely have to adjust his behavior to meet her expectations. With this in mind, he gave Tiffany an 11/20.

4. **Mild-Mannered**: John saw himself as a bit of an old-fashioned guy, naturally gravitating toward women who were gentle and reserved. He wasn't too keen on women who were very outspoken, perhaps even feeling a bit daunted by them. He preferred the quiet strength of women who could maintain their poise under pressure. Unfortunately, Tiffany didn't quite embody this. She wasn't shy about voicing her displeasure toward him, occasionally

in a tone that came off as rather forceful. Reflecting on this, he gave her a Score of 8/20.

5. **Emotionally Independent**: John was naturally attracted to women who stood strong on their own, those who didn't need his constant attention or presence. However, Tiffany didn't quite give him that impression. While she came across as kind-hearted, he couldn't shake the feeling that she might end up being overly attached, wanting more of his time and affection than he was willing to give. Taking this into account, he gave her a 10/20.

Table 3: *John's Partner Traits Score for Tiffany*

Traits	Importance (%)	Partner Evaluation
Physical Appearance	20	19
Spontaneousness/ Open-Mindedness	20	9
Forgiving	20	11
Mild-Mannered	20	8
Emotional Independence	20	10
Partner Traits Score	= 100	**= 57**

John struck a healthy balance between the importance of Values and Traits in a partner, choosing to divide his focus equally at a fifty-fifty ratio (Table 4).

Table 4: *John's Priority Allocation*

Values	50
Traits	50
Total	**= 100**

His calculation for his Partner Score looked like this:
Partner Values = (80) ÷ 100 x (50) **= 40**
Partner Traits = (57) ÷ 100 x (50) **= 28.5**

Table 5: *John's Partner Score for Tiffany*

Partner Values Score	40.0
Partner Traits Score	28.5
Partner Score	**= 69** (rounded from 68.5)

Table 6: *John's Love Formula Score*

John (Self Score)	= 92%
Tiffany (Partner Score)	= 69%
Love Formula Score	**= +23%**

John rated Tiffany 23% below his Self Score, which is clearly too large of a gap for a successful relationship. This realization led him to conclude that pursuing further dates with her wouldn't be wise. Opting for the most practical approach, he decided against continuing their interactions, believing it best to avoid wasting both their time.

As this example illustrates, a single encounter can lead to vastly different perceptions, with one individual feeling they've discovered their ideal partner, while the other perceiving no potential future. This disparity highlights the power of the Love Formula. It offers a systematic, objective framework for assessing compatibility within a relationship, safeguarding the individuals involved against the whirlwind of emotions that often accompany a first date.

In other words, first dates might have you feeling on top of the world or utterly perplexed, but the Love Formula is your tool for making informed and grounded decisions about your relationship.

Chapter 9

Stephanie and Wayne's Story of Love and Loss

Stephanie and Wayne shared many years of blissful marriage, welcoming two children into their lives. Their paths first intersected thanks to mutual friends, sparking an immediate and powerful attraction that made them feel like they were perfect for each other. Like many couples, their love story followed a traditional path: dating, engagement, marriage, buying a home, and then starting a family.

However, as Stephanie and Wayne navigated major life milestones, they each experienced personal growth, albeit in different directions. Over time, it became clear that this growth led them to drift apart, ultimately resulting in their breakup. In this case study, we'll examine the evolution of a couple's Love Formula, contrasting their initial compatibility from ten years ago with their situation today.

Love Formula Ten Years Ago

Stephanie

Ten years ago, when Stephanie was twenty-seven years old, she felt ready to settle down. Meeting Wayne only deepened her desire to get married and begin a family. She believed she had found her soulmate—a conviction that made her all the more eager to move forward with her life plans. Her Love Formula Scores in that year are shown below:

Table 1: *Stephanie's Self Score (Ten Years Ago)*

Values	Importance%	Self-Evaluation
Financial Choices	30	20
Career	25	20
Family	20	20
Social Status	15	12
Dependability	10	10
Self Score	**= 100**	**= 82**

Here Stephanie meticulously prioritized her list of Values in a clear hierarchy. Financial choices topped her list, even though she felt she hadn't achieved the success she desired in this area. Conversely, she exuded full confidence in the areas of family and dependability, which are arguably among the most essential Values for a long-term relationship. Initially hesitant to include social status as one of her Values, she ultimately decided to be true to herself and her evaluations. She understood that others might judge her for this choice if they knew, but she needed to be true to herself in this process.

Table 2: *Stephanie's Partner Values Score for Wayne (Ten Years Ago)*

Values	Importance (%)	Partner Evaluation
Financial Choices	30	25
Career	25	25
Family	20	11
Social Status	15	15
Dependability	10	5
Partner Values Score	**= 100**	**= 81**

Overall, Stephanie evaluated Wayne to be a very good match for her. Where she felt she was lacking, Wayne scored higher. Notably, in areas where she felt strong, such as *family* and *dependability*, he seemed to fall short. However, despite these differences, he was an almost perfect match in terms of Values, and she respected him wholeheartedly.

Table 3: *Stephanie's Partner Traits Score for Wayne (Ten Years Ago)*

Traits	Importance (%)	Partner Evaluation
Physique	20	20
Humor	20	20
Intelligence	20	20
Extroversion	20	15
Kindness	20	10
Partner Traits Score	= 100	**= 85**

Stephanie rated Wayne at 85%, indicating a strong attraction to him. However, his Score was noticeably lower in areas such as *extroversion* and *kindness*. She sometimes wished he were more outgoing and less selective about whom he socialized with. Additionally, she had witnessed a few instances of him displaying somewhat mean tendencies, which frankly turned her off. Despite these issues, she was highly emotionally attracted to Wayne overall.

Table 4: *Stephanie's Priority Allocation (Ten Years Ago)*

Values	50
Traits	50
Total	**= 100**

Here Stephanie was notably balanced in her priority allocation, giving equal importance to both Values and Traits.

Stephanie's Love Formula for Wayne's Partner Score looked like this (ten years ago):
Partner Values = (81) ÷ 100 x (50) **= 40.5**
Partner Traits = (85) ÷ 100 x (50) **= 42.5**

Table 5: *Stephanie's Partner Score for Wayne (Ten Years Ago)*

Partner Values Score	40.5
Partner Traits Score	42.5
Partner Score	**= 83**

The Partner Score she calculated for Wayne was 83%, taking into account both Values and Traits (Table 5).

Table 6: *Stephanie's Love Formula Total Score (Ten Years Ago)*

Stephanie (Self Score)	82
Wayne (Partner Score)	83
Love Formula Score	**= -1%**

Ten years ago, Stephanie rated herself at 82% and Wayne at 83%, indicating only a 1% difference (Table 6). To her, this suggested a remarkable match. No wonder she was ready to tie the knot with him and embark on a journey of marriage, children, and a lifetime together.

Now let's see how Wayne evaluated Stephanie ten years ago.

Wayne

At thirty-five, Wayne had grown weary of the bachelor lifestyle and was ready to settle down. Meeting Stephanie was a turning point; he felt he had finally found someone who matched him in all the important ways. He believed she would be an excellent partner and mother. Beyond his affection, Wayne also developed a deep sense of trust in Stephanie. His Love Formula Scores for that year, outlined below, reflect these feelings.

Table 1: *Wayne's Self Score (Ten Years Ago)*

Values	Importance (%)	Self-Evaluation
Communication/Manners	30	25
Family	25	23
Dependability	20	17
Education	15	15
Self-Care	10	10
Self Score	**= 100**	**= 90**

Wayne's Top 5 Values are listed in a clear hierarchy, each one distinctly ranked by importance. At the top of his list is *communication/manners*, though he acknowledges there is room for improvement in this area. While he rated himself slightly lower in *family* and *dependability*, he still scored an overall 90%, reflecting strong self-respect and a sense of "winning" in life (Table 1).

Table 2: *Wayne's Partner Values Score for Stephanie (Ten Years Ago)*

Values	Importance (%)	Self-Evaluation
Communication/Manners	30	27
Family	25	23
Dependability	20	19
Education	15	12
Self-Care	10	10
Partner Values Score	**= 100**	**= 91**

Wayne believed that Stephanie excelled in *communication/ manners* and *dependability*—more so than him. He considered himself more accomplished than her in *education*. Overall, though, he thought they balanced each other out quite well and had a very strong sense of respect for her, as reflected in his Partner Values Score of 91% (Table 2).

Table 3: *Wayne's Partner Traits Score for Stephanie*

Traits	Importance (%)	Partner Evaluation
Physique	20	17
Mild-Mannered	20	20
Humor	20	20
Generosity	20	20
Sensuality	20	15
Partner Traits Score	= 100	**= 92**

Wayne had a clear understanding of his ideal type, and all the traits held equal importance to him in terms of attraction. Stephanie fit his type almost perfectly. He gave her top marks in the *mild-mannered*, *humor*, and *generosity*. However, he docked some marks for *physique*, as he was accustomed to more athletic women, while she was the petite, feminine type. He also deducted significant points for *sensuality*, perceiving her to be more reserved than what he generally preferred. Overall, he rated her at 92%, indicating a very strong attraction (Table 3).

Table 4: *Wayne's Priority Allocation (Ten Years Ago)*

Values	40
Traits	60
Total	**= 100**

Wayne placed a slightly higher priority on attraction over lifestyle alignment, as the stimulation it provided was very important to him. For that reason, he did a sixty-forty split in favor of Traits (Table 4).

Wayne's calculation for Stephanie's Partner Score looked like this (ten years ago):

Partner Values = (91) ÷ 100 x (40) **= 36.4**

Partner Traits = (92) ÷ 100 x (60) **= 55.2**

Table 5: *Wayne's Partner Score for Stephanie (Ten Years Ago)*

Partner Values Score	**36.4**
Partner Traits Score	**55.2**
Partner Score	**= 92** (rounded from 91.6)

Wayne assigned Stephanie a 92% Partner Score, which means he felt she was a real catch and that he was lucky to have her (Table 5).

Table 6: *Wayne's Love Formula Score (Ten Years Ago)*

Wayne (Self Score)	= 90%
Stephanie (Partner Score)	= 92%
Love Formula Score	**= -2%**

Wayne's Love Formula calculations resulted in a -2% difference (Table 6), solidifying his belief that Stephanie was indeed the right person for him. With such closely matching Scores, Stephanie and Wayne seemed to be each other's ideal partners. They not only shared the same outlook on life but also felt an undeniable attraction to one another. Their connection seemed like destiny at work! Now let's turn our attention to their current Love Formula Scores to see how things have evolved.

Love Formula Present Day

Stephanie

After years of dedication to the man she had chosen as her life partner, Stephanie started sensing a void. The past decade had been a journey of profound wisdom, personal development, and significant changes. She still held a deep affection for Wayne, but her passion for him had faded. Doubts had started creeping in, leaving her questioning if Wayne was truly the one meant for her. Table 1 illustrates her current Love Formula.

Table 1: *Stephanie's Self Score (Current)*

Values	Importance (%)	Self-Evaluation
Dependability	30	30
Pursuing a Greater Purpose	25	20
Family	20	20
Financial Choices	15	10
Education	10	5
Self Score	= 100	**= 85**

Over the last ten years, she had experienced significant changes. While Wayne was her ideal match at the beginning, she realized that her interests, hobbies, and values were evolving year after year. Though she loved Wayne and couldn't imagine life without him, she gradually found herself settling into a relationship that no longer aligned with her evolved values. For instance, financial stability was always a top priority, but she now longed for adventure, travel, and cultural experiences. *Dependability*, which was her fifth most important Value, had now become her top priority. *Social status*, once a significant value, had completely disappeared from her Top 5 list. Instead, she now prioritized *pursuing a greater purpose*, a value that wasn't even on her list a decade ago. *Education* had also become important, whereas it wasn't a priority before. *Financial choices*, previously her number one value, had dropped to fourth position in her list. Clearly, her priorities had shifted as she matured.

Table 2: *Stephanie's Partner Values Score for Wayne (Current)*

Values	Importance (%)	Partner Evaluation
Dependability	30	15
Pursuing a Greater Purpose	25	15
Family	20	17
Financial Choices	15	15
Education	10	10
Partner Values Score	= 100	**= 72**

Stephanie's growth also revealed that she had "outgrown" Wayne, with a 13% difference emerging between them in Values. As *dependability* became increasingly important to her, she meticulously analyzed her relationship with Wayne. In the beginning, Wayne was not the steadfast partner she had hoped for, losing half his previous Score in this area. Over the years, he remained the same person and made little effort to improve. Unfortunately for Wayne, as Stephanie grew, so did her need for a dependable partner. With her expanding life experiences and a growing desire for a greater purpose, she also evaluated Wayne in this regard and found him lacking. Interestingly, she observed an improvement in his *family* category, noting that he had become a better father and took good care of their children. She considered him a rockstar in *financial choices*, though this Value had diminished in importance for her. Ultimately, Wayne was no longer a genuine match for the Values she now held dear.

Table 3: *Stephanie's Partner Traits Score for Wayne (Current)*

Traits	Importance (%)	Partner Evaluation
Physique	20	15
Humor	20	16
Intelligence	20	20
Extroversion	20	15
Kindness	20	10
Partner Traits Score	= 100	**=76**

In the beginning, Stephanie was completely smitten by Wayne and couldn't wait to cuddle up in his arms. However, over the years, she realized she was craving something more—more stimulating, less predictable, and more fun. Watching other couples laugh together and show constant affection made her realize the spark she once had with Wayne had significantly dwindled.

Interestingly, the list of Traits she found attractive hadn't changed in the last ten years; she still got attracted to the same "type" of guy. However, Wayne's physique seemed to have slipped in her eyes, and she no longer gave him top marks, docking him from his previous Score. Humor too had lost its charm; what had once captivated her now seemed predictable, childish, and sometimes even offensive. Despite these changes, she still deeply admired Wayne's intelligence and quick-wittedness, giving him full marks in this area and considering it his most attractive quality. Finally, she gave him the same Score for kindness, as she didn't perceive him as having evolved or devolved much in that regard.

Table 4: *Stephanie's Priority Allocation (Current)*

Values	60
Traits	40
Total	**= 100**

Ten years later, Stephanie's priorities began shifting more toward Values than Traits (Table 4). In other words, she started seeking lifestyle alignment slightly more than physical and emotional attraction.

Stephanie's Love Formula calculations for Wayne's Partner Score look like this now:
Partner Values = (72) ÷ 100 x (60) **= 43.2**
Partner Traits = (76) ÷ 100 x (40) **= 30.4**

Table 5: *Stephanie's Partner Score for Wayne (Current)*

Partner Values Score	43.2
Partner Traits Score	30.4
Partner Score	**= 74** (rounded from 73.6)

Table 6: *Stephanie's Love Formula Score (Current)*

Stephanie (Self Score)	= 85%
Wayne (Partner Score)	= 74%
Love Formula Score	**= +11%**

In her current Love Formula evaluation, there's a significant shift in Stephanie's feelings toward Wayne. Previously, he had a slight 1% advantage, but she is up by 11% (Table 6).

Wayne

Over the years, Wayne's core Values and Traits remained largely the same as when he first met Stephanie, with only minor shifts occurring over time. Below is his summary for the present day:

Table 1: *Wayne's Self Score (Current)*

Values	Importance (%)	Self-Evaluation
Communication/Manners	30	25
Family	25	25
Dependability	20	13
Education	15	15
Self-Care	10	10
Self Score	**= 100**	**= 88**

Wayne, a creature of habit, had not evolved much from his list of Values over the past ten years. They remained the same, with the same hierarchy of importance. He acknowledged that his *communication* hadn't improved and that he hadn't made significant efforts in this area either. Remarkably, his Score in this category didn't change at all. Over the years, he perceived himself as getting better in his *family* category, especially since he perceived himself as an awesome dad. Although his intentions were always good, he recognized that he could have been a better husband to Stephanie and that he had failed to be her rock in many moments throughout their relationship. Because of this, he lowered his Score substantially for *dependability*, and now it was even lower than it was ten years ago. Finally, *education* and *self-care* remained unchanged. Overall, he still respected himself strongly, though his Score was 2% lower than it had been ten years ago.

Table 2: *Wayne's Partner Values Score for Stephanie (Current)*

Values	Importance (%)	Partner Evaluation
Communication/Manners	30	30
Family	25	25
Dependability	20	20
Education	15	12
Self-Care	10	8
Partner Values Score	**= 100**	**= 95**

Over time, Wayne felt that Stephanie aligned more closely with his Values, especially in *communication/manners*, *family*, and *dependability*. She had truly proven herself to be a strong partner and a reliable rock during times of crisis. However, he noticed that her *self-care* had slipped compared to ten years ago. He understood this, given the demands of raising their kids, but he couldn't ignore the change altogether. Still, his respect for her had grown even more over the years. He admired how she excelled in many areas and felt proud to have her by his side. Overall, he rated her 95% (Table 2), a remarkably high Partner Values Score.

Table 3: *Wayne's Partner Traits Score for Stephanie (Current)*

Traits	Importance (%)	Partner Evaluation
Physique	20	20
Mild-Mannered	20	19
Humor	20	20
Generous	20	20
Sensual	20	14
Partner Traits Score	= 100	**= 93**

Wayne's type didn't change over the years. According to his Love Formula, Stephanie became even more attractive to him. There was a slight drop in her *mild-mannered* Trait, perhaps because her approach and demeanor had shifted slightly in his perception. Interestingly, he increased her physique Score from 17 ten years ago to 20 today. Although she hadn't changed much physically, her feminine and petite build had grown on him, making him far more attracted to it than the athletic type he preferred back then. He became enthralled with her. For *sensuality*, he gave her a slightly lower Score, possibly due to a lack of physical intimacy. However, overall Wayne remained as mesmerized by her as when they first met.

Table 4: *Wayne's Priority Allocation (Current)*

Values	50
Traits	50
Total	**= 100**

Over the years, Wayne balanced his priorities between Values and Traits. He believed that both lifestyle alignment and attraction were equally important, so he allocated his focus with a fifty-fifty split (Table 4).

In the present day, Wayne's Love Formula calculations for Stephanie's Partner Score look like this:
Partner Values = (95) ÷ 100 x (50) **= 47.5**
Partner Traits = (93) ÷ 100 x (50) **= 46.5**

Table 5: *Wayne's Partner Score for Stephanie (Current)*

Partner Values Score	47.5
Partner Traits Score	46.5
Partner Score	**= 94**

And so Wayne gave Stephanie an overall 94% Partner Score (Table 5), which is 2% higher than ten years ago.

Table 6: *Wayne's Love Formula Score (Current)*

Wayne (Self Score)	= 88%
Stephanie (Partner Score)	= 94%
Love Formula Score	**= -6%**

Ten years ago, Wayne had scored himself 2% lower than Stephanie. Today, he scored himself 6% less than her. It's clear from the results that Wayne's love for Stephanie had deepened and was now stronger than ever. After a decade together, his feelings of love and respect for her hadn't diminished in the slightest. His admiration for her continued to grow as the years passed, which made the end of their relationship all the more devastating.

So what changed? With each passing year, Stephanie outgrew him as both her Values and Traits evolved. Regrettably, it's a common scenario for one partner to grow and evolve while the other remains unchanged. Stephanie's professional achievements, personal growth, and changing outlook on life contributed to her evolution. She pursued new interests, developed different perspectives, and set higher goals for herself, all of which gradually created a distance between her and Wayne.

Wayne, on the other hand, remained relatively static in his personal development. He found comfort in the familiar and was perhaps less inclined to seek new experiences or challenge his existing beliefs. This disparity in their growth trajectories created a subtle but widening gap in their relationship.

Wayne and Stephanie's story shows us that there are times when both individuals in a relationship undergo significant development. Love has the capacity to survive these evolutions if the changes, particularly in Values, are in harmony. Couples who grow together often find that their shared experiences and mutual support strengthen their bond. They adapt to each other's changes, celebrating their partner's growth as part of their collective journey.

Yet, it's not unusual for couples to drift apart when their paths of growth don't align. When one partner evolves and the other remains the same, it can lead to feelings of frustration, alienation, and dissatisfaction. The once-shared goals and dreams may no longer resonate with both partners, causing a rift that can be difficult to bridge. In Wayne and Stephanie's case, despite Wayne's unwavering love and admiration, the divergence in their personal growth ultimately led to their separation. Their story underscores the importance of synchronized growth and the challenges that arise when one partner's evolution outpaces the other's.

The tale of Stephanie and Wayne serves as a poignant reminder that although love is a potent and wonderful force, it demands ongoing care and the willingness to adapt. Relationships represent a fine equilibrium of shared experiences, evolving personal identities, and the resilience required to manage the alterations life brings. Recognizing the complex relationship between personal development and love can offer crucial insights into forging lasting, satisfying relationships with our partners.

As we wrap up the discussion on how personal growth affects relationships, it's important to understand that our perceptions of Scores aren't set in stone. In the next chapter, we'll explore how day-to-day variations, influenced by both good and bad days, can impact your Love Formula.

Chapter 10

Understanding Your Default Range and Fluctuations

Life is a series of ups and downs, featuring both good and bad days. On the good days, you'll experience joyful and uplifting moments that brighten your mood. But on the tougher days, negative thoughts can creep in, making you think, *Life really sucks right now*.

But what happens when life's ups and downs impact you? Positive and negative fluctuations greatly influence how you see the world, yourself, and your relationship with your partner. Small or big life events can shift your perceptions, potentially changing your Love Formula Scores and even those of your partner.

With this in mind, let's explore how these changes relate to your "Default Range."

Your Default Range refers to the typical range of Self Score and Partner Score you assign based on your Top 5 Values. These Scores can vary in intensity and frequency, changing daily, weekly, or even yearly. There's no set pattern for when these fluctuations occur—they can happen within a specific category or impact your entire set of Top 5 Values.

Now, what does it mean to be in your "low range" as opposed to your "high range"? Being in the low range typically means experiencing a drop in self-esteem, even when nothing significant in your life has changed. Consider that time you had a disagreement with a coworker, employee, or business partner. Recall the frustration you felt over the absurdity and unfairness of the situation. You might have felt undervalued or insulted by the other person's dismissive tone. During these times, your negative mood can cloud your judgment, making it hard to maintain objectivity, likely leading you to assign yourself a lower Score.

So, what happens next?

Minor incidents can set off a cascading effect, leading you to obsess over them and convince yourself that your value has plummeted. A small event might trigger a series of self-sabotaging thoughts, causing you to adopt harmful narratives like the ones listed below:

- "Why doesn't anyone like me?"

- "Why do my coworkers pick on me?"

- "Why are my ideas either ignored or stolen?"

- "I remember feeling this way back in high school. Why do I keep falling into these same old patterns?"

- "Screw this! I'm done with everyone."

These thoughts can quickly spiral, significantly affecting your Self Score. Take Tommy, for example, who has an average daily Self Score of 75%. On tough days, like when he argues with his spouse, faces criticism from his boss, or receives negative feedback at work, his Self Score might drop to around 70%. This frustration from repeated setbacks affects his mood and negatively impacts how he views himself, resulting in a lower Self Score.

Unfortunately, when Tommy's Self Score is at its low end, he risks damaging his relationship. His self-doubt can make him feel inadequate, which in turn affects how he interacts with his partner. He might start to question his worthiness, thinking, "I'm not good enough for them" or "They deserve better." These thoughts can significantly influence his behavior and how he engages with his partner.

Meanwhile, Tommy's partner might notice his emotional withdrawal and mood changes, which could lead them to respond differently, adding to the confusion or concern. This situation highlights the importance of self-awareness and open communication in managing these mood swings. It also emphasizes the need for mutual support to sustain a strong and healthy relationship.

So, what if you find yourself in a low-range situation? It can feel disheartening, but remember that this is not an accurate reflection of your worth. Don't let a minor incident shake your self-esteem or alter your perception of your value. These situations can make you doubt whether you're living up to your own standards. It's important to stay rational and put things in perspective. Maintaining a consistent Self Score depends on emotional stability and mental resilience, which help minimize the swings between your high and low ranges.

Boosting your Self Score can often come from small, affirming events that remind you of your unique qualities and the positive impact you have on others. It might be something as simple as a gym trainer complimenting your progress, your partner making a thoughtful gesture, or your boss acknowledging your hard work. These positive experiences can reignite your self-esteem and help elevate your Love Formula Scores.

External events can influence how we see ourselves, but it's important to understand the interplay between these external factors and our internal responses. Our environment doesn't solely dictate our emotions and self-perception; our thoughts and beliefs play a significant role too. Ultimately, you are in control of your journey; *you* decide whether you navigate toward the lower or higher end of your default Self Score range.

The concept of a default range applies not just to a Self Score but also to a Partner Score, which can also fluctuate. For example, if *creativity* is one of your Top 5 Values, and one day your partner surprises you with a beautifully crafted piece of art, their display of talent might impress you so much that you give them the highest possible Partner Values Score for *creativity* in that moment.

However, there might be times when your partner tries something new, like playing a guitar solo they've been practicing all week, and it turns out to be predictable and underwhelming. In such instances, your impression of their *creativity* might diminish, and their Partner Values Score could temporarily drop, reflecting your disappointment that day.

It's normal for Scores to fluctuate, but in a healthy relationship, they should generally stay within a consistent range.

While short-term changes might happen due to mood swings or small incidents, it's important to recognize and understand the underlying patterns over time. Frequent and significant shifts in how you view yourself or your partner can lead to instability in the relationship, leading it into risky Relationship Zones (discussed in Part III) or even Distortions (discussed in Part V).

To illustrate how lifestyle choices and external factors can impact your default range, consider the following case study.

The Default Range: A Case Study

Brendan had just come back from a wild weekend in Vegas with his friends, where they had indulged in plenty of alcohol, junk food, and recreational drugs. Needless to say, his brain chemistry was completely out of whack when he returned home: He was very irritable, grumpy, and difficult to deal with. Upon returning, he carelessly tossed his shoes aside, left his luggage full of dirty clothes in the living room, and collapsed into bed, still smelling of alcohol.

His live-in girlfriend Janine thought, *Oh, hell no!* She had spent all weekend cleaning the house while he was out with his boys, and he was coming home a mess like that? No way! She asked him to pick up his things, start the laundry, and at least change his clothes before getting into bed. Unfortunately, given his current state, Brendan was uncooperative and immediately shut her out.

Then he started pestering her and, shockingly, labeled her a control freak, something she had never heard him say before. The argument escalated quickly, and Brendan found himself reminiscing about the carefree days before he had relationship responsibilities. Meanwhile, Janine started to wonder if she might be better off with someone who wasn't rude and irresponsible.

After spending the night in separate beds, the situation was tense. Janine was deeply disappointed by Brendan's behavior, and Brendan felt criticized and nagged.

That night, Brendan felt his attraction to Janine wane mainly because he found her behavior "controlling." However, his reaction was largely a projection of his irritation from the weekend's excesses. By the next day, as the effects of the alcohol wore off, so did his resentment. Once his mood stabilized, Brendan recognized that he had overreacted. Seeing things more clearly, he no longer viewed Janine as a threat to his independence, and his appreciation for her returned to normal.

While Brendan behaved poorly, Janine's attraction to him diminished. She found it unfair that he directed his drunken irritability at her over a reasonable request, one he typically had no problem fulfilling. Fortunately, Brendan realized his mistake and apologized, preventing any lasting damage to their relationship. Hopefully, he'll remember to behave better on future trips and leave Vegas in Vegas!

In the example provided, the shift in attraction wasn't due to anything Janine had done but rather Brendan's inability to manage stress rationally. His indulgent weekend disrupted his emotional balance. This highlights the importance of maintaining our mental and emotional well-being to retain attraction between partners and ensure our relationships remain harmonious.

On the other hand, there are "outlier" events. In the context of Scores, these are significant, unexpected life events that come out of nowhere. They are impactful and often unpredictable, with the potential to permanently alter Scores beyond their typical default ranges.

For example, discovering that your partner has cheated is a devastating outlier event. This all-too-common scenario can deeply wound your self-esteem and drastically alter how you see your partner. If such a significant breach of trust directly violates one of your core Values, such as *fidelity*, it might cause irreversible damage to the Partner Score.

It's not only the Partner Score that suffers a significant drop; you might also start to question your own value, which can lower your Self Score. The once-solid trust between you two has been shattered, disrupting the harmony you previously enjoyed. The consequences of this outlier event can be long-lasting, fundamentally altering the dynamics of your relationship and necessitating a period of healing and rebuilding.

An example like this demonstrates the deep impact betrayal can have on your Scores. It's a stark reminder that recovery after such a significant event is tough and complex, requiring time, effective communication, and a strong commitment to the Values that bind you together.

On the flip side, think about a positive event like receiving a job promotion. This milestone can greatly enhance self-esteem by affirming your capabilities and (typically) boosting your income. While primarily affecting one partner, the benefits can positively ripple through the relationship, enhancing both partners' lives.

With the financial boost from a job promotion, significant questions come into play. *Can we finally afford to start a family? Is it time to make our dream home a reality?* The excitement grows as you consider taking that long-awaited vacation. There might also be a newfound confidence in your retirement plans, allowing you to picture a future of retiring together, perhaps in a condo by the beach or in a quaint Tuscan villa.

In this scenario, receiving a promotion can boost your confidence and fill you with positivity. This emotional uplift can have a wonderful effect on your relationship. Your improved mood and the shared excitement about future possibilities can bring you and your partner closer together.

The key takeaway here is that both minor and major life events have the power to influence how you perceive your Self Score and your Partner Score, as well as how aligned you feel with each other. Large differences in Scores can strain the relationship—it's important to maintain a level-headed approach when minor events occur. To effectively use the Love Formula, we need to stay tuned to the ups and downs of each other's lives, adjusting and fine-tuning Scores through the different stages of our relationships.

Part III

Relationship Zones and the Path to Connection

The Love Formula can be a real game changer because it gives you a clear, no-nonsense look at how you and your partner vibe, helping you correct any issues messing with the good times. This isn't just about avoiding arguments or misunderstandings; it's about building something stronger where both of you feel happy and connected. It's about teamwork, figuring things out side by side, and moving toward something great.

In Part III, we'll explore how your perception of your Self Score and Partner Score might be keeping you from achieving relationship happiness. Understanding Score dynamics will help you see the big picture concerning your relationship and align with your partner.

As you dive into this section, it's important to remember Scores aren't the be-all and end-all for determining the course of your relationship. They're more like a catalyst to get you thinking about yourself and how you relate to your partner, acting as a starting point for emotional growth and better mutual understanding. The goal is, of course, to help you maintain the spark in your relationship.

Below are the three key relationship dynamics:

- **The Red Zone** where tensions and conflicts dominate.

- **The Yellow Zone** where caution and uncertainty are prevalent.

- **The Green Zone** where harmony and connection thrive.

The Red Zone is where things get pretty toxic, and unfortunately, it's a spot many of us find ourselves in at one point or another. In this Zone, both people are dealing with low self-esteem and tend to fall into harmful patterns.

The Yellow Zone isn't as bad as the Red, but it's still far from ideal. It can leave you feeling pretty worn out. Here one partner feels confident with a high Self Score, while the other is on the opposite end with a low Self Score. This imbalance can create a lot of tension and leave both partners wanting more from the relationship.

Finally, the Green Zone is where you want to be. It's the picture of a healthy, thriving relationship, with both partners scoring high, showing deep mutual respect and admiration for each other. This is where relationships are at their best.

At the same time, transitioning away from the Red and Yellow Zones isn't a quick fix but rather an ongoing effort. Achieving and upholding the Green Zone status requires continuous dedication as well.

Ultimately, the Zone you and your partner find yourselves in boils down to your choices. However, it's important to note that this excludes individuals grappling with mental health issues, substance addiction, or those exhibiting dangerous or unethical behavior. As highlighted earlier, emotional well-being and self-esteem significantly influence relationship dynamics. Prioritizing mental health and addressing any related concerns is essential before fostering healthy connections with others.

Chapter 11

The Red Zone

Red Zone: A relationship where both people assign a low Self Score and a low Partner Score, resulting in toxic dynamics.

Just as red lights on the road serve as universal signs to stop and exercise caution, indicating potential danger ahead, the "Red Zone" in relationships symbolizes their most perilous phase. It's a territory fraught with challenges and complications that most, if not all, couples encounter at some stage in their journey together. This chapter is dedicated to shedding light on the underlying causes that trap relationships in this challenging stage.

Based on our surveys, the average person's Self Score is 73%. Any self-assessment lower than this may indicate issues related to self-esteem and a higher likelihood of slipping into the Red Zone.

When both partners give low Partner Scores, it suggests they see each other as lacking in important areas, leading to diminished respect and affection. This lack of mutual appreciation can fuel insecurity and toxicity within the relationship. Understanding the core reasons behind the "Red Zone" is pivotal in learning how to steer clear of it.

One might wonder, "Why would they stay together if they both give low Scores to the other and there's a lack of respect between them?" Well, according to their calculations, they are a match—a match of low Scores.

Let's look at Suzie and Jake, a prime example of Red Zone calculations.

Suzie's Love Formula Score

Self Score	60%
Partner Score	63%
Love Formula Score	**= -3%**

In this instance, we can see that Suzie's Self Score is 60%, while she gives Jake a slightly higher Partner Score of 63%. While it is a close match, the low Scores also indicate she views herself and her partner as lacking.

Jake's Love Formula Score

Self Score	64%
Partner Score	68%
Love Formula Score	**= -4%**

Here we can see that Jake has given himself a Self Score of 64%, while he gives Suzie a higher Partner Score of 68%. Both Scores fall significantly below the threshold of healthy self-esteem and healthy relationship dynamics.

Compared to the average person, Suzie and Jake display lower self-esteem, as their Self Scores indicate. They've also rated their partners less favorably, which prompts the following question: *What's going on?*

Our analysis uncovers that Suzie and Jake are both trapped by a deep-seated lack of confidence. This profound doubt in their own worth leads them to the mistaken belief that they don't deserve, or simply can't attain, a fulfilling relationship. As a result, they stick to their current, unsatisfying situations, convinced that it's the best they're ever going to have.

At the heart of what makes Red Zone dynamics so toxic is a critical insight: It's all about the insecurities and life positions of the partners involved. In an effort to soothe their own insecurities, each person tries to boost their self-esteem by putting down their partner. This makes them feel temporarily superior. Simply put, this approach is a fast track to a relationship catastrophe.

Interestingly, Red Zone couples start off with a glowing view of their partners, convinced they've each found "The One." This burst of passion serves as a mutual attraction, temporarily masking their insecurities with an intense connection. Initially, it feels like a perfect solution to their low self-esteem.

But when the honeymoon phase starts coming to an end, the true nature of the relationship emerges; joy changes to irritation and discord. Suddenly, those once-charming quirks morph into significant irritants, as seen through a new, less forgiving lens.

The intense dedication your partner once showed to their creative endeavors, which used to inspire you too, now seems like a heavy load to bear. The allure of your passionate partner, who has been "working on" a divorce with their ex for three years, no longer seems like the stuff of fairy tales. And their once-admired ability to make friends with ease? Now it appears more as a glaring plea for attention.

The outcome? You find yourself trapped in a situation that repeatedly makes you cringe, reaching a point where it's simply unbearable.

It's important to note that these issues can arise in the Green Zone as well. The distinguishing factor in this case is that in the Red Zone, when conflicts and power struggles emerge, repairing the relationship becomes very difficult. Partners in this zone tend to be less healthy on social, emotional, and psychological levels, which results in conflicts that are both more frequent and more severe.

Individuals stuck in Red Zone dynamics usually bear the scars of unresolved childhood wounds, feeling unloved or undeserving of love. They are often their own worst critics and tend to project their feelings of failure onto their partners. Without a conscious effort toward self-love, self-respect, and personal growth from both sides, the relationship quickly degenerates into a cycle of blame and shame.

In the Red Zone, the path to self-love becomes a daunting challenge for partners. Moreover, showing respect and appreciation toward each other and sustaining a healthy emotional bond feels nearly impossible. For instance, after a tough day, he might find fault with how she vacuums, or she could snap at him for monopolizing the TV remote. What starts as trivial verbal spats quickly spiral into intense disputes, exacerbating the toxicity of the Red Zone dynamic.

Deep-seated insecurities often breed a fear of being vulnerable, making open and honest communication difficult. Egos take center stage, with neither partner willing to back down. Apologies become increasingly rare as both individuals compete for control through tactics such as gaslighting, shouting, hurling insults and profanities, interrupting their partner, and giving each other silent treatment. Manipulation becomes a standard tool in this tumultuous dynamic. For instance, consider the following scenarios:

- "If you don't give in to me, no sex for you."

- "I might ignore that honey-do list."

- "I'll express my frustration by slamming doors and drawers."

- "I'll simply walk out while you're speaking."

Unsurprisingly, such behaviors cultivate extreme resentment in both partners, leading to heightened anger and, at times, even fostering feelings of hate.

At the worst of it, there is a complete disconnect between the partners; they're miserable, and deep down, they both long to just leave the relationship and find someone better. You may have already guessed it—trust issues are *highly* prevalent in such situations because neither partner is giving or receiving healthy love. They are completely shut off from each other as neither partner has had their needs met for a long time. In fact, they may not even be aware of their own essential needs anymore because they have been stifled for so long.

The key is to recognize that trust issues can surface in any relationship. Even in the most harmonious unions, like those in the Green Zone, challenges can emerge. However, the Red Zone is particularly prone to these issues exacerbating, leading to greater escalation and volatility. This environment often fosters irrational accusations and excessive drama, with suspicions of infidelity typically acting as manifestations of one's own insecurities. Such a climate is likely to provoke controlling behaviors within the relationship.

In the Red Zone, there's a common misconception equating control with love, where individuals believe that exerting control over their partner signifies caring. This is especially true for those who feel insecure in different facets of their lives and look to their partners for affirmation and validation.

An example of controlling behavior in the Red Zone is saying, "*If* you really love me, you'll skip your best friend's birthday and stay home with me." Can this behavior be attributed to love? No.

This is, in fact, very manipulative. The tendency to control may also manifest as codependence, where each person unduly depends on the other to fulfill their emotional and social needs.

In the toxic Red Zone, burdens become overwhelming, completely dampening the relationship's vibe. It leaves partners feeling suffocated, with no room to breathe, enjoy independent activities, or maintain connections with family and friends. Their sense of freedom is compromised, and the relationship becomes an obstacle to personal development, self-worth, and joy. Instead of lifting each other, they end up dragging each other down.

The most troubling times in the toxic Red Zone emerge when one partner begins to dominate the other. This might start with critiquing clothing choices, persistently expecting uninterrupted communication, or stripping one partner of their autonomy. At its extreme, this dominance can result in one partner being cut off from their social support network, leaving them isolated from friends and family.

Disturbingly, at the far end of the spectrum, this situation can escalate to domestic violence, making the healing process even more challenging.

So, why do people stay together in such a dreadful situation?

Well, they're a match—even if it's due to low self-worth. They've become used to the (dis)comfort of this dysfunctional relationship and think it's better than being alone.

In the Red Zone, it's common for couples to fall into a cycle of separation and reconciliation. Initially, they split due to the intolerable dysfunction within their relationship. Yet, they frequently find themselves drawn back together, mistaking their longing for each other as a sign of true love. On a deeper, perhaps subconscious level, some may even find the relationship's turmoil and intensity strangely exhilarating, wrongly interpreting these emotions as evidence of genuine love.

After enduring a fierce and stormy dispute, one that may even escalate beyond mere shouting, the couple might find their way back to each other, sharing tender moments of closeness. This cycle is doomed to recur. This pattern, prevalent in relationships marred by deep psychological struggles or substance misuse, can intensify, becoming really dangerous. During the "second honeymoon phase," the abusive partner might display remorse and affection, followed by the inevitable crash, further fueling the cycle's volatility.

Furthermore, both partners might be misled into believing that their situation is on the mend, remaining oblivious to the fact that they are ensnared in a Red Zone dynamic until the cycle repeats itself.

Keep in mind that abuse extends beyond the physical realm. Emotional, verbal, financial, and sexual abuse can inflict equally profound devastation and mental exhaustion.

Moving through the Red Zone can feel like navigating a minefield, with the trauma level varying based on how deep and dark the relationship gets. It's critical to spot the warning signs early and make a move—whether that means fixing things or walking away. Bringing the Love Formula into the mix can serve as your roadmap to a healthier, happier relationship territory.

The Red Zone: A Case Study

Jake and Suzie's upbringing was marked by a challenging home environment filled with frequent arguments, emotional disconnection, stress, and a noticeable absence of affection. As they transitioned into adulthood, the impact of their troubled childhoods became evident in their romantic lives. Prior to finding each other, both had navigated their way through a series of disappointing and harmful relationships. These experiences further eroded their self-esteem and sense of self-worth over time.

The instant Jake and Suzie met, they felt an intense and immediate bond, as if they had finally found the missing piece in their lives. They found comfort and deep affection in one another's presence, feeling an instinctive reluctance to part ways. It was as though they were two puzzle pieces that fitted perfectly. In their hearts, they felt destined to be soulmates in what they believed would be an enduring love story.

Unfortunately, the initial bliss of their relationship was short-lived. Barely a month in, Jake and Suzie found themselves frequently caught up in intense arguments. What started as small disagreements quickly spiraled into significant disputes, with neither partner willing to accept responsibility for their actions or engage in any form of self-reflection.

In the face of disagreements, Suzie's reaction was to unleash uncontrollable outbursts, losing her temper and lashing out at Jake with insults without regard for his feelings. Jake's response to this onslaught was to retreat; he would withdraw into himself and vanish, seemingly for eons, cutting himself off from everything. These reactions served only to deepen their insecurities, fueling a relentless cycle of daily conflicts. As time passed, their fights grew more intense, and the respect they once held for each other was steadily eroded.

Despite numerous attempts to part ways, Jake and Suzie found themselves repeatedly drawn back to each other. It was as if they were addicted to the tumultuous cycle of their relationship, unable to stay away despite the glaring unhealthiness of their connection.

The love was almost gone. Jake and Suzie were in the Red Zone.

Moving Out of the Red Zone

It's common to underestimate the severity of being in the Red Zone, frequently dismissing the genuine damage such dynamics can cause. For those who were raised in environments rife with toxic relationship patterns, have friends caught in the Red Zone's grasp, or consistently experience these unhealthy interactions across their relationships, there's a risk of adopting the flawed perception that this turmoil is just the standard state of affairs—that such chaos is what relationships inherently entail.

In situations like these, acknowledging the reality of unhealthy relationships is crucial. It's important to understand that healthier, more loving forms of relating to others are not only possible but should be expected. The key question to ask yourself is whether you see parts of your own experiences in this scenario and can firmly say, "This isn't right; I deserve something better!"

The first crucial step is acknowledging the true condition of your relationship. If you identify that you're entrenched in a Red Zone relationship, there are practical approaches both you and your partner can undertake to transition toward a healthier Green Zone dynamic. However, if the relationship has escalated to the point of danger or abuse, or if you find yourself devoid of hope for any positive change, then prioritizing your safety and well-being by leaving becomes paramount.

Let's explore how the Love Formula can serve as a tool for personal and relationship development, offering a pathway out of the persistent turmoil characteristic of Red Zone dynamics. This approach can empower you to cultivate a healthier, more fulfilling partnership.

1. Reality Check

Exiting the Red Zone starts with a clear and truthful evaluation of where you stand. Pause for a moment to reflect. Did any of what you've read so far strike a chord? Maybe you found yourself wincing involuntarily or nodding along in quiet acknowledgment, feeling a deep connection to the scenarios described. Most importantly, has this reflection led you to recognize that your current relationship situation might be less than healthy?

Let's be honest: Change is hard. It feels like moving a mountain, especially when you're ensnared in the Red Zone. It's easy to fall into the blame game, pointing fingers at your partner and declaring them the sole cause of all issues—all while excusing yourself of any wrongdoing. But here's the catch: It's a two-player game in the Red Zone. Both partners are reacting to each other's insecurities and diminished self-worth. It's a textbook case of "it takes two to tango."

Acknowledging that your relationship dynamic is unhealthy marks the crucial first step. Deciding what you want to change about being in the Red Zone—be it trying to enhance the relationship or opting to separate—is a pivotal decision that sets the stage for healing and retaking control of your life.

If you find yourself caught in the Red Zone, you might have assigned yourself a low Self Score. This prompts the question: *But why?*

Yet, an even more important question looms: Are you prepared to shift your perspective on both yourself and your partner?

Keep in mind that choosing your partner was a decision you made. Yet this decision doesn't condemn you to a perpetual cycle of unhappiness. There's a way out of what feels like an endless bad dream. You have the power and control to change the narrative of your life.

2. Elevate Your Self-Worth

Assigning yourself a low Self Score signals a struggle with low self-esteem and a lack of acknowledgment of your own value. The critical question then becomes, "What's driving these negative views you hold about yourself?"

The adage that you can't truly love someone else or accept their love until you love yourself holds a lot of truth. According to our surveys, having a Self Score below 75% means you view yourself less positively than the average person views themselves.

Before taking steps to enhance your relationship or escape the Red Zone, it's crucial to focus on elevating your self-esteem. Persistently indulging in negative self-talk can lead to projecting your insecurities onto your partner, resulting in an unfair focus on their imperfections.

Do those persistent negative thoughts ring a bell? Perhaps they echo criticisms from your parents, previous partners, a strict boss, or others whose approval you've yearned for. Such messages can deeply impact your self-worth and influence your relationships over time. Remember, it's vital to recognize that these messages don't define you—they are not your own voice.

When you find yourself reacting intensely to your partner—be it through arguments, jealousy, clinginess, or attempts to control—it's important to pause and consider where these behaviors stem from. Psychologists use a powerful strategy known as "cognitive reframing" to help shift your viewpoint and the story you tell yourself about a given situation. This method can include practices such as creating positive affirmations, engaging in guided meditation, writing in a journal for self-reflection, or undergoing psychotherapy. At its heart, reframing aims to transform negative self-talk into positive affirmations and foster a more hopeful perspective on life. Let's explore some examples to understand how reframing can be applied in real-life scenarios.

Suppose you've assigned yourself a low Self Score regarding education, feeling that you're not knowledgeable enough and that you frequently find it challenging to keep up in conversations. This might lead to feelings of inadequacy, with the hope that others perceive you as smarter and more informed.

Now let's see how cognitive reframing can make a difference. Perhaps you haven't considered the fact that education isn't confined to conventional academia. If you're critical of yourself for not adhering to traditional educational standards, it's important to acknowledge that knowledge can come from a wide array of life experiences and engagements with the world around you. Interestingly, many notable figures, such as Oprah Winfrey, Benjamin Franklin, Abraham Lincoln, Steve Jobs, Bill Gates, Walt Disney, and Albert Einstein, reached astounding levels of success without pursuing standard educational routes.

Consider another example: your self-image. If you've rated yourself poorly in this area, think about whether you've been influenced by people who overemphasize physical looks or constantly draw comparisons to social media influencers. It's crucial to remember that regardless of how you look, your age, or your situation, there's someone out there who will value and appreciate you for the person you are right now.

At this point, pause to reevaluate your Self Score, considering adjustments based on this exercise of reframing and enhancing your self-esteem. If your past includes experiences of verbal or emotional abuse, childhood bullying, or any form of neglect, seeking therapy becomes a critical step. Healing these early traumas is key to fostering a healthier self-view and developing fulfilling, healthy relationships.

As the Persian poet Rumi so wisely stated, "Through love, all pain will turn to medicine." Remember, the most important source of this transformative love should be your own self-love.

3. Show Support for Your Partner

Keep in mind that existing in the Red Zone impacts how you see not just yourself but also your partner. Essentially, you may not view your partner in a positive light, which can stem from two main reasons:

1. Your partner indeed has specific shortcomings and a history of unfavorable behavior.

2. You could be misunderstanding their actions, overlooking their positive attributes, or adopting a negative perspective toward them.

If you're experiencing any form of abuse—be it physical, sexual, financial, verbal, or psychological—you need to seek support, ensure your safety, and get out of that situation quickly.

In other scenarios, it's important to reflect on whether your negative view of your partner is actually a projection of your own insecurities. Could it be that your critical opinion of them mirrors aspects of yourself you're not fond of, or is it a reflection of past hurts from previous relationships, family dynamics, or others who've caused you pain? For instance, if you've been betrayed by a past partner, it's natural to transfer that mistrust onto your current partner, irrespective of their actions or trustworthiness. Evaluating your emotional responses is an effective method to determine whether you're projecting onto your partner. If you find that your feelings are more intense than what the situation or your partner's behavior seems to justify, it's likely that you're overlaying past experiences onto the present moment and your partner.

Looking down on your partner or harboring negative thoughts about them doesn't help either of you grow. Being their ally is crucial. This doesn't mean you excuse or enable harmful behaviors or lack of effort. Instead, it's about showing empathy, seeking to understand their perspective, engaging in open and honest dialogue, and offering your support and love. For instance, if your partner is falling short on household duties, instead of assigning blame, initiate a constructive conversation to explore solutions together. Their reluctance to do laundry or dishes might stem from deeper issues. When they do contribute or go above and beyond, make it a point to recognize their efforts and verbally appreciate them. This approach not only fosters a supportive environment but also encourages positive behavior.

This is what it means to show support for your partner.

Escaping the grips of the Red Zone involves more than just enhancing your own self-esteem; it also requires actively seeking out reasons to respect your partner. In a thriving relationship, mutual admiration and compassion are essential. It's this reciprocal appreciation that lays the foundation for both partners to uplift and support each other's growth.

Does this mean you should support a partner who's not making an effort or is emotionally draining? Definitely not.

As you commit to self-improvement and begin advancing in your personal journey, you may start to view your partner as an anchor slowing you down. The reason for feeling compelled to move on often stems from the growth in your self-esteem and self-love, which in turn makes the differences between you and your partner more evident. With this newfound clarity and sense of self, it's natural to gravitate toward seeking a relationship that resonates more closely with the positive dynamics of the Green Zone.

But what if you're thinking, "Why should I put in all this effort for personal growth and our relationship when my partner isn't doing anything?" This leads us to...

4. Mutual Effort and Getting Support

For a relationship to truly flourish and escape the Red Zone, both partners need to be fully committed to taking the steps required for improvement. It's not enough for just one person to make an effort. This is where the importance of a growth-oriented mindset comes into play, alongside the significance of choosing a partner who shares a similar perspective on personal development. While nobody is flawless, if both of you are willing to engage in self-reflection and dedicate yourselves to becoming the best versions of yourselves, your relationship has a significantly better chance of evolving into the healthier dynamics of the Green Zone.

The Love Formula is all about teamwork. It's designed for you and your partner to sit down, go through it together, and really dive into each other's answers. It's a powerful way to kickstart honest conversations about what's really going on in your relationship, pinpointing the root of conflicts—be it jealousy, snide comments, trying to control each other, or something else entirely. Both of you owning up to how you might be adding fuel to the fire sets the stage for real, constructive change. It's about getting real with each other, understanding the deeper issues, and working together to fix them.

Bluntly asking, "Why the hell are you going to happy hour with your work buddies?!" might not get you the response you're hoping for. Instead, expressing your true feelings about the issue can make a world of difference. Try saying something like, "Honey, I've been feeling neglected lately because it feels like we haven't been spending quality time together." This kind of open, vulnerable communication tends to encourage a more understanding and sympathetic reaction. Remember, showing your vulnerability can really change the dynamics for the better.

If you find it tough to tackle these issues by yourselves, turning to a professional can be a smart decision. Relationship therapists frequently point out that couples tend to wait longer than they should to get help. It's critical to address problems early on; delaying can make things much harder to resolve. Both partners need to be committed to their own personal growth and to collaboratively address their issues. This means recognizing and changing negative thoughts and behaviors.

Mutual growth and healing are within reach when you first use the Love Formula on your own and then come together to share what you've learned. This process demands humility, authenticity, and the courage to be vulnerable. By sharing your deepest fears and wishes, you open the door to understanding and empathy from your partner. Ideally, this exchange is met with an open heart, compassion, and unconditional love, setting the foundation for a stronger, more connected relationship.

Remember, this is all about making progress, step by step, and not about transforming your relationship overnight. Hitting some sensitive spots while you're working through this together is totally expected. But, keep in mind, the whole reason you're doing this—sparking those real, raw conversations—is because you're trying to heal together. You want to reach a place where you genuinely enjoy each other's company, feeling like a true team. The journey comes with its ups and downs, but it's about moving forward together.

Breaking free from the Red Zone is unlikely if either partner lacks the willingness or emotional capacity for the deep work required, including having respectful, open discussions. In such situations, you're essentially faced with two options: Stay and continue to suffer or find the strength and courage to liberate yourselves. But what exactly does it take to successfully navigate out of the Red Zone? Let's explore that further!

Transitioning Out of the Red Zone: A Case Study

Returning to Jake and Suzie, we find them taking significant steps to leave the Red Zone behind. The first crucial step was initiating a brutally honest dialogue, both with themselves and each other, acknowledging that their current dynamic was failing. They realized the importance of compassion, understanding, and a willingness to change for the sake of a healthier partnership. Agreeing to seek couples counseling, they committed to fully investing in the process of mending their relationship. They set a checkpoint of three months to reassess their relationship, marking a clear timeline for their journey of healing and improvement.

Jake and Suzie took on the Love Formula as a team and made some eye-opening discoveries. A key insight was their mutual low self-scoring, which shed light on a shared struggle with self-love. This realization led them to understand that their personal insecurities might be getting unfairly projected onto each other. Recognizing the need for change, they committed to improving their self-esteem. To support this, their counselor suggested weekly check-ins, each to be capped off with an enjoyable activity. They enthusiastically agreed to this plan.

The second revelation came from recognizing their shortcomings in the eyes of their partner. Suzie learned that Jake's respect for her had waned because he highly valued family connections, and he felt that Suzie wasn't making enough effort to bond with his family. He viewed her as aloof and detached, raising doubts about their compatibility. Conversely, Jake found out he didn't meet Suzie's expectations regarding reliability, primarily because of his habit of retreating into silence after disagreements. This lack of dependability was a significant issue for Suzie.

Suzie took a deep dive into understanding why she acted the way she did. She discovered that her behavior mirrored the dynamics she had observed in her parents' marriage. Growing up, her parents argued frequently, and her father often left home for days at a time. This pattern left a lasting mark on Suzie, instilling a deep-seated fear of abandonment. This fear had significantly shaped how she engaged with those she cared about, including Jake.

Jake came to realize that his habit of withdrawing after arguments further worsened Suzie's fear of abandonment. He also recognized that he hadn't been equipped with healthy communication or conflict resolution skills, reflecting on his own upbringing. His parents were conflict-avoiders, choosing to bury their grievances until they erupted in resentment. They were "stuffers"—avoiding confrontation at all costs, only to later explode in resentment. Jake acknowledged this pattern and realized its impact on his behavior. He admitted to becoming defensive whenever Suzie expressed dissatisfaction or was upset with him, taking responsibility for his part in their communication breakdown.

The third revelation came when they discovered each other's struggles with self-esteem. This awareness fostered a deeper sense of empathy between them, encouraging them to be more open and vulnerable. Jake confessed to rating himself poorly in the area he valued most—finances. This admission prompted Suzie to express her compassion and support. She reassured him that, even though his career wasn't at the point he aspired to yet, she was incredibly proud of his efforts and had unwavering faith in his potential to reach his financial goals. This support from Suzie boosted Jake's confidence significantly and strengthened their connection. For the first time, he truly felt that Suzie was supporting him unconditionally.

Seeking the help of a couples counselor proved to be a game changer for Suzie and Jake, providing them with the tools to confront their issues directly. They committed to honest communication, choosing to face uncomfortable truths head-on instead of resorting to avoidance or projection. This newfound approach not only lessened the frequency, intensity, and duration of their arguments but also fostered deeper trust between them. As a result, both Suzie and Jake saw improvements in their self-esteem and experienced a significant enhancement in their relationship's overall quality.

Three months down the line, at the time of their reassessment, Suzie and Jake both felt a newfound sense of security within their relationship. Remarkably, they had successfully navigated their way out of the Red Zone and were now progressing toward the Green Zone.

Before delving into the characteristics and benefits of the Green Zone, let's take a closer look at the intermediary phase—the Yellow Zone.

Chapter 12

The Yellow Zone

Yellow Zone: A relationship where it is implicitly understood that one partner holds a higher Score than the other, leading to imbalanced and unhealthy dynamics.

Let's delve into the Yellow Zone. This stage might not be as infamous for wreaking havoc in relationships as the Red Zone, but it still poses a significant risk to the quality of your connection with your partner. Within the framework of the Love Formula, the Yellow Zone is characterized by a relationship in which there's a tacit understanding that one partner is deemed to have a higher Score than the other. This leads to an unhealthy imbalance in the relationship dynamic.

Contrary to the Red Zone, where both partners grapple with low Scores, the Yellow Zone presents a clear disparity: One partner has a higher Score, indicating a stronger sense of self-worth, than the other. Although this scenario might seem like a step up from the Red Zone dynamics, it's far from perfect. The core issue in the Yellow Zone is the underlying, unacknowledged consensus that one partner is somehow more valuable than the other. This imbalance, while not openly addressed, can lead to significant friction and challenges within the relationship.

To dive deeper into how dynamics in the Yellow Zone are quantified, let's examine the case of Brooke and Charlie. We'll start with Brooke's calculations.

Brooke's Love Formula Score

Self Score	69%
Partner Score	81%
Love Formula Score	**= -12%**

Through the lens of the Love Formula, Brooke sees herself as not quite measuring up to her partner. Her Self Score is on the lower side, which makes her feel like she's not as valuable in their relationship. This kind of self-view naturally leads to a skewed dynamic where Brooke, perhaps without fully realizing it, sees herself as the "lesser" partner and assumes that her partner, in this case Charlie, carries more weight and significance in their union. Let's turn our attention to Charlie and see how he fits into the picture.

Charlie's Love Formula Score

Self Score	87%
Partner Score	77%
Love Formula Score	**= +10%**

In the context of the Love Formula, Charlie perceives himself as bringing more to the table compared to Brooke. With a higher Self Score, he feels that he contributes more value to their relationship. This belief can create an imbalance, where Charlie sees himself as the more significant partner.

In the case of Brooke and Charlie, there's an unspoken consensus that Charlie is somehow "more valuable" than Brooke. This dynamic starkly highlights the potential for codependency to emerge, with Brooke, who has the lower Score, becoming overly reliant on Charlie for her sense of worth and fulfillment. It raises a critical question: Why would they stay together when there's such a notable disparity in how they view themselves and each other?

It's important to understand that relationships usually start with the best of intentions. Each partner genuinely wants to be loving and supportive, aiming for what they believe could be an ideal relationship—a "match made in heaven."

Yet, as time goes by, it's natural for Scores to change as individuals undergo personal growth and transformation. This development can result in shifts in personal Values and Traits, which in turn can cause variations in how partners view each other's Scores. If these differences continue to grow and aren't addressed, they can accumulate and eventually lead to the relationship ending.

Even when confronted with compatibility challenges, numerous couples opt to remain together, especially if they've built a long history. This decision is influenced by multiple factors, including the fear of being alone, shared responsibilities such as family and finances, and health issues, among others. For those in the Yellow Zone, whether they stay in or leave the relationship depends on their specific situation. Yet, a universal aspect of these relationships is the clear absence of fulfillment for both parties involved.

Couples stuck in the Yellow Zone often find themselves in limbo, feeling that their relationship isn't bad enough to warrant leaving. However, they regularly question whether staying is a mistake, caught in the dilemma of whether they're settling for less than they deserve or compromising too much.

The Yellow Zone, situated midway through the relationship spectrum, acts as a transitional space where couples can move among the three zones with relative ease. Moving from the Red Zone into the Yellow Zone often demands just a small push or minimal effort, making it a feasible step toward healthier dynamics.

Likewise, couples who are comfortably situated in the Green Zone might find themselves slipping into the Yellow Zone from time to time. This change can result from a range of issues such as depression, stress or dissatisfaction at work, unexpected accidents, difficult dynamics with in-laws, financial hardships, and other external pressures. These challenges have the potential to nudge a once-harmonious couple out of the Green Zone, leading them into the Yellow or even Red Zones.

Let's examine two scenarios showing how the Yellow Zone dynamics can unfold.

Scenario 1: The Low Scorer's Insecurity Pushes the Confident High Scorer Away

A partner with a low Self Score might inadvertently elevate their significant other, placing them on a pedestal. This dynamic can awaken a profound fear of loss, compelling the lower-scoring partner to adopt behaviors that, although unintended, can drive a wedge between them, further complicating their connection.

It's crucial to highlight an important aspect of this dynamic. At the onset of their relationship, the couple typically begins on equal ground. Yet, as time progresses, a sense of inequality may gradually emerge if one partner starts to view themselves as "lesser" than the other. This skewed perception can foster behaviors that are detrimental to their self-esteem, gradually eroding it and causing their Self Score to diminish.

Imagine a scenario where a woman's marriage dissolves because her husband persistently tells her, "You're way too good for me. Someday, you'll wake up, realize you can do better, and leave me." Despite her ongoing efforts to reassure him of her love and his value, his prophecy ultimately comes true. She finds herself overwhelmed by his incessant need for reassurance and validation, leading to a point where he no longer holds the same appeal to her.

Unfortunately, a partner suffering from low self-esteem might inadvertently set in motion a self-fulfilling prophecy. Their own unhealthy behaviors, driven by their insecurities, can lead to their partner pulling away and ultimately rejecting them.

In various situations, a partner with a low Self Score might resort to manipulation in an attempt to keep their higher-scoring partner from leaving. Ironically, these manipulative actions often have the opposite effect, pushing the more confident, high-scoring partner further away.

Manipulation in relationships can show up in sneaky ways. Take, for instance, someone who pretends they are in high demand, hinting at interest from others to make their partner see them as more desirable. While it might seem like a quick fix to boost their standing, it's a shaky foundation for any relationship. Continually chipping away at your partner's trust isn't just unattractive—it's outright damaging. Those who are truly looking to cultivate a deep and lasting connection will quickly lose patience with such games. Over time, these manipulative moves just push them away, as genuine, strong relationships are built on honesty and mutual respect, not deception and insecurity.

In the same vein, independence can become a contentious issue, especially when it uncovers the manipulative streak in a partner with low self-esteem. The moment the more independent, high-scoring partner seeks some space or autonomy, it can trigger deep-seated fears of abandonment in their partner. This fear often leads the lower-scoring partner to adopt controlling behaviors in a bid to keep their partner close. A classic warning sign is when they start to restrict their partner's time with friends, morphing from a supportive companion into a possessive one. Driven by their insecurities, they might demand constant attention, particularly in social settings, and some may even stir up drama to keep the focus on themselves. These actions not only strain the relationship but also highlight a shift toward unhealthy control rather than mutual respect and trust.

Make no mistake: Insecurities can push people to use some pretty intense tactics to get what they want in a relationship. A favorite method is guilt-tripping, which could sound something like, "Lately, I feel like you just don't care about me. You're always glued to your work. Don't I deserve more of your time than your job?" This approach uses guilt to try and manipulate their partner into prioritizing them over other commitments, playing on their emotions to gain more control and attention.

While these manipulation tactics might seem effective at first, they rarely hold up in the long run. Sooner or later, the high-scoring partner starts to see through the facade, categorizing their partner with labels such as "insecure," "needy," and "controlling." This realization can significantly erode the foundation of trust and open communication within the relationship, leading the high-scoring partner to pull away.

In the Yellow Zone, just like in the Red Zone, trust issues are a huge problem. People with lower Scores often struggle to trust their partners, feeling deep down that their partners could do better. When their usual tactics—like guilt-tripping or trying to manipulate—don't ease their worries, they might start invading their partner's privacy. This could mean going through their messages, checking their phone when they're not around, or obsessively tracking who interacts with their partner on social media. Questions like "Who's this person liking all your photos?" become common. This kind of behavior isn't just a one-off; it's driven by ongoing, deep-seated insecurities and a fundamental lack of trust.

This is a big problem for the confident, high-scoring partner, especially when they harbor genuine feelings for the person who constantly questions themselves to oblivion. Nevertheless, the constant accusations of infidelity take a toll on their well-being. Attending social events and gatherings or even innocently checking their phone becomes a source of anxiety, eroding their overall quality of life. The perpetual dread of character attacks forces them to navigate their relationship with extreme caution, and quite frankly, it sucks.

For high-scoring partners, this kind of relationship presents a problem. While they care deeply for their partner, the cycle of clinginess, jealousy, control, and insecurity can wear people down pretty fast. Sadly, this may result in them feeling trapped in the relationship, and inevitably, they will long for something more fulfilling. Now let's learn more about Charlie and Brooke.

The Yellow Zone: Case Study #1

Charlie, an ER doctor, and Brooke, a young nurse, were captivated by each other from the very start, swiftly moving into a relationship. Brooke admired Charlie greatly; he was widely regarded as a handsome, charismatic, and compassionate doctor. She considered herself lucky to be with him, especially knowing how many other women envied her position, often voicing how much they wished they could be in her shoes.

They fell in love instantly, and the honeymoon stage was nothing short of a dream for the both of them.

As time went on, Brooke began to grapple with feelings of insecurity, doubting her worthiness for someone like Charlie. By placing him on a pedestal, she inadvertently set the stage for self-doubt, turning into her own most severe critic. This shift in perception had devastating impacts. Brooke started to view her educational achievements as insignificant, her physical appearance as merely average, and her intellectual capabilities as lacking. In her eyes, every other woman possessed the qualities or attributes she believed she was missing.

This growing insecurity in Brooke manifested as jealousy, becoming apparent in her reactions whenever other women engaged with Charlie. She found herself constantly wondering if their interactions were flirtatious or if she was being sidelined. Over time, this jealousy intensified, transforming into a mix of irritation, anger, and an even deeper sense of insecurity each time she noticed other women paying attention to Charlie.

With Charlie's Top Values including *communication*, *manners*, and *poise*, it was clear that Brooke was no longer making the cut. To avoid causing drama, Charlie vehemently denied all accusations and walked on eggshells around the female staff at the hospital. There was a period when his affection for Brooke was undeniable, and he went out of his way to make her feel like she was the most important person in his life. However, Brooke's growing insecurities, her unreasonable behavior, and the frequent guilt trips she embarked on were far from what he had envisioned in a lasting relationship. Despite these challenges, Charlie chose to stay, clinging to the hope that they would somehow recapture the magic of their early days together and that Brooke would revert to the woman he had originally fallen for.

At last, her biggest fear—that he no longer wanted to be with her—became a reality. Brooke's insecurities had ultimately started pushing Charlie away. Charlie and Brooke were in the Yellow Zone.

Scenario 2: The Confident High Scorer Exploits the Vulnerable Low Scorer

In this scenario, the partner with the lower Score goes to great lengths to prove their value to their significant other. They spare no effort, pouring their heart and soul into fulfilling their partner's needs and prioritizing them above everything else. In doing so, the low-scoring partner often neglects their own well-being, desires, and self-care routines. Why do they exhibit such selflessness?

Because their sense of joy is deeply tied to their partner's happiness. Yet, this level of devotion doesn't come without its drawbacks.

In this setup, the partner with the higher score takes on a commanding role, displaying a sense of entitlement and insisting on having things their way. They take the reins on decisions ranging from dividing chores, choosing vacation spots, deciding on meals and entertainment, and, most significantly, determining who wins in disputes. This creates a clear power disparity in the relationship. Intriguingly, both partners find a degree of satisfaction in this arrangement: The Low Scorer feels privileged to be associated with their more dominant partner, while the High Scorer views their partner's acquiescence as a testament to their own desirability. The *irony* (cue: eye roll).

As a result, the High Scorer often displays behaviors that are controlling, inflexible, emotionally distant, or even abusive. This individual may show a significant lack of compassion, empathy, and respect toward their partner. Yet, the low-scoring partner expresses such gratitude that the high-scoring partner doesn't fear losing them, even if they know they're being a jerk.

The high-scoring partner dominates the relationship, making all the decisions. When the low-scoring partner dares to point out the imbalance, they're met with a dismissive ultimatum—"Okay, you're free to leave"—with the high-scoring partner showing no interest in mending the relationship. This leaves the low-scoring partner in a tough spot, struggling to voice their unhappiness with the clear disparity. This unwillingness to tackle the issue reflects the high-scoring partner's conviction that they won't have trouble finding a more suitable match. They stand their ground, unwilling to compromise, convinced that they deserve someone better.

In the dynamics of the Yellow Zone, the partner with the lower score moves carefully, always mindful of their high-scoring partner's wishes and preferences. They crave acknowledgment, to be seen and cherished, longing for their partner's love. They seek validation and a silent acknowledgment of their value in their partner's eyes. Unfortunately, beneath this longing lies a struggle with feelings of not being good enough, a belief that they're unworthy of their partner. Driven by this, they're willing to go to great lengths to ensure their partner's happiness, often at the expense of their own needs. This relentless pursuit of approval leads them to put their partner's well-being ahead of their own, even when it compromises their self-care.

Imagine a situation where the High Scorer doesn't like the Low Scorer's friends. In response, the Low Scorer doesn't hesitate to cut off these friendships, sacrificing their social life to make their partner happy. If the High Scorer wants luxury items, exotic vacations, or gourmet meals, the Low Scorer will find a way to fulfill these desires. They pour their energy into satisfying their partner's expensive tastes, often neglecting their own needs in the process. Despite bending over backward to please their partner, the Low Scorer often accepts minimal acknowledgment in return. The sad irony is that they find some measure of satisfaction in this imbalance, content with any small sign of appreciation, no matter how disproportionate to their own efforts and sacrifices.

And here's the ultimate cherry on top: If the High Scorer decides they're not ready for a formal relationship but still seeks sexual intimacy with fewer strings attached, the Low Scorer will agree to these terms, even if it causes them significant pain. In such situations, the Low Scorer faces a tough internal battle, torn between the hurt this arrangement causes them and their desire to maintain a "drama-free" relationship. This internal struggle highlights the lengths to which they're willing to go, sacrificing their own emotional well-being in an effort to keep their partner satisfied.

Under these circumstances, the Low Scorer's self-esteem inevitably suffers a significant blow. The realization that their partner's feelings don't match the intensity of their own is hard enough, but when the High Scorer openly acknowledges this disparity without any attempt to address the imbalance, it adds insult to injury. This blatant acknowledgment, devoid of any effort to even the emotional playing field, can be particularly damaging.

Consider this scenario as a prime illustration of the intricate blend of our emotions, thoughts, and behaviors. It highlights how, in situations that appear unbalanced, there's usually a complex undercurrent at play; indeed, it takes two to tango. However, before delving deeper into this example, it's crucial to make a key distinction. The presence of Traits like selfishness, entitlement, and a lack of empathy in a high-scoring partner doesn't automatically label them as "narcissists."

Narcissism is defined as a profound personality disorder marked by an overarching absence of remorse and empathy, which affects a person's interactions across all relationships. While a high-scoring partner might display certain concerning behaviors, this doesn't necessarily mean they are indifferent to their partner's feelings or intend to cause harm.

This distinction is crucial. The objective here isn't to label individuals within this dynamic as narcissists; instead, it's to shed light on how disparities in Scores can result in behaviors that are selfish and lack emotional connection.

The Yellow Zone: Case Study #2

Silvia and Kathleen crossed paths through mutual friends at a point in life where both were eager to settle down. For Silvia, the certainty was absolute—Kathleen was the piece she had been missing in the puzzle of her life, and she was determined to do whatever it took to build a future together.

On the other hand, Kathleen wasn't sure she felt the same way. In her last relationship, her partner couldn't keep up with her luxurious lifestyle, and she wanted to be sure her next partner would fulfill those needs. In other words, wealth mattered to her, and her heart wouldn't be open to someone who couldn't provide for her.

Still, Kathleen stayed in a relationship with Silvia because she recognized she had nothing to lose. Without other potential partners in sight, it seemed like a fun way to fill the time.

Silvia and Kathleen had an open discussion about the latter's expectations, a conversation that left Silvia feeling somewhat lacking. Deep down, they both recognized that Silvia couldn't meet Kathleen's desires for a luxurious lifestyle. Despite this, Silvia made extraordinary efforts to show her worth in other ways. She treated Kathleen to lavish dinners, gave her thoughtful presents, made grand gestures of affection, and constantly complimented her. Silvia dedicated herself to making Kathleen happy, cautiously steering clear of anything that might upset her.

To anyone looking in, Kathleen might have appeared to be incredibly fortunate with Silvia's display of unconditional love. However, Kathleen believed she deserved it; after all, Silvia was fortunate to be with her. Whenever Silvia stumbled, Kathleen swiftly moved to end the conflict by ending the relationship until Silvia pleaded for reconciliation and begged to win her affection back.

Kathleen's expectations were unjustly high, placing constant demands on Silvia. She was excruciatingly unfair, always demanding Silvia do as she said, with no room for error. Due to their dynamic, Kathleen and Silvia found themselves in the Yellow Zone.

Moving Out of the Yellow Zone

So, let's talk about how to get *out* of the Yellow Zone and into a better place—that is, the Green Zone. If any of the situations described in this chapter strike a chord with you, it's a sign that your relationship might not be providing the joy and fulfillment you deserve, prompting you to recognize the need for a shift. Deep within, we all seek balance. We yearn to be with someone we hold in high regard and who reciprocates that admiration. We desire a mutual connection where our partner is as enthusiastic about us as we are about them.

If we do find ourselves in such a scenario, it might be because we believe there are no better alternatives, or we've simply become accustomed to the dysfunction. Regardless of the reasons you find yourself here, remember, you're not stuck. There's a path to improvement, and the Love Formula offers a way forward. Here's how it can guide you:

1. Honest Self-Talk

If you think that you and your partner are lingering in the Yellow Zone, and you're longing for a way to jump into the Green Zone where your relationship can truly thrive, the secret lies in gaining self-awareness. Recognizing your relationship in any of the scenarios described means it's time to acknowledge where you're at and make a conscious decision to change.

The initial move is for the low-scoring partner to admit to themselves that they have certain insecurities that make them feel less than their partner. Recognizing this is the critical first step on the path to dealing with and ultimately overcoming these feelings.

Put plainly, the Low Scorer has, in a way, sold themselves on the idea that they're not good enough. What's particularly telling is that their significant other often doesn't see things the same way, as seen in the scenario with Charlie and Brooke. The rift in their relationship isn't a result of the high-scoring partner feeling they're better than the Low Scorer. Rather, it's the detrimental behaviors and beliefs held by the Low Scorer that create the divide.

If you relate more with Scenario 2, where you are the Low Scorer, it's time to have an honest conversation with yourself. Ask yourself these questions: Are you your own worst critic and feel overwhelmed by negative self-talk? Do you often feel like you don't measure up to your partner? Are you frequently grappling with feelings of jealousy, neediness, or a desire to control them? Is there a relentless pursuit for attention, along with an insatiable need for reassurance and validation from your partner?

You may feel like you've hit the jackpot, convincing yourself that you're lucky to have such an incredible partner. Yet, there's a real danger of losing this relationship if you don't start to see your own value and believe in your worth. Once you get a taste of what the Green Zone has to offer, you'll understand the Yellow Zone isn't the highest form of love attainable for you.

In the Green Zone, relationships thrive on mutual respect, healthy self-esteem, and confidence between partners. Yet, achieving this level of harmony requires both individuals to commit to a journey of self-discovery and personal growth.

For the Low Scorer, embarking on this path means coming to terms with and actively working through their insecurities. It involves silencing the inner critic and fully embracing their own value. This journey is rooted in the understanding that their partner's choice to be with them wasn't out of pity or obligation but was driven by recognizing something truly special in them.

The High Scorer's role in the journey is to offer steadfast support, patience, and encouragement as their partner navigates through this period of transformation. They need to help build up their partner's self-esteem and assist them in seeing their own worth and greatness.

Moving from the Yellow Zone into the Green Zone isn't an overnight process; it takes time, dedication, and concerted effort. Yet, with a commitment to growth and a mutual aspiration for a healthier, more affectionate partnership, this journey is not only feasible but also immensely fulfilling. Therefore, if you recognize you're currently in the Yellow Zone, embrace that crucial first step toward self-awareness. Begin your journey toward the lush, fulfilling Green Zone, where love and happiness flourish.

2. Elevate Your Self-Worth

If you see yourself as a Low Scorer within the Yellow Zone, your first move should be deep introspection. This requires you to explore your emotions and thoughts comprehensively, with the aim of improving how you view yourself. The goal is to reach a point where you see yourself as equal to your partner. It's at this juncture that you'll truly gain the respect and admiration of your significant other.

The Love Formula offers the low-scoring partner a set of tools to accurately identify where they feel deficient. With this clarity, they can embark on proactive measures to enhance their inner dialogue and transform how they see themselves. It's vital to keep in mind that these Self Scores are inherently subjective and intimately personal; they are *not* universal truths.

In this context, cognitive reframing becomes an indispensable tool. As discussed in earlier sections, cognitive reframing involves looking at a situation through a new lens, effectively changing the story you tell yourself. Remember: You are more than enough. Your value is indisputable. You inherently deserve love, respect, and admiration. Accepting these truths is crucial for your journey of change.

As you nurture your self-respect, you'll find yourself setting healthy boundaries in your relationship. This change will, interestingly enough, increase your attractiveness and desirability to your partner. It's crucial to grasp that accepting disrespectful behavior only leads to more of the same, creating a harmful cycle that neither of you wants to continue. By enhancing your self-esteem, you'll encourage a positive reaction from your partner, moving both of you toward shared satisfaction and a more robust, joyful relationship.

Transitioning from the Yellow Zone into the harmonious Green Zone is a journey of intentional self-betterment. This path requires facing your insecurities head-on, fostering a habit of positive self-dialogue, and developing a profound sense of self-value. By embarking on this process, you're not only improving your own life but also strengthening the bond with your partner, creating a more loving and resilient partnership. Your view of yourself wields immense influence, with the power to transform both your personal experience and the nature of your relationship. Approach this journey of self-enhancement resolutely, as it paves the way to a brighter, more rewarding future together.

3. Stand by Your Partner

For those who identify as High Scorers in the Yellow Zone, introspection is a crucial step. If you find yourself in the position of the high-scoring partner in Scenario 2, it's important to pause and reflect. Question whether you're truly satisfied with how things are and think about whether the imbalance in your relationship might be leading you to treat your partner unfairly. Believing that you're above your partner and not treating them with the respect and equality they deserve can damage both your personal growth and the health of your relationship.

Now is the moment to embark on your Love Formula journey. Start by identifying the areas where you excel. Then, show kindness and forgiveness to your partner in aspects where they might fall short of your expectations. For example, if their income is lower, take the time to understand their perspective on it. They might value the tranquility and flexibility of a less demanding job over the high-pressure environment of a better-paying role. It's possible they're deeply committed to supporting you, your children, and perhaps your aging parents or to maintaining a peaceful home for the benefit of everyone's well-being.

If you're a High Scorer in the Yellow Zone looking to support your partner, especially if they're grappling with depression and seeking help through therapy or medication, you can be there for them in constructive ways. They might not always be in high spirits, but showing empathy and patience as they work through their condition is crucial. Openly ask them how you can be supportive in their journey toward recovery, demonstrating your willingness to stand by them through thick and thin.

Another positive approach is to recognize and celebrate your partner's efforts. Provide encouragement and express your appreciation. For instance, if your partner usually feels jealous when you make plans with friends but shows understanding instead, take a moment to acknowledge their progress and thank them for being flexible. Such acts of positivity foster an environment where both partners can feel valued and understood, enhancing the relationship's overall warmth and supportiveness.

Making your partner feel valued and cherished is key. Remind them of their inherent worth and that they are just as deserving of love and respect as you are. By demonstrating empathy, patience, and gratitude, you contribute to a more balanced and harmonious relationship where both of you can feel equally appreciated and supported. Love is fundamentally a partnership flourishing most when both partners collaborate to cultivate a nurturing and fulfilling connection.

4. Mutual Effort

Just as with the Red Zone, transitioning from the Yellow Zone to the Green Zone is a collaborative effort, requiring both partners to be dedicated to fostering growth and improvement. If you both see untapped potential in your relationship and aim for happiness together, diving into the Love Formula journey can be transformative. This process serves as a potent catalyst for enhancing communication, sharing your deepest insecurities, identifying mutual areas of admiration and respect, and ultimately, strengthening your bond as a couple.

The Love Formula acts as a mirror, allowing both you and your partner to reevaluate the fairness of your self-assessments. Discovering, through this tool, that you may have been too hard on yourselves opens the door to fostering greater self-compassion and understanding. It illuminates the aspects of yourselves and your relationship that require care and development, guiding you toward a more nurturing and balanced stage of your partnership.

It's understandable if your partner initially hesitates about using the Love Formula, but it's crucial to highlight the potential benefits of tackling it as a team. If you both genuinely aim for personal betterment and are dedicated to improving your relationship, then meaningful change and a happier, more fulfilling partnership are not just feasible—they are a promising outcome that's well within your grasp. By pooling your efforts and using the Love Formula as your roadmap, you can navigate your way to the Green Zone together.

Transitioning Out of the Yellow Zone: Case Study #1

Charlie and Brooke turned to the Love Formula to tackle the disparities straining their relationship and guide their journey from the Yellow Zone into the Green Zone. Through this process, Charlie discovered Brooke's insecurities about her education and her tendency to undervalue her own knowledge. He made it a point to express his profound respect for her profession as a nurse, emphasizing that in many respects, her expertise matched that of doctors. This revelation was a surprise to Brooke and helped her see things in a new light—she realized Charlie truly valued her and believed she brought substantial value to their partnership.

Charlie also opened up about the elements in their relationship that were faltering. He pointed out Brooke's communication style, which had become defensive and accusatory, and shared how he felt like he was walking on eggshells around her. To his surprise, Brooke revealed that his behavior had made her suspect he was hiding something, which had only fueled her defensive stance. In response, Charlie reassured her that he had nothing to hide, aiming to dispel her fears and suspicions.

Charlie and Brooke agreed to regularly revisit the Love Formula, setting aside time every few weeks to engage in open dialogues about their feelings and experiences. Two months into this committed practice, their ongoing communication helped them both gain a clearer perspective on their relationship's state and the strides they had made toward stability. This approach paved the way for transparent and harmonious interactions, deepening their bond significantly. The consistent reevaluation and assessment of their relationship through the Love Formula not only enhanced their mutual respect but also solidified their confidence in the enduring strength of their love.

Brooke took steps to boost her self-esteem by signing up for a seminar on confidence and public speaking. Additionally, she began guitar lessons, embracing a new skill that she hoped would further elevate her self-confidence. On the other hand, Charlie committed to having more transparent discussions about his interactions at work, aiming to clear up any misconceptions about his female colleagues by reassuring Brooke that these relationships were strictly professional and platonic. Together, these proactive measures helped fortify their relationship and were key in their journey toward the Green Zone.

Transitioning Out of the Yellow Zone: Case Study #2

Silvia and Kathleen found themselves perpetually stuck in the Yellow Zone. While Silvia was eager to collaborate and cultivate a healthy relationship, Kathleen lacked the same willingness to invest the necessary effort. This difference in their commitment to the relationship served as a substantial barrier, preventing them from moving forward together.

The dynamic between Silvia and Kathleen became even more challenging due to Silvia's struggles with confidence and self-esteem, which in turn seemed to justify Kathleen's diminishing respect for her. It became evident that their aspirations and core values were fundamentally misaligned. Kathleen sought a partnership defined by luxury and material abundance, while Silvia yearned for a healthy, supportive relationship. With Silvia being unable to fulfill Kathleen's material desires and Kathleen being reluctant to adjust her expectations, the rift between them only widened.

The emotional strain of their situation led Silvia to a crucial realization: She needed to reclaim her self-respect and pursue a relationship within the Green Zone to find true, lasting happiness. Understanding that the fulfilling partnership she longed for could not be realized with Kathleen prompted Silvia to make a bold and brave choice—to end the relationship. This decision, though difficult, was guided by her desire for a healthier, more rewarding connection in the future.

Choosing to part ways, while certainly a tough decision, stands as a testament to the value placed on personal well-being and the quest for a relationship that resonates with one's own values and desires. By deciding to walk different paths, Silvia and Kathleen opened themselves up to the possibility of meeting partners whose visions and values were more in harmony with their own. Such a move paves the way for potential future relationships that are happier, healthier, and more fulfilling, marking a positive stride toward realizing their individual Green Zone dreams.

Now Silvia was ready for her next adventure, where she'd hopefully be in a loving Green Zone—let's explore what that looks like.

Chapter 13

The Green Zone

Green Zone: A relationship where there is a mutual understanding that both partners have high and relatively equal Scores, resulting in healthy and balanced dynamics.

The "Green Zone" is the ideal relationship territory where love thrives and minor issues don't disrupt your bond. This zone signifies a partnership where both individuals equally recognize and appreciate each other's worth. Being in the Green Zone means you are with someone who not only values you but truly deserves your love. It means you have found a partner who is as grateful for your presence in their life as you are for theirs.

So how can you use the Love Formula to determine whether you're in the Green Zone? It's simpler than you think. If your Self Score is soaring high *and* is neck and neck with your Partner Score, it's a clear sign of mutual respect and admiration. That's the sweet spot where both of you appreciate your own and the other's worth fully.

To illustrate what being in the Green Zone looks like, let's explore Sarina and Kweku's calculations in this ideal relationship dynamic.

Sarina's Love Formula Score

Self Score	89%
Partner Score	89%
Love Formula Score	**= 0%**

According to the Love Formula, it's clear that Sarina has high self-worth and also thinks highly of her partner.

Kweku's Love Formula Score

Self Score	90%
Partner Score	93%
Love Formula Score	**= -3%**

Kweku's Love Formula shows he has high self-worth and believes the same about Sarina.

The Green Zone is like the gold standard for an ideal relationship—a partnership where you've got peace of mind, and your connection is built on mutual love and respect. But it's not always as simple as it looks, is it?

One defining feature of those in Green Zone relationships is a strong sense of self-worth. According to our surveys, these individuals assign themselves an average Self Score of 76% and a Partner Score of 81%. Despite their high self-esteem, they stay humble, avoiding arrogance or a sense of entitlement, and they do not view themselves as superior to their partners. It's important to note, though, that self-confidence on its own isn't sufficient to achieve Green Zone status; it demands committed effort, vulnerability, and deep self-reflection.

In the Green Zone, partners possess a strong sense of self-worth without veering into cockiness. They understand that acknowledging their imperfections strengthens their bond. Humility plays a crucial role, with both individuals admitting when they're wrong, apologizing, and showing vulnerability. This authenticity fosters a deep connection built on mutual respect and understanding, leading to a truly fulfilling relationship.

Conflict is a natural part of any relationship, but how you handle it can make all the difference. In healthy relationships, conflicts are resolved through compassion and effective communication. Both partners are committed to working through disagreements in a constructive manner, guided by their shared values and love for each other.

In the Green Zone, the relationship evolves into a genuine partnership, where both individuals actively support each other's growth and success. They celebrate each other's triumphs and provide unwavering support during challenging times. They view love as a journey they embark on together, rather than as a competition between them.

Achieving and maintaining balance and centeredness is essential for sustaining a relationship in the Green Zone. When there's an equilibrium between values and traits in your Love Formula calculations, it often indicates potential harmony in the Green Zone. Individuals who prioritize both values and traits equally in their Love Formula are more likely to achieve and sustain balance in the Green Zone.

In the Green Zone, partners adeptly balance independence and interdependence. They value personal space, pursue individual interests, and maintain separate friendships while also embracing interdependence. They rely on each other for various aspects of their lives, share responsibilities, and provide emotional support. Operating as a unified team, they draw strength from their cohesion and mutual respect.

In this scenario, one partner working outside the home while the other stays at home is a common arrangement that reflects the balance and interdependence characteristic of the Green Zone. While the working partner contributes financially, the stay-at-home partner provides invaluable support by managing household responsibilities, childcare, and other essential tasks. Both roles are essential for the family's sustainability and well-being, highlighting the mutual respect and appreciation present in a Green Zone relationship.

In the Green Zone, communication is the cornerstone of the relationship dynamic. Partners prioritize open, honest, and respectful dialogue, avoiding manipulative tactics or acts of reprisal. They create an environment where expressing concerns or feelings is welcomed and met with understanding, nurturing a deep sense of trust and mutual respect between them.

Drama has no place in the Green Zone. Partners understand that a calm and harmonious environment is essential for a fulfilling life together. They prioritize the well-being of the relationship over personal ego and pride, recognizing that maintaining open, honest communication is crucial for nurturing a healthy and stable partnership.

One of the most valuable rewards in the Green Zone is the deep trust that partners have in each other. Minor issues are quickly resolved, and trust remains steadfast. Partners don't harbor suspicions or insecurities, creating a peaceful and secure atmosphere in the relationship.

However, maintaining a position in the Green Zone can be challenging. Many couples may occasionally find themselves slipping into the Yellow or Red Zones.

For instance, when faced with adversity, such as one partner losing their job and experiencing depression, a couple can transition into the Yellow Zone. One partner may grapple with feelings of inadequacy while the other's self-esteem remains intact. Without intervention or improvement, this situation can lead to discouragement, disempowerment, and unfair behaviors directed toward the "more successful" partner.

In certain instances, external factors can also trigger shifts into the Yellow or Red Zones. For example, the loss of a loved one can induce anxiety and depression, leading one partner to exhibit behaviors associated with these Zones. In such cases, if the other partner offers patience, love, and compassion, it often paves the way for a return to the Green Zone.

Let's look into how Kweku and Sarina worked together toward the Green Zone.

Navigating the Green Zone: A Case Study

Before Sarina and Kweku met, they were both healing from painful breakups. After leaving their partners, they were heartbroken, each determined not to repeat the same mistakes in their next relationship.

When Kweku and Sarina's paths crossed, there was an unmistakable spark, a hint that this could be something special. But they didn't rush, instead choosing to approach their budding relationship with a blend of care, respect, and genuine affection. Having learned from past experiences, Kweku vowed to be more giving this time around. Sarina, on her end, recognized the importance of cherishing herself more.

Together, they applied these lessons, crafting a relationship that felt beautifully balanced and deeply fulfilling. It was as if they had found the perfect recipe for a healthy partnership, enjoying each moment they shared with a sense of completeness.

Was there ever trouble in paradise? Did they get into arguments? Yes, of course. Nonetheless, they were both mindful not to fall into the same patterns they had experienced in their past relationships. They wholeheartedly dedicated themselves to treating each other with love and respect, even in moments of disagreement. They made a concerted effort to request 100% of what they desired while also expressing 100% gratitude for what they already had.

Staying in the Green Zone

If the story of the Green Zone sounds like your love story, then take a moment to give yourselves a well-deserved pat on the back! You've built an extraordinary relationship, laying down a strong foundation of mutual growth, respect, and enduring harmony. Remember, landing in the Green Zone is no walk in the park. It's a badge of honor you earn after navigating through countless storms and challenges. Achieving personal growth is a formidable journey, and you've shown remarkable dedication to reaching this state of bliss. You're not just surviving together; you're thriving, and that's a rare and beautiful thing to celebrate.

Yet it's crucial to remember that staying in this Zone requires continuous, unwavering commitment. To ensure that you remain on this fulfilling path, here are a few strategies to consider:

1. Practice Gratitude

Treading the dating landscape can often feel like an endurance test, riddled with competitiveness and, at times, a cynical outlook. Landing in a meaningful relationship is a victory worth celebrating. If you've weathered the trials and tribulations, you know all too well that this journey is anything but straightforward. And if, after countless attempts, you've finally settled into the cherished Green

Zone, you're probably overwhelmed with a sense of gratitude for breaking free from the vicious cycle of past errors. This achievement marks not just a new chapter in your love life but also a profound moment of personal victory and growth.

It's common to fall into a state of complacency, where you might start to take your relationship for granted. There might be moments when you catch yourself "coasting" along or thinking, "There are plenty of other fish in the sea." While it's normal to have these lapses, swiftly shaking off this mindset is also essential. These periods of taking things lightly can sneak up on you, but recognizing and addressing them quickly ensures they don't undermine the solid foundation you've built together. Remember, the grass isn't greener on the other side; it's greener where you water it. Stay vigilant in nurturing your relationship, and it will continue to thrive.

Arriving at the Green Zone represents a significant achievement. This level of love and connection isn't something you stumble upon with just anyone. Both you and your partner have poured considerable effort and commitment into reaching this stage. Hence, it's crucial to be vigilant against undermining your progress by overlooking the importance of gratitude. Recognizing and appreciating each other's contributions helps maintain the strength and health of your relationship. It's the daily acts of acknowledgment and thankfulness that reinforce your bond and ensure you don't take this hard-earned place of harmony for granted. Keep the flames of appreciation stoked, and your relationship will continue to flourish in the Green Zone.

Make it a habit to express appreciation, extending this gratitude not just toward your partner but also toward yourself for the journey that has led you both to the Green Zone. Take time to celebrate the effort, personal growth, and depth of love that have molded your relationship into something truly exceptional. This sense of gratitude acts as a crucial pillar in safeguarding and fostering the precious connection you've cultivated together. It's this foundation of appreciation that ensures your relationship continues to thrive, deepening the bond and enriching your shared experiences in the Green Zone.

2. Infuse Your Relationship with Excitement

Once you're in the Green Zone, life adopts a new tempo—steady, predictable, mature, and fulfilling. Yet, it's an intriguing part of our human makeup that we sometimes hunger for excitement, drama, and an additional spark, especially when our surroundings feel too comfortable, too straightforward, and too stable. This yearning for a bit more "zing" is natural, reflecting our complex desires for both security and adventure. It's a reminder of the delicate balance we seek in our lives and relationships: A place where stability does not mean stagnation and where comfort doesn't extinguish the flames of passion and novelty. Recognizing this duality is key to navigating the peaceful waters of the Green Zone without losing sight of the vibrant energy that keeps love alive and exciting.

Many who have maneuvered their way through the tumultuous territories of the Red and Yellow Zones in past relationships might find themselves craving the excitement, drama, and intense energy they've grown accustomed to. This longing can be almost like a drug addiction, where the rollercoaster of extreme highs and lows, the allure of constant change, and the thrill of novelty become familiar chaos. In the face of this, the calmness and predictability of stable relationships might, unfortunately, be dismissed as "boring." This perspective reflects how experiences in our relational history can shape our expectations and desires, sometimes leading us to overlook the beauty and depth found in a peaceful, stable relationship. Recognizing and adjusting these expectations is crucial for fully appreciating the serene harmony of the Green Zone without mislabeling its tranquility as monotony.

The essence of the Green Zone largely lies in its smooth and consistent flow. However, to sidestep the snare of monotony, it's crucial to avoid becoming too settled in routines, like spending excessive time lounging on the couch or sticking strictly to the familiar repertoire of home-cooked meals. Embrace the chance to venture out and inject new experiences into your life. Delve into activities that awaken your senses and ignite your passion. Whether it's trying out a new hobby together, exploring unseen places, or simply switching up your daily habits, these ventures can refresh and energize your relationship. By keeping the spirit of adventure alive, you ensure that your journey in the Green Zone remains vibrant and fulfilling, far from the realms of boredom.

3. Prevent Regression into Yellow or Red Zones

Navigating your way to and sustaining a place in the Green Zone is no small feat, and it's common for couples to occasionally find themselves drifting into the Yellow or Red Zones. This ebb and flow through the zones, transitioning from Green to Yellow, dipping into Red, and then perhaps back to Green, is a part of many relationships' natural cycles. However, to anchor your relationship firmly in the Green Zone, a continuous, dedicated effort is needed.

Spotting potential stressors that might cause you or your partner to regress is crucial:

- Are there ongoing disputes with your partner's family that resurface occasionally?

- Do the stresses of a toxic workplace follow you home?

- Are irritability or mood swings often the result of hunger, lack of sleep, too much noise, or overwhelming situations?

- Could financial worries threaten your sense of balance?

Awareness of these triggers can help you both to preemptively manage or mitigate their impact. Common stressors include financial pressures, work-related stress, health issues, differences in parenting styles, communication breakdowns, and lack of quality time together. By identifying these stress points early on, you can develop strategies to address them.

Rather than perceiving these challenges as setbacks, consider them as chances for growth and deeper understanding. Tackle them with empathy and a united determination to discover solutions. This approach not only fosters resilience but also fortifies your relationship, turning potential obstacles into powerful moments of collective triumph and enlightenment.

Maintaining your place in the Green Zone is an ongoing journey that relies on self-awareness, clear communication, and mutual support. It involves a deliberate choice to uphold love, respect, and growth, even when faced with the inevitable challenges and setbacks of life. This commitment to navigating life's ups and downs together is what keeps the relationship vibrant, resilient, and deeply fulfilling.

4. Communicate, Communicate, Communicate

Keeping your relationship within the Green Zone demands that both partners develop profound self-awareness and continually recommit to themselves, each other, and the relationship as their highest priorities. In this context, using the Love Formula and exchanging your insights plays a pivotal role. This practice fosters open communication, ensures alignment of values and goals, and reinforces the bond that sustains the relationship's health and vitality.

Often, we might not fully grasp how our partners see us or even how they view themselves. Our wants and needs can shift as we journey through life, occasionally catching us off guard when it comes to our true desires. In such situations, the Love Formula serves as a revealing tool, shining a light on vulnerabilities and pinpointing areas where your partner, or even you, might see potential for growth. The key goal is to create an environment where open and sincere dialogue flourishes, rather than misusing this insight as a means to undermine or assert dominance over each other. This approach is fundamental in building trust and understanding within the relationship.

Lean into vulnerability and clear openness as you communicate your needs. Engage in these conversations with a spirit of kindness, ensuring that each partner has the space to both speak fearlessly and listen attentively. After you've each filled out your Love Formulas separately, start and end your discussion with sincere expressions of gratitude. This method can be thought of as "sandwiching," where even constructive feedback, if delivered with respect and care, tends to be embraced more willingly within a context of warm, positive affirmation. This technique not only facilitates a smoother exchange of potentially delicate insights but also reinforces the bond of mutual respect and affection.

As a couple, it's beneficial to establish regular check-in meetings, whether they be weekly or monthly. These sessions are a strategic way to make sure you both stay on the same page, are happy with how the relationship is developing, and remain attuned to each other's emotions. Adopting this proactive stance acts as a preventive measure, effectively nipping any budding problems that might otherwise grow and shift you into the Yellow Zone. By consistently dedicating time to assess and nurture your relationship, you reinforce its strength and resilience, ensuring that you continue thriving in the Green Zone.

Even in the most joyful of relationships, setbacks can emerge if individuals don't stay true to themselves and their partners about experiencing boredom or if needs, wants, and desires are going unmet. This lack of openness can lead to feelings of being undervalued, regardless of whether it's an intentional oversight by their partner. Thus, keeping communication channels open and active is crucial for the health and vibrancy of the relationship. It ensures that both partners feel heard, valued, and understood, preventing misunderstandings that could otherwise drive a wedge between them. This commitment to transparency is a key ingredient in nurturing a relationship that not only survives but flourishes.

Imagine your relationship as a garden. Much like how a garden needs consistent weeding, watering, and daily care to flourish and flower, your relationship demands regular attention and care to prosper. This analogy underscores the importance of actively engaging in the maintenance and growth of your partnership. By dedicating time and effort to address issues, communicating effectively, and nurturing your bond, you create a thriving environment where love can bloom and grow, just as a well-tended garden becomes a source of beauty and sustenance.

To sum up, the framework of Red, Yellow, and Green Zones offers a valuable roadmap through the complex landscape of human relationships. The Red Zone highlights areas of deep conflict and distress, serving as a stark reminder of the emotional battlegrounds we strive to avoid. The Yellow Zone, meanwhile, signals a time for caution and introspection, where, following the principles of the Love Formula, individuals and couples come to terms with their flaws and acknowledge the need for healing and growth. The ultimate goal, however, is to reach the Green Zone. It is in this space that the ideals of the Love Formula flourish—mutual respect, love, and the journey of self-discovery lay the groundwork. Relationships in the Green Zone are not just sustained; they thrive, powered by an equation that encourages both personal development and collective harmony. Embracing these insights and the tenets of the Love Formula equips you with the tools necessary for a fulfilling and peaceful voyage through love's varied terrains.

Part IV

Personality Types

The Love Formula's effectiveness lies in its recognition that each individual is uniquely wired, with distinct personal beliefs and experiences influencing their approach to love and relationships. For example, some people prioritize caution and safety in their relationships, while others seek something exhilarating and will not settle for anything less.

Based on our one-on-one interviews, it became clear that participants demonstrated remarkably unique approaches to their calculations, showcasing their dynamic personalities and diverse perspectives. This observation led to the formulation of four distinct Personality Type scales:

1. **Practical vs. Emotional**

2. **Critic vs. Optimist**

3. **Safety Seeker vs. Risk-Taker**

4. **Alike vs. Diversified**

Just as the Love Formula assists individuals in achieving greater self-awareness, these Personality Types serve as tools for a more refined understanding of oneself. It's crucial to recognize that these classifications are not about labeling behaviors as inherently good or bad. Instead, it's the "Extreme" within each type that warrants careful consideration. Each Personality Type exists on a spectrum, and we will examine what constitutes a "Healthy" expression versus an "Extreme" manifestation within each category.

To understand how you and your partner view and approach relationships, we use a scale to categorize and understand your personalities. The scale below ranges from one Extreme to the other, with a healthy balance in the middle.

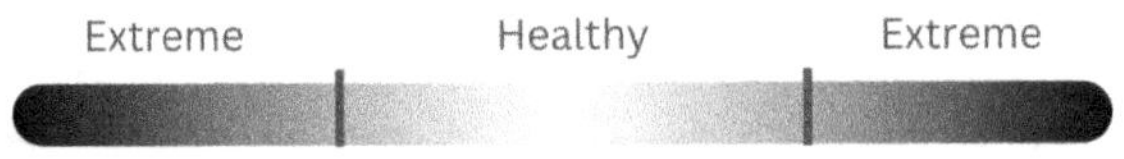

On the far left, we identify behaviors and inclinations that are overly intense or rigid. As we move toward the center, these characteristics become more balanced. Here individuals exhibit a well-rounded and adaptive personality.

In the chapters ahead, we'll explore each Personality Type in detail, focusing on their strengths and challenges. Understanding and managing these differences is key. Each chapter ends with a questionnaire designed to give you deeper insights into your relationships, encourage self-reflection, and help you better navigate the complexities of interpersonal interactions.

Let's get into it.

Chapter 14

The Practical vs. the Emotional

Do you find yourself swept away by the whims of your heart, or do you take a more pragmatic approach, letting logic guide your romantic decisions? The Love Formula recognizes how each of us is wired uniquely, acknowledging that some may navigate love with a heart-led emotional approach, while others may adopt a more practical, reasoned perspective. Gaining insight into where you and your partner fall on this emotional-practical spectrum is crucial for a deeper understanding of each other. It facilitates empathy, promotes better communication, and helps in navigating the differences and similarities between partners with greater awareness.

To help you and your partner better grasp where you each stand, we'll delve into both the Healthy and the Extreme sides of each personality aspect.

The Healthy Practical

Healthy Practical: A Values-leaning individual with a more pragmatic approach to relationships.

Meet the "Healthy Practical"—a person who places the crown of importance on Values rather than getting lost in the labyrinth of Traits. For them, a partnership must first and foremost "make sense."

From their perspective, a relationship is deemed impractical or unlikely to endure if there's a significant discord in fundamental beliefs and lifestyles. Their aim is to connect with a partner whose Values align closely with their own, someone who not only fits effortlessly into their lifestyle but also serves as a dependable ally. This preference for practical advantages over purely emotional attractions is vividly captured in their Love Formula (Step 4: Priority Allocation), where Values receive a greater emphasis than Traits.

When using the Love Formula, the Healthy Practical will give a Priority Allocation of 30% to Traits and 70% to Values (Table 4), respectively. This balance highlights their pragmatic approach to relationships, prioritizing shared principles and compatibility in core beliefs and lifestyle. However, if the priority allocation in favor of Values exceeds 70%, it shifts them toward the "Extreme Practical" end of the spectrum.

Imagine a long-distance relationship where two people go to great lengths to keep their connection alive with texts, calls, FaceTime, and the odd physical visit. The driving force behind their dedication to navigating this tough situation is the deep emotional connection they've built and their readiness to make sacrifices for one another.

But life is full of twists and turns. Imagine if one partner lands a promotion—meaning they must remain in their city despite earlier intentions to move closer to their significant other. This scenario can lead to the need for tough, rational decisions over emotional ones. If one or both partners take on a Healthy Practical perspective, they might conclude that the relationship no longer aligns with their evolving paths due to these differing life directions.

When faced with complex situations, the Healthy Practical knows when to step back and evaluate whether the relationship aligns with their Values. If it does, they will continue to invest further time and resources. It's not that the Healthy Practical doesn't seek an emotional connection; they can be just as enthralled and smitten as anyone else. The critical difference is that this person avoids making *impulsive* relationship decisions driven by overpowering emotions and desires. They won't rush into commitment for the sake of partnership. People in this personality bracket often want peace of mind and predictability. They remain pragmatic and focused, looking for a relationship that complements their desire for a balanced life.

A relationship with a Healthy Practical is marked by a distinctive combination of stability, compatibility, and a focus on teamwork toward shared goals. In such a partnership, you can look forward to

- **Steadiness**: Your relationship is built on a solid foundation, where unexpected upheavals are rare, and security is a given.

- **Alignment**: You and your partner will likely share key life goals and Values, making it easier to dream and plan for the future together.

- **Pragmatic Love**: Emotions are important, but decisions are made with a balanced view, considering both partners' long-term well-being.

- **Mutual Support**: Whether it's career ambitions or personal growth, expect encouragement and backing from each other.

- **Effective Communication**: Conversations tend to be open, honest, and solution-oriented, aimed at resolving differences constructively.

- **Quality Teamwork**: Working together seamlessly, both in everyday tasks and in achieving larger life goals, is a hallmark of your relationship.

In essence, being with a Healthy Practical means embarking on a journey where love is both felt and thoughtfully considered, creating a nurturing environment for both individuals to thrive.

The Healthy Practical: A Case Study

Karl's childhood was spent in a home where financial stability was always just out of reach, leaving him with memories of opportunities missed because there simply wasn't enough money. Now having grown up, Karl has transformed his circumstances through education and hard work, securing a corporate position that pays a six-figure salary. This achievement has allowed him to find the financial stability that was absent during his formative years, something he values immensely and considers a significant personal triumph.

One day, he meets Mitra at a coffee shop, and her humor and beauty captivate him almost instantly. Over the next month, they spend more time together, deepening their connection, becoming intimate, and getting to know each other better.

But soon Karl learns that Mitra has racked up a substantial credit card debt of $50,000, and she appears to have no desire to repay it. Despite his strong feelings and attraction for her, Karl wonders if Mitra's lifestyle aligns with his own. He had always dreamed of sharing a comfortable lifestyle with a partner, but now he is unsure if Mitra can be that person.

And so Karl finds himself at a crossroads, torn between continuing the relationship or breaking up with her. *What if he ends things with Mitra and never finds someone who makes him feel like she does?* On the other hand, if he chooses to be with her and build a life together, he worries about the possibility of them having to live paycheck to paycheck due to her financial choices. It is a tough decision, but after careful consideration, Karl makes a prudent choice, ultimately ending the relationship—a hallmark of his "Healthy Practical" mindset.

In Karl's case, his Love Formula places a higher importance on Values, particularly *financial stability*, as a cornerstone of his decision-making process. This example shows how a person's Values, shaped by their life experiences, can have a significant impact on their relationship choices.

The Extreme Practical

Extreme Practical: A Values-focused individual with a rigid approach to relationships.

It's time to meet the "Extreme Practical"—someone who is *so* focused on Values that they exclusively make head-over-heart decisions without any wiggle room. This person either doesn't consider their emotions or represses them entirely to rationalize their rigid thought process.

When using the Love Formula, the Extreme Practical's Priority Allocation in favor of Values will exceed 70% (Table 4). This imbalance highlights their strict approach to relationships and their unwillingness to compromise their shared Values and lifestyle. Here's what an Extreme Practical may sound like:

- "You want to travel and chip away at my retirement savings? Hell no!"

- "You won't provide for me while I complete my PhD program? Goodbye."

- "You can't have kids because of physical health issues? To the curb!"

Ouch, right? While this Personality Type is relatively rare—with most of our survey participants falling within the middle range—an individual who excessively emphasizes Values can be damaging to any relationship. Unlike Healthy Practicals, Extreme Practicals place such exceptional importance on Values in their Love Formula that anything short of perfection is considered nonnegotiable.

Individuals falling within this category have crystal-clear goals and are determined to achieve them. The Extreme Practical is resolute and will go to great lengths to ensure they succeed in their aspirations.

So are people with this personality simply robots, unable to feel guilt, remorse, shame, or love? Absolutely not. But they *are* dead set on their priorities, which are far more important to them than any one individual. Hence, they seek the highest Partner Values Scores, leaving no room for compromise. The instant they detect their partner falling short in Values, they step back significantly or terminate the relationship, regardless of commitments, familial ties, circumstances, or emotional attachments.

Those involved with Extreme Practicals often perceive their relationships as transactional, akin to a business agreement. It's a continuous exchange along the lines of "I provide this, and you provide that." The partner's experience can be characterized by an absence of love and passion, leaving them to question whether any romantic sparks exist. In addition, you can expect the following from an Extreme Practical:

- **Lack of Spontaneity**: Spontaneous, romantic gestures may be less common as they tend to plan and calculate their actions meticulously.

- **Emotionally Reserved**: Their display of emotions and affection may be sporadic, focusing more on practicality than emotional attachment.

- **High Expectations**: They might have a set of specific expectations that need to be met, and any deviation from these standards can lead to dissatisfaction.

- **Analytical Approach**: They tend to analyze the pros and cons of the relationship and may make decisions based on a cost-benefit analysis rather than emotional factors.

If you happen to be in love with an Extreme Practical and find yourself falling short of their set of Values, proceed with caution. This person might end up breaking your heart.

The Extreme Practical: A Case Study

Robert identified himself as a pragmatic person, deeply trusting in his logical and goal-oriented approach to life. He had a clear vision of where he wanted to be in the next five years: in a committed relationship, co-owning a home, raising two children, having saved at least $100,000, and traveling every two years. Robert was unwavering in his pursuit of these goals and was not willing to compromise on them. He had resolved to only date people who shared and fitted into his meticulously outlined five-year plan, believing that this strategy would lead him to the fulfilling life he had envisioned.

When he met Sarah, it wasn't just about the sparks; it was as if he had found someone who truly fit into the picture he had in his mind for the future. She was everything he valued: dependable, focused on her career, and always honest. Together, they shared Values that made the first few years feel just right, moving steadily toward the goals they dreamed of achieving as a team. But life threw them a curveball when Sarah faced a DUI charge, leading to the loss of her law license. This wasn't just a bump in the road; it was a seismic shift for Sarah, leaving her to face the reality of a future that suddenly seemed shaky and uncertain.

After hearing the news, Robert, who had always been the type to think practically above all, quickly started weighing the new reality. Questions started racing through his mind: How would Sarah keep earning without her license? Was going back to school for a new career even on the table, considering the time, money, and debt it would entail? Unfortunately, looking at things through his pragmatic lens and what he considered *his* Love Formula, Robert couldn't see any logical reason to stay together. So within a week after Sarah lost her license, he made the tough decision to end their relationship.

What led Robert to become so emotionally guarded, to distance himself from his feelings, especially after three years with someone by his side? It could be a number of things: Maybe past heartaches, tough experiences in his early years, or deep scars left by neglect or abandonment played a part in building those walls. It's possible that facing one too many letdowns had pushed him to lean more on logic than on his heart as a way to protect himself from more hurt. No matter the cause, his approach as an Extreme Practical meant he found it hard to give that unconditional love or support when times got tough. Robert's situation really highlights how crucial it is to strike a balance in relationships to ensure that both partners feel supported and understood.

The Healthy Emotional

Healthy Emotional: A Traits-leaning individual with a more emotional approach to relationships.

Let's talk about the "Healthy Emotional" Personality Type. When using the Love Formula, the Healthy Emotional will give a Priority Allocation of no less than 30% to Values, and no more than 70% to Traits. This balance highlights their emotionally connected approach to relationships, emphasizing affection and attraction. However, if the Priority Allocation in favor of Traits exceeds 70%, they shift toward the "Extreme Emotional" end of the spectrum.

For this group, emotional connection is key. They're the ones who can look past a not-so-great Partner Values Score if they feel emotionally fulfilled. When making decisions about their relationships, they go with their gut feeling over cold, hard logic. It's all about what feels right in the heart, not what looks perfect on paper.

Imagine someone who cherishes affection more than anything else—because, truly, what's more powerful than love to keep the world spinning? Those who fall into the Healthy Emotional category put a huge emphasis on the emotional bond and the depth of their interactions. Their relationships thrive on chemistry, physical connection, deep talks, and shared excitement for life's adventures. Yet, they haven't thrown caution to the wind; they still keep a solid grip on practicality and reason. They're concerned about finding that sweet spot between following their heart and using their head.

Here's a distinguishing characteristic of the Healthy Emotional: They're rockstars when it comes to communication, which is absolutely key to keeping that emotional intimacy alive and well. It's probably no surprise that these folks have emotional intelligence in spades. In their relationships, you'll find a lot of open and honest conversations—this openness not only brings them closer to their partner but also cements their emotional bond. They're not shy about sharing how they feel and they create a space where their partner feels just as comfortable doing the same.

It turns out that the bulk of those who took our survey identify with the Healthy Emotional Personality Type. And that's really encouraging! It means a lot of us naturally seek out those deeper, more emotionally fulfilling connections in our relationships. We're talking about a preference for the kind of richness that comes from genuine emotional experiences. This shows a common desire for meaningful interactions and a deeper understanding and appreciation of one another.

Being in a relationship with a Healthy Emotional can provide deep emotional satisfaction, making one feel genuinely wanted and loved by their partner. You can expect this person to offer

- **Genuine Affection**: Expect abundant displays of affection and care. They enjoy physical touch, loving gestures, and words of affirmation, ensuring you feel genuinely wanted and loved.

- **Loving Support**: They are your biggest cheerleaders. They unwaveringly support your pursuits, dreams, and challenges, making you feel confident, empowered, and loved.

- **Emotional Safety**: They help you feel safe in this relationship. You can be authentic, express your emotions without judgment, and know you are genuinely cared for and appreciated.

- **Intimate Connection**: Intimacy is an essential aspect of your relationship. Whether it's physical intimacy, deep conversations, or sharing vulnerabilities, Healthy Emotionals feel intimately connected on various levels.

The Healthy Emotional Personality Type is all about empathy, top-notch communication skills, and a solid commitment to both personal and relationship growth. These are the folks who bring a priceless depth of feeling and understanding to their connections, making their relationships richer and more fulfilling. Their empathy allows them to really get where their partner is coming from, while their communication skills ensure that issues don't just sit—they get addressed. And their dedication to growth means they're always working on making things even better, both for themselves and for the relationship. It's these qualities that help build a deep, lasting bond with their partners.

The Healthy Emotional: A Case Study

Richard's single life had been a worrying topic for his parents, especially when he had moved into his forties without settling down with someone for the long haul. But then Lynn came into the picture—a delightful woman in her mid-thirties, also on the lookout for a serious relationship. To his parents, she was just what they had been hoping for Richard: She valued family, stood on solid financial ground, and had a rich appreciation for culture. In their view, Lynn was the perfect fit for Richard, someone who would not just join their family but truly become part of it.

After his parents introduced the two, Richard found himself sharing coffee with Lynn, and it didn't take long for him to think, "Mom and Dad might be onto something here. She really is a wonderful person." On paper, the match seemed almost too good to be true. Keeping an open mind, Richard decided to give this a fair shot, agreeing to go on three more dates with Lynn to explore where this connection might lead.

As Richard and Lynn spent more time together, he increasingly saw her as "wifey material." They found that their Values aligned beautifully, which was something Richard took seriously when considering a future together. The idea of choosing Lynn as a long-term partner, and maybe even as the mother of his future children, started to feel like not just a heart-led decision but a smart, practical one too.

Yet there was a significant hiccup in Richard's budding relationship with Lynn: The spark just wasn't there. Their first kiss didn't set off any fireworks, holding hands felt oddly mundane, and hugging her felt more familial than romantic. Despite his willingness to let attraction grow over time and the comfort he felt in Lynn's company, Richard couldn't shake off the feeling that their relationship was missing the excitement he had longed for. To make matters more complex, he realized that laughter was scarce between them, which was a dealbreaker for him. Laughter and shared joy were vital to Richard, and their sparseness marked a significant gap in what he needed from a relationship.

As someone who identified closely with the "Healthy Emotional" type, Richard placed significant importance on the Traits and both the emotional and physical connections within a relationship. Despite everything seemingly fitting well on the surface, and to the surprise of those around him, Richard made the difficult decision to end the relationship at this juncture. For him, the lack of passion and the inability to share laughter—a key Trait he valued deeply—outweighed the logical reasons to stay together. This move underscored his belief in the importance of a deep emotional and physical connection as the foundation of a lasting relationship.

Richard's decision to end things with Lynn was rooted in a thoughtful and measured approach. It wasn't a snap judgment but rather the result of careful deliberation, keen self-awareness, and an attempt to strike a balance between what's desired and what's present. Far from being an "extreme" reaction, it was a calculated move informed by his personal needs and relationship ideals. Although he appreciated the Values he shared with Lynn, the absence of a robust physical or emotional connection was something he couldn't overlook. For Richard, these connections are fundamental, not just nice-to-haves, in building a relationship that's both fulfilling and enduring.

The Extreme Emotional

Extreme Emotional: A Traits-focused individual with an overly emotional approach to relationships.

The "Extreme Emotional" individuals exhibit intense sensitivity and often find it hard to anchor their decisions in logic. It's a classic scenario—despite all rational signs pointing one way, they'll say, "But I love him/her!" Their emotions are the driver, the map, and the destination, making it challenging for them to navigate the waters of love with a clear head.

When using the Love Formula, the Extreme Emotional's Priority Allocation in favor of Traits will exceed 70% (Table 4). This imbalance highlights their emotionally intense approach to relationships, where they are blinded by their attraction to their partner. They often become overly forgiving of a low Partner Values Score if the Partner Traits Score is high, focusing too much on certain qualities at the expense of a well-rounded view of the relationship.

You might wonder, "What's the problem? They love others for their true selves, right?" While that's a valid perspective, let's consider a different scenario: What if *being reliable* is one of their Top 5 Values? In this case, is it truly beneficial to overlook the actions of someone who consistently shows up forty-five minutes late to dates, cancels plans at the last minute, or fails to keep their promises? This brings up an important question: Where do you draw the line to ensure that your most important standards aren't being compromised?

"But they're SO sexyy!" you might still argue. If that's your main sticking point, then, my friend, you've ventured deep into the territory of the Extreme Emotional. Brace yourself because this is where hearts don't just break; they shatter into a million tiny pieces. It's a poignant reminder of the high emotional stakes involved when attraction overshadows other critical aspects of a relationship.

People who lean into Extreme Emotional tendencies generally find it hard to focus on the long haul or think practically about the future. They tend to weave this idealized story in their minds, something straight out of a flawless Romeo-and-Juliet narrative. Yet, as time passes, it becomes painfully clear that their envisioned love story was doomed from the start. This pattern is often a sign of a youthful, immature, and hopelessly romantic view of love. In essence, it's like being addicted to the idea of love itself, resulting in a belief in perfect, fairy-tale relationships that simply don't exist in reality.

For those deeply caught up in Extreme Emotional inclinations, the idea of a balanced, stable love often seems unappealing— too mundane for their taste. They crave the constant flutter of butterflies in their stomach. For them, a relationship must be a source of ceaseless emotional stimulation, regardless of whether it brings joy or pain. This craving for intensity often leads them into a cycle of turbulent, "on again, off again" relationships, or into those murky, complex "it's complicated" situations. Their emotional highs and lows, combined with unpredictable behaviors, make it challenging to maintain steady, healthy relationships.

They have a habit of projecting their own fantasies onto their partners, setting the stage for potentially painful misunderstandings. Even when they recognize the destructive patterns in their behavior, gaining control over these impulses can be a daunting challenge. And when that self-awareness slips even slightly, they find themselves drawn back into the seductive grip of their emotional fantasies, struggling to differentiate between what's real and what's wished for. This cycle not only strains their relationships but also hampers their emotional growth and self-understanding.

Keep in mind that a Trait can be beneficial, neutral, or harmful. Traits such as emotional unavailability, controlling behavior, dominance, and abusive tendencies are decidedly in the harmful camp. When an Extreme Emotional sets their sights on someone embodying these destructive Traits, the outcome can be catastrophic. This combination can result in the normalization or even romanticization of detrimental behavior, leading to the acceptance of toxic patterns. Because of their propensity to prioritize intense feelings over logical assessment, Extreme Emotionals are more vulnerable to abusive relationships. This vulnerability stems from their willingness to overlook their core Values and endure unacceptable behavior, all under the guise of love.

Starting a relationship with an Extreme Emotional often results in instant excitement followed by a rapid deterioration. You may also find

- **Intense Initial Attraction**: They will sweep you off your feet with intense passion and enthusiasm. Their love can be all-consuming, making you feel incredibly desired and cherished.

- **Obsessive Love**: Their love can sometimes border on obsession, leading to possessiveness and jealousy. This can contribute to toxicity in the relationship and lead to issues of trust and control.

- **Difficulty Managing Autonomy**: They can make you feel overwhelmed and lose your sense of independence, as they often prioritize constant togetherness.

- **Inability to Let Go and Move On**: They often linger after a breakup, struggling to detach emotionally, and might engage in unhealthy actions to maintain a connection with you.

While a relationship with an Extreme Emotional can have moments of passion and excitement, it can also be challenging for those who prefer a more balanced and calmer approach to love and relationships. To make this partnership work, there must be open communication, boundaries, and a mutual understanding of each other's needs.

The Extreme Emotional: A Case Study

At the age of twenty-six, Tracy found herself repeatedly drawn to the so-called "bad boys"—those with an irresistible allure, sweeping her into whirlwinds of initial thrill and passionate moments. Yet time and again, these relationships took a dark turn, becoming toxic landscapes of jealousy and baseless accusations. Fresh from the aftermath of her latest relationship disaster, Tracy was more resolved than ever. She was determined to break this cycle and steer clear of relationships with men whose charm concealed destructive tendencies.

One day, as Tracy was in line at the DMV, she noticed a tall man behind her, clad in ripped jeans and a fitted shirt. The moment their gazes met and smiles were shared, she felt that all-too-familiar flutter of butterflies in her stomach. Her instincts immediately sent up red flags, whispering, "This guy is *definitely* trouble." She tried to stay focused on the line ahead, but he got her attention by making her laugh with a joke.

After some conversation, she learned that his name was Seth. They flirted and exchanged numbers. Tracy could already sense herself melting at the thought of him. But during the early stages of dating, she discovered some concerning details about Seth: He had lost custody of his two young children due to issues with alcohol, he worked for an oil company, and he harbored strong negative opinions about Middle Eastern cultures. These revelations took Tracy by surprise, as they clashed significantly with her core Values. As an environmentalist and a stanch anti-racism advocate, she found herself at a crossroads, confronted with the reality that Seth represented everything she stood against.

Despite the stark contrast between Seth's lifestyle and her Values, Tracy's approach to love—her Love Formula—urged her to give priority to the Traits she found attractive in a partner, even at the expense of her core beliefs. The challenge of resisting the powerful attraction she felt toward Seth proved difficult because he embodied the Traits she was drawn to. Given her Extreme Emotional inclinations, Tracy chose to keep seeing Seth, deciding to navigate the tumultuous waters of her attraction despite the compromises she had to make on her Values.

The Practical vs. the Emotional Personality Type Questionnaire

Where do you find yourself on the spectrum between pragmatism and passion? Reaching the middle ground between choices grounded in practicality and those led by our emotions is crucial.

This questionnaire is designed to help you reflect on your tendencies and preferences when navigating a relationship's practical and emotional aspects, a core component of the Love Formula's philosophy. By answering these questions, you'll uncover valuable insights about your own decision-making processes, your communication style, and how you manage and understand relationships.

Please check the box next to each statement that generally applies to your relationships.				
	A	B	C	D
I mostly base my relationship decisions on what makes the most logical sense.		☐		
I mostly base my relationship decisions on what feels right.			☐	
I know when to call it quits.		☐		
I try not to allow my emotions to guide my relationship decisions.	☐			
I stay in relationships longer than I should.			☐	
I pay close attention to the practical benefits of a relationship.		☐		
Emotional benefits are important to me in relationships.			☐	
To me, compatibility is more important than chemistry.		☐		
To me, chemistry is more important than compatibility.			☐	
I won't settle for anything less than a fairy-tale relationship.				☐
I often jump into relationships quickly and deeply.				☐
My partner has to be solidly on track with my life goals. I'm not giving up my lifestyle or future plans for anyone, period.	☐			
It takes a very long time for me to let go of an ex.				☐

Relationships are transactional. I won't settle for anything less.	☐			
I tend to have intense, instant chemistry with people who are not good for me.				☐
It doesn't matter much to me if my partner and I have a history or have made a long-term commitment. The moment it stops making practical sense to stay in the relationship, I'm out.	☐			

Breaking Down Your Answers

Mostly As

If you checked mostly As, you are an Extreme Practical. For you, emotions play a minor role, if any, in the dynamics of a relationship; the union of two individuals must be logical and purposeful above all. You are steadfastly committed to your long-term objectives and will not consider a partnership with someone who doesn't share or support these goals. For you, the spark of chemistry and emotional connection is secondary; instead, you prioritize assessing compatibility with a potential partner based on tangible contributions and shared life plans.

Mostly Bs

If you checked mostly Bs, you are a Healthy Practical. For you, entering into a relationship is contingent upon your potential partner aligning with your core Values. You see the essence of long-term compatibility in having shared goals, similar lifestyles, and perhaps even matching daily routines. While you regard the relationship through a practical lens, you also recognize the significance of having a genuine connection. In your view, emotional elements take a backseat in the relationship equation, as practical considerations are paramount.

Mostly Cs

If you checked mostly Cs, you are a Healthy Emotional. For you, feeling a strong attraction is nonnegotiable. A partner who may tick all the boxes in terms of compatibility or future planning but lacks that vital emotional connection doesn't cut it for you. A true partnership, in your eyes, is deeply rooted in the emotional bond shared between two people. Should that connection start to wane, you find it increasingly difficult to stay committed to the relationship.

An Equal Number of Bs and Cs

If you checked an equal number of Bs and Cs, you straddle the middle ground between Healthy Practical and Healthy Emotional. Your approach to relationships is adaptable, significantly influenced by your partner's qualities and what they evoke in you. It also varies with your current life phase and whether you prioritize shared goals, lifestyles, and achievements over the emotional connection at certain times. This balance indicates a healthy approach to relationships, characterized by flexibility and an appreciation for the nuances of partnership dynamics.

Mostly Ds

If you checked mostly Ds, you are an Extreme Emotional. You have a deep yearning to be in love, often finding that your heart remains fiercely loyal to partners who may not necessarily be the right match for you. In relationships, your heart is all in, anchored by the belief that true love is the foundation of a successful partnership. Your dedication to the person you love knows a few bounds, occasionally even leading you to put their needs above your own. It's also likely you often find yourself reflecting on past relationships, as the process of moving on from someone you've loved deeply can be a profound challenge for you.

Chapter 15

The Critic vs. the Optimist

In our exploration of Personality Types, we uncover the fascinating contrast between the "Critic" and the "Optimist." In my work, this distinction emerged from careful analysis of interviews, where it was observed that some individuals were exceptionally generous in their self-assessment and evaluation of their partners, awarding perfect scores with an optimistic flair. Yet as we dug deeper, it became clear that people's approach to evaluations varied broadly—ranging from those with a generous tendency to see the best in everyone and everything to those who apply a more skeptical lens. This chapter delves further into this dichotomy, with the aim of offering insights that help you pinpoint where you might fall on this spectrum between generosity and critical judgment.

The Healthy Critic

Healthy Critic: An individual who exercises caution when assessing their Self Score and Partner Score.

Introducing the "Healthy Critic"—a Personality Type particularly relevant when it comes to evaluating the Values list. This individual approaches ratings with intention and caution, never quite willing to award themselves or others a Partner Values Score above 85%, even in instances where the performance being assessed reaches near-perfection levels. The rationale? They hold a firm belief that there is always room for growth and improvement—that a perfect 100% Score is unachievable.

Make no mistake—they are well aware that perfection is a myth, be it in education, financial matters, communication skills, or even mastering a yoga pose. To them, it's these very imperfections that add richness and depth to life. They recognize that excelling in every area is unrealistic, yet this acknowledgment doesn't deter their commitment to continual growth. Instead, it fuels their desire to keep improving.

The Healthy Critic exercises a methodical approach in assigning Scores. If they value *dependability*, a high Score isn't something they hand out lightly. Instead, they undertake a thorough evaluation, questioning the consistency of their partner's support during crucial times and pondering over potential areas for enhancement in their partner's conduct. This meticulous assessment isn't reserved for their partner alone; they turn the same critical eye on themselves, asking, "Am I living up to my own expectations? What steps can I take to improve?" What sets the Healthy Critic apart is their ability to also recognize and see the strengths in both themselves and their partner.

Unsurprisingly, these individuals maintain relatively high standards when it comes to selecting a partner, making them more discerning than others. You might wonder if this is problematic. The answer is "No, it's not!" They simply tend to be more analytical than their counterpart, the Optimists. They base their Partner Score on concrete observations and actions, steering clear of emotional biases or wishful thinking. They take their time in deciding whether a high Score is deserved; they don't believe in giving it away easily. For example, they might say, "Just because you go to the gym once a week doesn't mean I'll give you an 18/20 for *fitness!*"

The Healthy Critic often shares common ground with the Healthy Practical, especially in their meticulous approach to choosing a partner. At first glance, it might seem as though they are hard to satisfy, but that's not quite the case. When they do decide to commit, their love is deep and full hearted, and they're keenly appreciative of their partner's virtues and achievements. Even if a drawback of being with a Healthy Critic is their tendency to spot imperfections, they handle these flaws with grace—both for themselves and their partners. They view these not as obstacles but as opportunities for growth. In this way, Healthy Critics embody realism while embracing the journey toward betterment.

They revel in the process of self-improvement, believing that personal growth fuels their confidence. For them, the essence of a healthy relationship lies in mutual motivation, where both partners inspire each other toward greatness. Expanding outside the comfort zone—whether through small, cautious steps or bold, decisive leaps—is very important.

The advantages of finding yourself in a relationship with a "Healthy Critic" include

- **Encouragement for Personal Growth**: They are frequently driven toward self-enhancement and personal development. With a passion for learning, they can inspire and encourage you to embark on your own journey of personal growth.

- **Goal Oriented**: They are perpetually engaged in self-improvement and expect the same from their partner. They establish objectives and aspirations, collaborating on strategies to achieve them.

- **Constructive Critics and Honest Advisers**: While they are gentle with their approach, they are honest about their views regarding your choices and potential areas for improvement. Their intentions are simply to support you in becoming the best version of yourself.

- **Power Couple Dynamic**: They foster shared development and accomplishments, inspiring pride and confidence as you both stride forward together.

Partnering with a Healthy Critic sets the stage for true teamwork, where both of you actively work toward achieving your goals and shared dreams. They become a steadfast support system, always offering encouragement and the occasional gentle push needed to overcome hurdles. They stand by you not just as a cheerleader but also as a true collaborative partner, ready to face challenges head-on and celebrate successes together.

The Healthy Critic: A Case Study

Carol epitomized the spirit of a go-getter, her mind perpetually racing ahead to the next milestone. Her thoughts were a whirlwind of to-do lists, productivity hacks, and strategies for boosting her well-being and financial prosperity. It was only natural that she expected her partner to embrace a similar ethos, setting the bar high for both their personal and professional lives.

Ritchie had all the qualities she respected. He was dependable, had a strong work ethic, and held firm to his family. For Carol, Ritchie wasn't just a partner; he was the cornerstone of the future she had envisioned.

Carol's ambitions fueled a relentless drive to not only better herself but to also encourage Ritchie to reach his utmost potential. Even though Ritchie exhibited exceptional qualities, Carol never granted him a full score for any specific Value in her Love Formula. Her philosophy was rooted in the belief that there is always scope for growth and development. In fact, she might never give a perfect Partner Score, even in areas where Ritchie excelled.

In their quest for personal and relational growth, Carol and Ritchie actively supported each other's passions. Carol encouraged Ritchie to explore his interest in photography, and Ritchie, in turn, motivated Carol to pursue her dream of learning a new language. These pursuits did more than just ignite their individual passions; they underscored the depth of their commitment to each other's personal growth.

The Extreme Critic

Extreme Critic: An individual who harshly evaluates and is radically conservative with their Self Score and their Partner Score.

Meet the "Extreme Critic." These individuals are unwilling to assign a Self Score or a Partner Score above 70%, which is below the threshold needed to maintain a healthy relationship.

Trying to meet their standards can feel like walking a tightrope—every step needs to be perfect, and even then, it might not be enough. They're the type to spot a single out-of-place thread on a perfectly tailored suit. When it comes to evaluating themselves and their partners, they're tough critics. It's not just about being hard to please; it's that their benchmark for what's acceptable—whether it's in themselves or someone they're with—is set incredibly high, often impossibly so.

Individuals with this Personality Type will scrutinize even the tiniest flaws. Whether it's evaluating themselves or their partner, they don't hesitate to decrease a Score for any imperfection they find. They're their own harshest critics, holding themselves to sky-high standards. This intense scrutiny means they're constantly on the lookout for ways to improve, but it also sets a challenging pace for personal and relationship growth.

Extreme Critics don't enter relationships very easily, if at all. Their search for perfection makes them exceptionally picky, always on the lookout for a mythical "unicorn" that, in reality, does not exist. On the rare occasions when they do decide to embark on a relationship, their critical nature doesn't take a backseat, always observing and assessing—the way their partner chews food, how punctual they are, or even how they choose to spend leisure time. This focus on minor imperfections can overshadow the more substantial, meaningful aspects of a relationship, making it difficult for them to appreciate the "good" amid their pursuit of the unattainable "perfect."

People grappling with an inferiority complex frequently find themselves under the Extreme Critic umbrella. They battle feelings of inadequacy, a struggle that often gets projected outward as a relentless drive for perfection. This mindset makes it hard for them to recognize and celebrate their own achievements, while appreciating their partner's successes becomes even more challenging. Their quest for perfection is, in many ways, an attempt to compensate for their own perceived shortcomings.

To better understand this behavior, it would be helpful to note that individuals raised in dysfunctional family environments, where parental affection was scant or conditional, often evolve into perfectionists as adults. During their childhood, they consistently received the message that they were not "good" enough and were constantly striving to earn their parents' approval. This relentless pursuit of validation can embed a deep-seated sense of inadequacy, which often does not fully manifest until later in life. This obsessive thirst for perfection, then, becomes a coping mechanism—a way to counteract feelings of unworthiness instilled in them from a young age.

People in this category are particularly vulnerable to depression and anxiety stemming from profound dissatisfaction with their lives and accomplishments. While it's easy to label this Personality Type as challenging to deal with, it's crucial to approach them with understanding and compassion. The struggle to see and appreciate the good in themselves and others can be profoundly damaging, trapping them in a cycle of perpetual dissatisfaction. It's no surprise that they experience depression because no achievement ever seems sufficient, and any accomplishment only briefly fulfills them. They quickly revert to the mindset of "That wasn't good enough; I need to do more."

Extreme Critics often find their sense of self-worth intricately tied to their productivity and achievements. This conditioning means their self-esteem is closely tied to their ability to produce tangible results or receive validation from the world around them. This reliance on external validation and success for self-worth sets a shaky foundation for their self-esteem, which fluctuates with their latest achievements or failures.

If they encounter a major life crisis—like losing a job, facing profound grief, or dealing with a serious illness or injury—their self-perception can spiral into something both unbearable and humiliating. In these times of intense vulnerability, the turmoil churning inside them often gets projected onto those around them. This projection can make Extreme Critics particularly tough to engage, cohabit, or maintain a loving relationship with.

Being in a relationship with an Extreme Critic can severely damage one's self-esteem because nothing will ever meet their standards. Other characteristics may include

- **Constant Doubt**: They may express significant doubts about the relationship, which can lead to feelings of insecurity and the fear of being abandoned.

- **Unrealistic Expectations**: Their deep-seated skepticism can sometimes lead them to set unreasonably high and negative expectations, which can cause ongoing feelings of uncertainty and unhappiness in the relationship.

- **Criticism and Scrutiny**: You might often find your actions and choices under close examination and critique. They will focus on the flaws and shortcomings, leading to a negative atmosphere in the relationship.

- **Constant Seeking of Assurance**: You might find yourself continually providing reassurance to address your partner's doubts and concerns.

Partners of Extreme Critics often find themselves feeling like they're constantly walking on eggshells, trying to tread the minefield of demanding expectations without causing offense or disappointment. This persistent state of tension can breed feelings of insecurity and anxiety, as they strive to reach standards that often seem entirely unreasonable and unattainable.

If this description resonates with you or your partner, as cliché as it may sound, love is the path to healing— a megadose of self-love. Seek the support you need daily, be genuine, and extend kindness to yourself and others.

The Extreme Critic: A Case Study

Ahmad was raised in a wealthy household where productivity defined success. His parents ensured he and his siblings were constantly engaged in activities like sports, homework, learning musical instruments, and watching documentaries— all intended to promote personal growth and development. Unfortunately, during their childhood, they never heard the simple words "Good job!" or "I'm proud of you." The absence of early validation led him to constantly question achievements and fostered a deep-seated need for perfection, both in himself and in his partners.

By the time Ahmad was twenty-eight, he had completed his PhD and was working at a university. His daily routine involved waking up at five in the morning, dedicating an hour to intense exercise, making breakfast, going to work, coming home to make dinner, practicing a new tune on his guitar, jumping into bed with a nonfiction, self-improvement or business book, and then finally going to sleep at half-past ten in the night. He followed this regimen five days a week.

On weekends, Ahmad invested his time in socializing with friends and family, participating in soccer matches with a recreational league, tending to household chores such as laundry and shopping, attending online workshops, and perhaps indulging in a brief moment of relaxation before another demanding week began.

Given Ahmad's impressive accomplishments and rigorous self-discipline, one might expect him to feel a sense of fulfillment and self-assurance. Yet the reality was starkly different. Ahmad struggled with severe depression and anxiety that was rooted in a relentless feeling of inadequacy. He perpetually undervalued himself, convinced that he had to keep enhancing his intellect, physical well-being, and career. No milestone or achievement brought him the much-anticipated satisfaction; there was always a next level he felt compelled to reach. This perpetual state of discontent wasn't confined to his self-perception alone; sadly, Ahmad projected these same unattainable standards onto his partner, Marie.

As much as she loved Ahmad, Marie felt very burdened by their relationship. While she admired his high energy and felt proud to be with him, she also felt immense pressure to match his productivity and ambition. His personal feelings of inadequacy spilled over onto Marie, along with his struggles with depression and anxiety. He expected her to utilize her time as efficiently as he did, viewing her explanations for not doing so—like being drained after a long workday, struggling to find time for reading, or juggling the kids' schedules with gym commitments—as excuses and not valid reasons. In essence, Ahmad demanded nothing short of perfection from both himself and his partner.

The Healthy Optimist

Healthy Optimist: An individual who generously awards a high Self Score and a high Partner Score.

Meet the "Healthy Optimist"—a person who lives by the motto "A for effort!" When it comes to evaluating themselves and their partners using their Love Formula, Healthy Optimists display a remarkable level of flexibility and generosity. This Personality Type is characterized by their willingness to see the best in themselves and their significant others, often assigning Scores of 90% or higher with ease and consistency.

Their standards are very reasonable and relatively easy to achieve. This means that even when they observe shortcomings or areas for improvement in their partner, a Healthy Optimist will readily assign a high Values Score, so long as the effort is there. For them, the commitment to trying and the willingness to grow and improve are more important than achieving perfection.

In fact, this Personality Type doesn't expect perfection. Their philosophy centers around authenticity and the genuine effort to be one's true self, without the pretense of trying to fit into a mold or embody something they're not. They encourage pursuing dreams with fervor, while maintaining that it's completely acceptable to be figuring things out or to not have it all mapped out. In their eyes and hearts, the mere fact that you're trying makes you perfectly lovable.

Healthy Optimists have a knack for finding the silver lining, consistently looking for and acknowledging the good in people. To them, what might be considered flaws by others are not drawbacks but unique characteristics that contribute to an individual's identity.

The Healthy Optimist moves through life with a patient disposition that understands growth and development take time. They steer clear of rushing themselves or others through these processes and are especially careful not to judge their partner's current stage in their personal journey. Embracing individuals as complete packages, they apply this ethos of acceptance equally to themselves and those around them. Although they too have ambitions and goals, Healthy Optimists possess a remarkable ability to find contentment in their present circumstances, celebrating life as it unfolds rather than fixating solely on future outcomes.

You might be thinking, "Wow, these folks sound like a dream to be around!" And you'd be right. Healthy Optimists are indeed wonderful companions, making any relationship with them feel like the ultimate safe haven. Imagine having a partner who not only supports you unconditionally but also walks alongside you as your most encouraging best friend at every step of your journey. A relationship with a "Healthy Optimist" is also marked by

- **Warmth and Affection**: They tend to express their love and appreciation openly, creating a nurturing and loving environment.

- **Shared Joyful Moments**: These individuals are skilled at finding joy in everyday life and often share this enthusiasm with their partner.

- **Confidence**: They will be happy with you regardless of your standing in life. Whether you're far from or close to your dreams and goals, their Score for you won't change, as long as you're putting in some effort.

- **Peace of Mind**: They will not push you outside of your comfort zone. You'll find yourself free from the relentless pressure to constantly improve or achieve more. They will provide a tranquil environment where you can grow at your own pace.

While the Healthy Optimist brings numerous positives to any relationship, it's important to acknowledge a potential downside: They can sometimes seem a bit unadventurous or complacent. The comfort and acceptance they offer, though profoundly reassuring, might occasionally lead to a lack of challenge or the incentive to step out of one's comfort zone—a crucial aspect of personal growth and development. For some partners, particularly those with a Healthy Critic personality, this might lead to a longing for more of a motivational push. They may crave a relationship dynamic that not only nurtures but also actively encourages taking risks and pursuing challenges for the sake of growth.

The Healthy Optimist: A Case Study

Most people who met Zachary thought he was an absolute sweetheart. Known as a man without a mean bone in his entire body, he was always in positive spirits and viewed as a highly encouraging friend and partner.

When conflicts arose, Zachary approached them with remarkable patience, acting as a peacemaker and problem solver. His friends and loved ones frequently looked to him in times of turmoil, confident that he would offer advice and support, driven by his empathetic nature.

Zachary had dreams and milestones he was chasing, but he was grounded by a simple yet powerful reminder to himself: "I am exactly where I need to be right now, and I'll reach my goals when the time is right. The journey's what matters most." This way of thinking wasn't just a mantra for staying calm; it deeply influenced how he viewed himself and his partner.

Zachary didn't hold back when it came to giving full Scores, whether while assessing himself or appreciating the people he cared about. This tendency was a testament to his belief in appreciating the moment and the growth happening within it, rather than fixating solely on the end goals.

Even when faced with partners who were harshly critical of themselves, Zachary's approach remained unwavering. He loved them wholeheartedly, not just for who they were at the moment but for the potential he saw in them. In his eyes, they were perfect exactly as they were.

Zachary epitomizes what it means to be a Healthy Optimist. He embodies an exceptional combination of unwavering positivity, humility, and genuine support for the people in his life. His approach to life and relationships serves as a shining example of how optimism, when grounded in authenticity and kindness, can have a profoundly positive impact on those around us. Zachary is a reminder of the power of genuine encouragement and acceptance in fostering personal growth and happiness in relationships.

The Extreme Optimist

Extreme Optimist: An individual who irrationally awards a high Self Score and a high Partner Score.

It's time to introduce the "Extreme Optimist." This Personality Type takes generosity to an extreme, assigning high Scores that might feel uplifting but don't always serve the best interest of the relationship. They wear rose-colored glasses, viewing their partnership with an optimism that borders on the unrealistic, pushing aside any doubts or concerns. In their eyes, their partner can do no wrong and is often hailed as the best thing since sliced bread. When it comes to their Love Formula, both they and their partners receive perfect Scores of 100%, regardless of the actual dynamics at play.

Extreme Optimists have a profound capacity to love, often extending their affection even in circumstances where it might not be deserved or reciprocated. They have a tendency to forgive and overlook bad behavior repeatedly, continuously elevating their partner to a pedestal despite clear signs that such admiration may not be justified. This boundless and unconditional love, while noble in its intentions, unfortunately makes them susceptible to being taken advantage of.

The friends and family of Extreme Optimists often find themselves concerned, not just because the latter tolerate bad dynamics within their relationships, but also because they seem oblivious to them. This Personality Type exudes loyalty to an extraordinary degree, unconditionally supporting their partner through thick and thin.

Forgiving a partner's imperfections is a hallmark of the Healthy Optimist—a commendable quality when the partner is actively working on improvement. However, the Extreme Optimist stretches the scope of forgiveness to an excessive extent, displaying leniency toward even the most destructive flaws and patterns. This tendency to overlook serious issues not only fails to address the root problems but also risks the Extreme Optimist's own well-being.

Like the Extreme Emotional, the Extreme Optimist is at a heightened risk of finding themselves in abusive relationships. Their tendency to set no boundaries and to permit their partners to speak to and treat them in any manner exacerbates this vulnerability. Their detrimental decisions regarding their relationships often raise alarms among their friends and family, who may feel powerless as they watch these toxic patterns unfold.

For instance, an Extreme Optimist might score their partner a perfect 30/30 for *faithfulness*, even in the wake of repeated infidelity. They might rationalize it this way: "It's all right. It was just three mistakes. Her reasons were valid, and she promised not to do it again. This is her life journey, and I must respect her process." This level of forgiveness and understanding, while reflecting a deeply compassionate stance, also illustrates the Extreme Optimist's tendency to overlook their own needs.

Moreover, these individuals are fully satisfied with their Partner's Score and don't try to encourage their partners to pursue personal growth. This absence of motivation—no gentle nudges to move forward, no wake-up calls to face reality, no reflective moments of self-assessment, and no prompts for self-improvement—can become a significant deterrent in the relationship. This passive attitude may inadvertently result in a stagnant dynamic where both individuals miss out on the enriching experience of evolving together.

If you find yourself in a relationship with an Extreme Optimist, you can expect the following characteristics to show up:

- **Conflict Avoidance**: They tend to shy away from confrontations and difficult discussions. They might find it challenging to address these issues head-on, often opting to downplay or outright avoid them instead.

- **Overlooking Issues**: They often overlook or underestimate real problems, which could lead to unresolved issues or delayed problem-solving measures.

- **Enabling**: Their excessively positive view of the relationship can result in a tendency to enable unhealthy behaviors by the partner, readily overlooking or quickly excusing them.

- **Boredom**: They don't encourage you to improve yourself, which can lead to a state of complacency and boredom. There may be a loss of drive to seek new challenges or engage in activities that foster growth.

While being optimistic is generally a positive attribute, for Extreme Optimists, this outlook can sometimes blur the boundaries in their relationships. Their constant idealization of their partners often means they miss the warning signs of a relationship that's not healthy or balanced. This approach can lead them into situations where they're not just overlooking minor flaws but also ignoring serious issues that could lead to emotional (and/or physical) hurt.

The Extreme Optimist: A Case Study

Marlon and Courtney had been in a whirlwind relationship for nearly a year. Every three months, Courtney would find a reason to break up with him, inevitably breaking Marlon's heart. But Marlon always told himself, "Courtney is just confused and scared. She loves me. She will come back." And he was right! She would indeed always come back—but every time they would restart their relationship, her behavior toward him became increasingly worse.

She would speak to him and treat him condescendingly, in ways bordering on emotional abuse. She would push his boundaries repeatedly, testing to see what she could get away with. And sure enough, she would get away with a lot. Marlon always made excuses for her: "She is confused or probably even depressed. She loves me so much. I know that. She's a wonderful person, deep down."

While they undeniably had an exceptional connection, Marlon's friends and family often noticed that Courtney treated him poorly. Several times, they tried to talk to him and open his eyes to what was happening. But it was pointless! Marlon defended Courtney, essentially telling others to "go to hell." *If you want to be my friend, you will accept my partner.* Period.

Marlon's Love Formula, as an Extreme Optimist, is at the core of his loyalty, unconditional love, and resistance to recognizing the negative aspects of his partner—and their relationship. While his optimism can be a positive quality, in this case it blinded him to the harmful dynamics in his relationship. Sadly, it inadvertently tethered him to a partnership that did not serve his best interests in the long run.

The Critic vs. the Optimist
Personality Type Questionnaire

Are you inclined to view your partner and yourself with a critical eye, or do you tend to see the best in both of you? This questionnaire will help you determine whether you lean toward being a Critic or an Optimist in matters of the heart. Your responses will shed light on your love style and its impact on your relationships.

Please check the box next to each statement that generally applies to your relationships.	A	B	C	D
I think my partner has room to improve themselves. Everyone does.		❑		
I am not very picky. I jump into relationships because I don't see flaws in people. I see the best in people.				❑
I am committed to personal growth and self-improvement and support my partner as well.		❑		
I've been told I'm blind to flaws and put up with too much.				❑
I love and appreciate my partner for who they are.			❑	
I expect myself and my partner to always do our best. Anything less is being a slacker.	❑			
I don't criticize my partner for their shortcomings but may point them out gently.			❑	
My standards are usually unreachable for everyone.	❑			
I am picky about who I will be with romantically.		❑		
I think my partner should actively work on their shortcomings.		❑		
I don't push my partner to rush their journey. Growth will come naturally.			❑	
I don't push my partner to grow because I am fully content with who they are. True love accepts people as they are, period.				❑

I focus more on appreciation and gratitude and try not to nitpick.			☐	
Maintaining long-term relationships is difficult because I get annoyed easily.	☐			
I've been told I'm judgy and overly critical of my partners.	☐			
I've been told I'm "too nice" and over-forgiving of my partner's flaws. It's hard for me to see anything bad about my partner, even if they're making mistakes. I see them as good.				☐

Breaking Down Your Answers

Mostly As

If you checked mostly As, you're an Extreme Critic. You're overly picky with relationships and oftentimes make your partner feel they're not good enough. You push yourself and your partner very hard to achieve excellence and are unforgiving of flaws. You may also have a tendency to end relationships quickly or take a long time to commit. However, remember that growth and change are possible, and by understanding your Love Formula and communicating openly, you can build a happy and lasting connection with your partner.

Mostly Bs

If you checked mostly Bs, you are a Healthy Critic. You believe there is always room to grow as individuals and as a couple. Your approach to partnership is constructive: You're there to cheer on your partner, encouraging them toward self-improvement and celebrating their successes right alongside them. Yet you also don't shy away from steering them back on track if they start to stray. Your role oscillates between being their biggest supporter and their gentlest guide, always pushing them (and yourself) toward mutual development and enrichment.

Mostly Cs

If you checked mostly Cs, you are a Healthy Optimist. As a partner, you're incredibly supportive and nurturing, always there to reassure your significant other of their inherent worth and lovability, just as they are. You understand that everyone comes with their own mix of strengths and weaknesses, and you believe in enhancing each other's best qualities. You foster a loving environment where both partners are committed to bringing out the best in each other.

An Equal Number of Bs and Cs

If you checked an equal number of Bs and Cs, you display the attributes of both a Healthy Critic and a Healthy Optimist, depending on the partner and the topics of concern. You maintain an excellent balance between both categories, possessing the insight to know when it's time to encourage your partner toward personal development and when it's more important to offer unconditional love and acceptance. Your ability to navigate these dynamics suggests you're well-equipped to foster and enjoy a healthy, harmonious relationship.

Mostly Ds

If you checked mostly Ds, you are an Extreme Optimist. You are overly forgiving of your partner's flaws, even to your own detriment. You are often blind to "reality" and give people far more benefit of the doubt than they deserve. You tend not to push your partners to grow, even accepting their destructive flaws. Your relationships may become abusive, which is hard for you to see while you're enmeshed in them. Your family and friends are probably worried about your relationship choices. If you fall into this category, there is hope for positive change and growth; awareness is the first step and can lead to healthier, more fulfilling relationships.

Chapter 16

The Safety Seeker vs. the Risk-Taker

The "Safety Seekers" and the "Risk-Takers" represent two fascinating Personality Types, each with their own unique approach to pursuing love and connection.

Safety Seekers, as the name suggests, prefer finding a partner who is a close match to their Self Score. They value security, predictability, and alignment in their relationships. They find comfort in the predictability of such relationships, where they can anticipate the thoughts and actions of their partner easily. These individuals thrive in the harmonious coexistence of shared Values, where compatibility is fundamental.

On the other side of the spectrum, we have the Risk-Takers. These individuals are exhilarated by the idea of being with someone with a higher Partner Score. They crave the kind of relationship that keeps them on their toes, where every day brings a new challenge or lesson. They seek the thrill of stepping outside of their comfort zone.

The Healthy Safety Seeker

Healthy Safety Seeker: An individual who prefers a relationship with a matching Self Score and Partner Score, or a Self Score that is slightly higher than the Partner Score.

Healthy Safety Seekers feel more comfortable in relationships where the Partner Score closely matches their Self Score or is slightly lower. This preference is rooted in their desire for a comfortable and stable relationship, rather than one that feels competitive or emotionally taxing. They tend to steer clear of partners they view as operating on a "higher" level, fearing such dynamics could introduce stress in their lives and challenge their sense of security. The Healthy Safety Seeker doesn't see the point in pursuing someone out of their league; it requires too much effort and puts them in a vulnerable position.

Take Todd, for example. He was pretty happy with how his dating life was going, especially now that he was in a relationship with a girl from his neighborhood. Todd didn't see the point in chasing after the stereotypical "hot cheerleader" that seemed to catch every guy's eye. He was well aware that jumping into that kind of competition probably meant facing rejection, and frankly, he was not down for that.

For Healthy Safety Seekers, landing a partner with a high Score doesn't always equate to relationship bliss. They might worry about not being stimulating or engaging enough for their partner, feeling constant pressure to keep up. However, this concern doesn't necessarily stem from low self-esteem. Quite the contrary! They often have a solid sense of self-confidence. It's more about their preference for stability and harmony over the potential stress of trying to keep up with or exceed a partner's accomplishments or dynamic lifestyle.

Imagine that an average Joe finds himself in a relationship with a celebrity of Reese Witherspoon's caliber. As thrilling as this might initially seem, the glaring differences in their public statuses could soon weigh heavily on him. He might feel the pressure to compare himself to her past high-profile relationships, such as with Ryan Phillippe, and wonder if he measures up, not just to Reese but also to the expectations of her fans. While Joe might have stepped into the relationship full of confidence, the relentless pace and visibility of celebrity life could challenge his sense of stability and fulfillment.

Some people love the spotlight and may rely on their high-scoring partner to draw attention—the Healthy Safety Seeker doesn't need that. They have no use for arm candies or trophy relationships to feel validated. Their preference leans toward simplicity and authenticity, desiring a partner who aligns closely with their Values, perhaps even someone who scores just a tad lower on the scale. For them, life isn't a competition for the most glamorous plus-one. They're content with where they are, appreciating their life in its current condition, and are in search of a partner who can blend into that existing happiness without introducing unnecessary drama or complexity. Their goal is harmony and shared happiness, and they look for someone who naturally complements their life rather than complicating it.

Being in a relationship with a Healthy Safety Seeker can be a fulfilling and harmonious experience. Here are some key characteristics:

- **Peace of Mind**: They place great importance on peace of mind and seek to create a tranquil and stress-free environment in their relationships.

- **Comfort Zone**: They typically stay within their comfort zone and may be cautious about venturing into unfamiliar territory.

- **Predictability**: They find comfort in predictability and routine. Establishing clear patterns and expectations in their relationships is important for maintaining the stability and security they seek.

A relationship with a Healthy Safety Seeker is characterized by a sense of tranquility and emotional security. They commit to preserving a stable, predictable, and harmonious partnership. While it may lack some of the excitement and spontaneity of other relationship types, it offers a secure and nurturing environment where both partners can experience emotional and long-term satisfaction.

The Healthy Safety Seeker: A Case Study

Evan approached love with thoughtful discernment. To him, the ideal relationship wasn't about dazzling displays of passion or the kind of love stories that movies are made of. Instead, he sought a woman whose presence felt like a natural extension of his daily life, someone who melded into his routine with ease and grace. Stability, security, and predictability were his relationship ideals, as he steered clear of tumultuous ups and downs. Confident and charismatic by nature, Evan wasn't looking for a partner to complete him; rather, he desired a relationship that brought a peaceful balance to his life.

Then, one day, Evan crossed paths with Jill. From the start, he noticed something about her that resonated deeply with his Love Formula. It wasn't just an attraction; it was a recognition, a sense of familiarity that went beyond the surface. Jill seemed to embody the qualities Evan had long sought in a partner—a calm demeanor, a mature approach to life, and an ease with which she navigated the world around her. There was a profound sense of connection, and Evan couldn't help but feel that this was different from any other encounter he'd experienced.

Evan and Jill didn't need grand gestures to feel secure in their relationship. In fact, evenings were a time for the couple to relax and connect. Both avid readers, they would often find themselves nestled on the couch, lost in the worlds of their favorite books, occasionally sharing snippets or interesting passages. This routine of exploring literary worlds together evolved into a cherished tradition for them, serving as a subtle yet profound testament to their connection.

Evan had found his perfect match. Their shared interests and the effortlessness of their relationship gave him the utmost security.

The Extreme Safety Seeker

Extreme Safety Seeker: An individual who prefers a relationship with a Partner Score that is significantly lower than their Self Score.

Now let's turn our attention to the "Extreme Safety Seeker." This person often rejects their Love Formula match and looks for someone whose Partner Score falls way below their Self Score. This is typically due to an intense fear of abandonment, perhaps from unhealed childhood wounds. By choosing partners they perceive as less likely to leave, they're attempting to shield themselves from potential pain, even if it means settling for a relationship that doesn't challenge or fulfill them.

The Extreme Safety Seeker often carries the weight of numerous rejections, a burden collected from both childhood experiences and adult relationships. To them, genuine love seems synonymous with heartbreak, and the thought of another heartbreak feels completely unbearable. As a result, they will go to great lengths to avoid it.

It's clear that Extreme Safety Seekers have been through significant emotional trauma, which has left them with a profound fear of falling in love again. The scars from their past have led them to a paradoxical approach to relationships: They find it safer to be with someone for whom they don't feel a deep affection. By choosing partners who score lower on their Love Formula, they aim to minimize their emotional investment, believing that this will protect them from potential heartache.

Being with a partner who scores lower in their Love Formula is a strategy to secure an unshakable sense of safety in the relationship. They operate under the belief that "They won't leave me because they cannot do better than me. They're lucky to have me, and they know it." This idea, coupled with a protective shield of "Even if the relationship were to end, it wouldn't matter much because my feelings were never deeply invested," acts as their defense mechanism. This approach allows them to maintain a distance, ensuring that they are shielded from the deeper emotional vulnerabilities and potential hurts that come from being fully committed to and invested in a partner.

When Extreme Safety Seekers are strongly drawn to someone, alarm bells start ringing in their minds. They are convinced that, just like past relationships, this new one will also inevitably crumble. This anticipation of heartbreak is so ingrained that they preemptively pull away from anyone who stirs strong emotions within them and could potentially offer genuine connection and love.

If they happen to enter a relationship, they will intentionally select one where true admiration is lacking. Consequently, they must make deliberate efforts to remain interested. They often push themselves to find humor, engage in conversations, and even initiate intimacy. These individuals are acutely aware that there's the potential for a more rewarding and fulfilling romantic experience in their life, but, in their view, the risks involved simply don't seem worth it.

If Extreme Safety Seekers do find themselves in a relationship, it's usually one where genuine admiration and deep affection are conspicuously absent. To compensate for this lack of natural interest and emotional depth, they put in considerable effort to keep the relationship afloat. Deep down, they're painfully aware that love could offer them a more enriching and fulfilling experience, one filled with genuine passion and connection.

But what does this mean for the partners of Extreme Safety Seekers? The dynamic within these relationships can significantly impact the partner's self-esteem. Given that Extreme Safety Seekers feel more secure when their emotional investment is minimal, their partners might never fully experience the depth of love, passion, and intimacy typically sought in a romantic relationship. The emotional distance maintained by the Extreme Safety Seeker, while serving as their protective mechanism, can leave their partners feeling undervalued and unloved and questioning their own worthiness. Here are some other critical aspects that a partner might encounter in a relationship with an Extreme Safety Seeker:

- **High Demand for Reassurance**: Partners will find themselves constantly pressured to provide reassurance, often needing to affirm their love and commitment repeatedly. This can become emotionally taxing.

- **One-Sided Effort**: The partner may find that they are putting in much more effort to maintain the relationship. The emotional labor often falls on their shoulders.

- **Longing for a Deeper Connection**: Partners may desire a more profound emotional bond, making them contemplate whether the relationship can provide the depth and passion they seek.

In such circumstances, the partnership will likely feel hollow, setting the stage for a potential disaster.

Consider Eve, a Love Formula interview participant who had just ended a two-year relationship with her boyfriend. The couple remained together despite a whopping forty-point difference between their Scores. Why would Eve stay with this person, given such a drastic difference in their combined Values and Traits? During the interview, Eve explained as follows:

- "I was forcing myself to be attracted."

- "I was afraid this was as good as it was gonna get, so I settled."

- "I believe that if I am dating someone who's cute, he must be a player. And if he isn't, he's a keeper."

- "I hadn't gotten attention and dedication from a partner in a long time."

- "I was worried I would miss out on a good-enough thing."

- "I was traumatized from prior relationships. I had just come out of one."

- "I was not in the space to be with anyone but willing to compromise because I saw dedication from him."

All this is quite revealing, isn't it? Eve's deep-seated traumas and fears led her to settle for someone with a much lower Partner Score—all for some peace of mind and comfort! However, this story has a happy ending. About three months after that relationship ended, Eve encountered someone new and embarked on a fresh journey. According to her Love Formula, her new partner is a much closer match.

The Extreme Safety Seeker: A Case Study

Omar was a beloved member of his community, adored by his friends, coworkers, family, and almost anyone who crossed his path. However, deep down, he always felt undeserving of love. Poisoned with thoughts of being unlovable, he faced a never-ending emptiness. Omar's fear of inadequacy largely originated from his parents not giving him much attention and emotional support during his childhood.

During Omar's initial dating experiences, he discovered that love could be challenging for him. His first relationship lasted six months until he got dumped for someone who was considered "more attractive." And his second girlfriend was rather cruel in the way she ended things. She spread a rumor that he was a terrible kisser and that his room "smelled funny."

His young adult years weren't any better. He endured rejection after rejection, heartbreak after heartbreak. By his early thirties, Omar had reached a breaking point; his heart simply couldn't take it anymore. Love had become synonymous with pain, and he dreaded experiencing more disappointments.

Then Omar met Sandra. She wasn't exactly his ideal type; she didn't particularly stand out either. Overall, she was just "okay" to introduce to friends and family. Yet it was this very ordinariness that gave Omar a profound sense of security. The fears of betrayal or abandonment that had haunted his past relationships seemed irrelevant with Sandra. Despite a noticeable lack of fulfillment, excitement, passion, admiration, and even attraction in their relationship, Omar chose to stay. He found comfort in the emotional safety that being with Sandra provided, a safety that outweighed his desire for a more passionate connection. This decision marked Omar as an Extreme Safety Seeker, someone who prioritizes emotional security over the depth and richness of a truly engaging partnership.

The Healthy Risk-Taker

Healthy Risk-Taker: An individual who prefers a relationship with someone whose Partner Score is higher than their Self Score.

Meet the "Healthy Risk-Taker," someone who prefers a relationship marked by a higher Partner Score than their Self Score. Dating individuals with a higher Partner Score gives them an invigorating challenge, allowing them to step outside their comfort zone and expand their beliefs and behaviors. Far from finding challenges draining, Healthy Risk-Takers thrive on them, seeing each new obstacle as a chance to evolve. Being with a partner who scores highly serves as a catalyst for this growth, pushing them to aspire to new heights and motivating them to continually improve themselves.

These individuals are always pushing their boundaries and seeking to experience things they've never done before. If *health and fitness* ranks among their Top 5 Values, they'll relish having a partner who can introduce them to various health and wellness techniques. When paired with a partner who scores high in *pursuing a greater purpose*, you can be sure they'll be inspired to join forces in making a meaningful impact in the world. They love getting to the next stage in life, whether it's related to finances, family, education, or anything else. In their eyes, a partner with a higher Partner Score doesn't just complement them; they represent a valuable source of knowledge and experience, someone from whom they can learn and with whom they can grow to reach new heights together.

Healthy Risk-Takers are known to be self-confident go-getters. They're the type who, once they've got a goal in sight, won't just sit back and hope for the best. They're on it, working tirelessly until they've ticked that box. They don't get intimidated by a high-scoring partner. For them, such a partner would be like a live-in mentor and motivator rolled into one. They're always picking their partner's brain, taking notes on how they do what they do, and trying out things they've never considered before. It's not about comparison for them; it's about inspiration. Their partner lights a fire in them to push harder, dream bigger, and be the best version of themselves.

Opting for a higher Partner Score doesn't imply they need someone completely out of their league. What's essential is a reasonable gap that gives them the chance to keep pace and elevate their own Self Score. It's about finding a sweet spot—a gap that's just wide enough to challenge them and inspire personal improvement but not so vast that it becomes discouraging. Take, for example, someone wanting to up their game in the kitchen; they don't necessarily need a partner who's a Michelin-star chef. A partner who's a tad more skilled in culinary arts than them could offer the perfect blend of motivation and achievable learning opportunities.

Healthy Risk-Takers are ready to jump at the opportunity to be with someone who not only shares their Top 5 Values but also has a slightly higher Partner Score. Imagine having a Self Score of 90% and a Partner Score of 94%. In this case, you consider your partner a great catch, but you also view yourself in a similarly positive light. They acknowledge their own worth and contributions to the relationship, creating a balanced and healthy dynamic where both partners feel valued and seen.

If your partner is a Healthy Risk-Taker, expect to be admired, appreciated, and loved; this person will be crazy about you! You can also expect:

- **Purpose**: With a Healthy Risk-Taker, your experiences, insights, and knowledge are not only valued but seen as integral to the partnership's growth and happiness.

- **Emotional Security**: You will feel the utmost validation in a relationship with a Healthy Risk-Taker, which will help strengthen your bond and foster an environment where you're both feeling emotionally secure.

- **Confidence**: Being with a Healthy Risk-Taker is an excellent ego boost. Their constant admiration and expressions of love can significantly raise your self-esteem and confidence. You'll feel valuable and worthy in their eyes.

- **Validation**: Healthy Risk-Takers will acknowledge and appreciate their partner's feelings, thoughts, and contributions, making them feel seen and heard in deeply resonating ways.

The Healthy Risk-Taker promises to take you on an exciting journey where you'll be cherished, inspired, and continually uplifted in a thriving and mutually fulfilling relationship.

The Healthy Risk-Taker: A Case Study

For a while, Mary had found herself stuck in a rut. It wasn't that she was happy where she was; it was more than convenience, and a certain lack of drive kept her from wanting more.

This year marked a turning point for Mary. She made a New Year's resolution to work on personal development and surround herself with people she admired. This shift extended to her choice of partners too. Mary committed to seeking out men who not only inspired her but also challenged her to grow, opting for those with a higher Partner Score than her own Self Score. It was a deliberate step toward her own evolution, a way to ensure she kept moving forward. Mary was no longer content with just settling. She yearned for a partner who was not just a companion but a standout individual from whom she could learn and with whom she could grow.

One day, she met Andrew, an athlete by day and a motivational speaker by night. Mary could see that Andrew was well-grounded and epitomized self-development and growth. Most importantly, Andrew had a higher Partner Score than her Self Score, and for that very reason, she wanted to be in a relationship with him. She was not only highly attracted to him but also greatly respected him. Mary had transformed into a Healthy Risk-Taker.

The Extreme Risk-Taker

Extreme Risk-Taker: An individual who only enters a relationship with a Partner Score significantly higher than their Self Score.

Meet the "Extreme Risk-Takers"—individuals who pursue only those with the highest Partner Scores, bypassing anyone who even remotely mirrors their level and aiming solely for those perceived as the "cream of the crop."

Why is this so problematic? After all, we all strive for the best, don't we? However, when presented with the opportunity to be with someone truly extraordinary—a millionaire celebrity, a supermodel, or an elite athlete—most of us remain grounded, understanding that such lifestyles might not align with our own. But not the Extreme Risk-Taker. They set their sights on nothing but the exceptional, dismissing anyone who doesn't shine with perfection. The most educated, the smartest, the most attractive, and positioned at the top of the hierarchy—these are all attributes this Personality Type seeks. As you may have guessed, many of these expectations are unrealistic.

The pull toward partnering with a star isn't just about glamour. It often stems from deep-rooted insecurities and the lasting impact of past criticisms. Those labeled as Extreme Risk-Takers might have grown up constantly hearing that they weren't good enough, facing judgment during their most formative years and sometimes even into adulthood. This kind of relentless negativity can hardwire a belief in their minds that they truly are "not enough." Consequently, they lean on the prestige of a high-scoring partner as proof of their worth and their place in the world.

Relying on a high-value partner to affirm your worth isn't a healthy way to approach love. Extreme Risk-Takers set themselves up for heartbreak by chasing partners who are, frankly, out of their league—not in terms of value but compatibility. There's often little common ground, and they find themselves drawn to people who possess the qualities and Partner Score they wish they had themselves. It's a risky game where the stakes are high and the odds of a genuine connection are low.

If Extreme Risk-Takers manage to enter a committed relationship, it's likely just a matter of time before their partner picks up on their deep-seated self-esteem issues. Soon, it becomes painfully clear that their partnership stands on shaky ground, teetering on the edge of toxicity. Believing their partner to be superior, Extreme Risk-Takers inadvertently set the stage for a self-fulfilling prophecy—where their partner might start to agree. This imbalance can lead to jealousy, trust issues, and a relationship fraught with drama and toxicity.

The biggest danger for Extreme Risk-Takers lies in the possibility that their high-scoring partner might eventually lose interest in them or feel that they've outgrown the relationship. Haunted by the constant fear of being seen as a fraud, they're stuck in a cycle of insecurity. If their partner doesn't show real appreciation and acceptance for them as they are, Extreme Risk-Takers end up in an exhausting race to keep their partner's attention, always trying to "level up" to meet them where they are. In their scramble to stay relevant, they might even twist the truth or put on a facade to seem more impressive or keep their partner interested.

The truth is that relationships with the "person of their dreams" often don't last for Extreme Risk-Takers. More frequently, they find themselves in relationships where they can't shake the feeling of settling. This perception not only impacts their own satisfaction but can deeply affect their partner's self-esteem. Here's what it might be like:

- **Challenge and Pressure**: The relationship, especially a new one, may come with a certain level of challenge and pressure. You might constantly need to excel and meet the expectations set by your Extreme Risk-Taker partner, which can be demanding.

- **Endless Criticism**: Criticism about your accomplishments may be a recurring theme. Constantly measuring your achievements against their high standards can create tension and insecurity.

- **Lack of Commitment**: This person may be looking for a unicorn, only the best of the best. They may be unwilling to commit otherwise.

This person always aims for the top: *the most educated, the smartest, the most attractive,* and so on. But these high standards are often more dream than reality, making any relationship feel like a never-ending search for the perfect partner. This can turn a partnership with Extreme Risk-Takers into an exhausting experience. Finding a middle ground where you acknowledge the difference between aspiration and reality is key to keeping the relationship healthy and rewarding.

The Extreme Risk-Taker: A Case Study

Tim was respected by his friends and colleagues, yet he battled feelings of inadequacy. Even though everyone around him considered him a person of integrity and worth, Tim saw himself in a harsher light, giving himself a low Self Score. Despite having an admirable job in marketing consultancy, Tim felt that something crucial was missing from his life. He believed he wasn't making a significant difference in the world or experiencing genuine happiness and fulfillment.

But Tim's world changed the day he met Patricia. He was immediately taken by her when she mentioned she had invented a technology that had revolutionized the distribution of medical supplies. To Tim, Patricia's accomplishment was not just impressive; it was the kind of meaningful impact he longed to make. In his eyes, Patricia was on a whole other level—she was the dream partner he had always hoped for. Yet this admiration came with a fear: Tim worried that Patricia might see him as less than enough.

Determined to win her heart, Tim made it his mission to impress her. He invested time and effort into courting her, date after date, week after week. Finally, his efforts paid off, and Patricia agreed to be in a relationship with him.

Tim was eager to tell his friends and family about Patricia, eager to boast that someone as successful as her had chosen him. Her achievements brought him a sense of pride and validation, seemingly filling the void of his own self-doubts. For a while, he felt that her purposeful actions compensated for what he saw as his own lack of significance. But over time, Patricia began to see the deep-seated self-esteem issues Tim harbored, which further led to unhealthy behaviors. Although she was initially open to the idea of a lasting relationship, the realization of their profound mismatch led her to end things.

Devastated, Tim moved on. And like a true Extreme Risk-Taker, he constantly compared his new partners to Patricia and her accomplishments.

The Safety Seeker vs. the Risk-Taker Personality Type Questionnaire

Are you a Safety Seeker or a Risk-Taker when it comes to love and relationships? This insightful questionnaire will help you uncover your unique Personality Type and how it influences your choices in love. Are you drawn to the security of what's familiar, or do you crave the excitement of connecting with someone who stands out from the crowd? The questions that follow will shed light on your preferences and patterns in romance.

Please check the box next to each statement that generally applies to your relationships.				
	A	B	C	D
I lower my standards a bit to be in a relationship.		❑		
I stay in relationships longer if I think my partner is better than me in some important ways. They challenge me to improve myself in a supportive manner.			❑	
I turn down suitable matches because I'm fixated on getting someone with a higher Partner Score.				❑

Statement	1	2	3	4	5
I make sure my potential romantic partner is interested in me before I get too involved.		☐			
I feel more secure in a relationship if I know I'm a little better than my partner.		☐			
I only get into relationships with people who meet or somewhat exceed my standards.			☐		
I stay in relationships longer if I think I have a bit more to offer than my partner.		☐			
I get a thrill from dating people who "do life" somewhat better than me.			☐		
I settle into relationships because I fear someone who closely matches my Self Score will leave me.	☐				
I will only date people I know would never cheat on me because they don't have many options.	☐				
I will not settle for anyone who doesn't stand out in some way (celebrity status or super high achiever).					☐
I feel more secure in a relationship with a partner who is a match or a bit better than me.				☐	
I've been told I have very unrealistic expectations for a partner.					☐
I only want to be with someone who is deeply dedicated and almost worships me. This gives me peace of mind.	☐				
I often force myself to be with someone, even if they have a low Partner Score because it's better than having nobody.	☐				
I love dating someone "out of my league" because it makes me feel so good.					☐

Breaking Down Your Answers

Mostly As

If you checked mostly As, you are an Extreme Safety Seeker. The idea of being with someone who matches or surpasses your desired Partner Score makes you feel vulnerable and scared of being left behind. To avoid this fear, you tend to pick partners with Partner Scores that are significantly lower than your Self Score. It's a strategy for emotional safety, ensuring that you feel secure and less threatened in your relationships.

Mostly Bs

If you checked mostly Bs, you are a Healthy Safety Seeker. You value stability and comfort in your relationships, preferring partners who seem more average because you believe these connections are more likely to endure. This approach brings you a sense of tranquility and reassurance, and you deeply value your partner for the security and peace they offer.

Mostly Cs

If you checked mostly Cs, you are a Healthy Risk-Taker. Growth is at the core of your relationship Values, and you're drawn to partners who challenge you to evolve by having a slightly higher Partner Score. You enter relationships with people you truly respect and feel proud to stand beside, seeking partners who inspire you to be your best self.

An Equal Number of Bs and Cs

If you checked an equal number of Bs and Cs, you seek a partner who exceeds you in some areas and perhaps falls short in others. You're looking for a partner who both challenges and supports you. You appreciate a relationship where you and your partner complement each other perfectly—celebrating strengths, providing support, and compensating for any weaknesses. For you, the essence of a relationship lies in being each other's backbone and balancing each other out in every way possible.

Mostly Ds

If you checked mostly Ds, you are an Extreme Risk-Taker. Your approach to relationships is focused on partnering with someone who excels in the Values you find important, to the point where 'matching' them is unrealistic. You tend to pass over partners who would otherwise be a good fit simply because they don't dazzle you or seem too ordinary.

Chapter 17

The Alike vs. the Diversified

The "Alike" and the "Diversified" add a fascinating dimension to the Love Formula. These dynamics shift the focus from shared Values to Trait preferences—do you gravitate toward a partner with similar personality and physical Traits, or do you find yourself drawn to differences?

The Alike are those who are drawn to partners with similar Traits as their own, such as shared generosity, a similar sense of humor, or both being extroverted. On the other hand, The Diversified are open to Traits unlike their own, like the pairing of an introvert and an extrovert, a tall person with a shorter partner, or someone with an alpha personality connecting with a beta. Just like the dynamics we've looked at before, the spectrum between Alike and Diversified ranges from Healthy to Extreme levels. The way individuals are placed on this spectrum plays a crucial role in shaping their approach to relationships and their love life.

The Healthy Alike

Healthy Alike: An individual who seeks a partner with Traits similar to their own.

The "Healthy Alike" seeks Traits that are similar and familiar, essentially looking for someone who "feels like home." For them, a deep sense of comfort is essential. Authenticity is also crucial for a Healthy Alike, as they find it easier to be themselves with a partner who shares similar Traits. This mutual understanding is what they cherish the most.

For the Healthy Alike, finding a partner with similar Traits is the secret to that electrifying "zing" they seek in a relationship. Their interactions are filled with effortless conversations, shared humor, and an undeniable connection. It's like they're perfectly in sync, often completing each other's sentences, laughing at the same quirky jokes, and fitting together like two pieces of a puzzle.

Take, for instance, a shy man who finds a deeper connection with a woman as reserved as he is. He's spared the stress of small talk and the pressure to be more outgoing than he's comfortable with. For partners like these, who share similar Traits, there's clarity and ease in their relationship—no need to decipher hidden meanings or adjust expectations. For Healthy Alikes, this predictability and the safety of staying within their comfort zone regarding Traits lay the foundation for a stable and fulfilling relationship.

It's important to note that the Healthy Alike does not look down on or hold any prejudice against those who differ in Traits. They value and respect diversity in others; it's just that, in matters of love and attraction, they're naturally drawn to those who mirror their own characteristics. This similarity is what truly ignites their romantic passion. Here's what being in a relationship with a Healthy Alike might be like:

- **Emotional Connection**: The strong emotional connection in the relationship is based on shared Traits. Partners relate to each other's emotional experiences and can provide mutual understanding and support.

- **Comfort and Reassurance**: The comfort that comes from shared Traits and the feeling of being with someone as similar as one's mirror image can be reassuring. Partners feel understood and validated in their personalities and Traits.

- **Balanced Bliss**: The relationship is characterized by stability and harmony. The strong similarity in personality fosters a sense of predictability and a peaceful, loving connection.

The partner of a Healthy Alike is likely to experience a relationship that feels incredibly homey and relaxed, where everything just flows. Imagine the comfort and ease that comes with such a harmonious match!

The Healthy Alike: A Case Study

Michael is a forty-three-year-old engineer from Brazil with an alpha personality. He's strong, dominant, and a natural-born leader. In the past, Michael dated women with calmer and more subdued personalities compared to his own. Although he appreciated the stability they brought into his life, he found himself longing for a partner who could match his assertive and leading nature.

During a dinner outing with friends at a well-known local eatery, Michael's attention was immediately drawn to Angelica the moment she entered the place. With her confident posture, head held high and shoulders back, and leading her group of three friends, she stood out. Adept at recognizing fellow go-getters, Michael wasted no time and approached her.

Meeting Angelica was a refreshing experience for Michael; he was thrilled to discover she was a kindred spirit. As they spent more time together, their similarities became unmistakably clear. Personality-wise, Angelica was a mirror image of Michael, reflecting his Traits and interests back to him. This realization only deepened their connection, highlighting how alike they truly were.

Being a Healthy Alike, Michael was drawn to individuals who reflected his own Traits. His connection with Angelica wasn't a stroke of luck but a predictable match, according to his Love Formula. Their relationship thrived on mutual understanding and aligned life goals, making Michael and Angelica's bond seem effortlessly perfect.

The Extreme Alike

Extreme Alike: An individual who is unbending about seeking a partner with the exact same Traits as their own.

Meet the "Extreme Alike," a Personality Type characterized by an unyielding determination to find a partner who mirrors their Traits to the last detail. This level of exclusivity can sometimes border on the dangerously narrow-minded, as they reject any Trait that deviates from their personal Love Formula. This aversion may stem from societal expectations, upbringing, or a fundamental aspect of their personality.

Social pressures, like family expectations, can push some toward becoming Extreme Alikes, fostering an "Us vs. Them" mentality. For example, they might limit their dating pool to people within their cultural, religious, or racial community. This behavior can lead to arrogance and a sense of superiority. They may also exhibit a strong dislike for unfamiliar Traits and pass judgment on individuals with characteristics different from their own. This pigeonholes them into seeking a *highly specific* partner profile.

The Extreme Alike mentality may be driven by a fear of the unknown and a discomfort with uncertainty. By choosing a partner with similar Traits, individuals may believe they can predict and control the course of the relationship, thereby creating a sense of stability and familiarity.

At times, these individuals may also feel compelled to conform to peer pressure to avoid being ostracized by their social groups. Therefore, the outgoing, adventurous, and loud individual would look for someone who mirrors those personality Traits. Likewise, the buff, sexy, six-pack enthusiast would also seek those same physical attributes in their partner.

Being in a relationship with an Extreme Alike can present several challenges and unique dynamics, such as the following:

- **Rigidity**: The Extreme Alike is typically inflexible regarding their Partner Traits. This can lead to conflicts and difficulties when navigating differences or changes within the relationship.

- **Peer Pressure**: The Extreme Alike may prioritize their social group's expectations over the relationship, leading to difficulties and tension with their partner.

- **Frequent Rejections**: Individuals who don't meet the stringent Trait standards of the Extreme Alike often face frequent rejections and criticism. This can erode self-esteem and lead to emotional challenges.

It's natural to feel frustrated by their rigid standards, and in the most likely scenario, only another Extreme Alike would truly get along with them. Other Personality Types would likely grow weary and want out quickly.

The Extreme Alike: A Case Study

Meet Emma, a twenty-eight-year-old teacher with an Extreme Alike personality. For Emma, the perfect partner was one who closely mirrored her Traits, especially in the realm of *intelligence*.

One sunny afternoon at a local park, Emma encountered Mark, an easygoing and kind-hearted guy who shared numerous interests with her. They struck up a conversation, and the connection seemed incredibly promising. However, Emma noticed one key Trait that set them apart: their wits.

Emma prided herself on being a quick-witted, sharp, and articulate woman. Finding a partner with high intelligence was very important for her. And while Mark was checking many of her boxes, he was lacking in this area. This difference in intelligence caught Emma's attention, and it troubled her. Despite their compatibility in numerous other areas, she believed this could be a major obstacle to a successful relationship.

Emma's Extreme Alike mindset made her hesitant to pursue a deeper connection with Mark because she genuinely felt that the contrast in intelligence was an insurmountable barrier. Ultimately, she rejected Mark as a potential partner based solely on this Trait preference.

This decision left Mark perplexed and disheartened, as he had genuinely enjoyed his time with Emma and felt that they had a strong connection. For Emma, it was another instance of her stringent standards overshadowing the potential for a meaningful connection. Her Extreme Alike approach to dating had once again limited her prospects, leading her to continue the search for someone who matched her criteria precisely.

The Healthy Diversified

Healthy Diversified: An individual who seeks Traits that are different from their own.

Typically, the "Healthy Diversified" won't claim to have specific preferences or types, as they are attracted to a wide range of Partner Traits. It could be someone tall, short, or anywhere in between, extroverted or introverted, funny or serious—what matters to them is how the connection *feels*.

These individuals are best described as "easygoing." They are incredibly accepting and have a special talent for making you feel appreciated for all your unique Traits. You can often recognize a Healthy Diversified by looking at their past relationships—if it's hard to find similarities among their previous partners, you've likely found one!

They see beauty in *all* people and enjoy newness, mystery, and novelty. They embrace diversity; any Trait that differs from their own sparks curiosity, adding some spice to their love life. They actively seek Traits that complement and enhance their own. Their open-mindedness means they embrace new experiences and different people. They thrive on both excitement and comfort, enjoying a mix of predictability and unpredictability.

They are truly indifferent to their partner's specific Traits; instead, they prioritize shared Values. They're perfectly fine if their partner has unexpected Traits, as long as their core Values align.

The Healthy Diversified often scores high on compassion. They are rarely judgmental about others' lifestyles and always seek to understand their partner better. For them, understanding differences is key to attraction and forming strong bonds.

Healthy Diversifieds are usually nonconformists who resist pressure from family or society to choose a certain type of partner. They are comfortable with who they are and freely express their true selves. They also don't try to make their partners fit any standards but appreciate them for their unique qualities. These individuals are open-minded and not overly picky, allowing their partners to be themselves and feel loved for it.

If you're in a relationship with a Healthy Diversified partner, here are some snapshots of what that adventurous ride might be like:

- **Embracing Unique Traits**: If you happen to possess unique or unexpected Traits, your partner readily accepts and cherishes these qualities, appreciating the diversity you bring to the relationship.

- **Non-conformity and Self-Expression**: They are comfortable with their identities and readily express their true selves. This self-assuredness extends to their partner, allowing them to be authentic and loved for their unique qualities.

- **Enhanced Self-Esteem:** By accepting their partners for who they are, these individuals often create a supportive and accepting environment that leads to their partner's enhanced self-esteem.

Being in a relationship with a Healthy Diversified partner is often an enriching experience characterized by mutual understanding, appreciation of differences, and the excitement of exploring a wide range of experiences together.

The Healthy Diversified: A Case Study

Meet Julie, a lively advocate for individuality who celebrates diversity in love. Ask her friends about her past boyfriends, and you'll hear a wide range of descriptions. Her partners have been physically different and had unique personalities and varied senses of humor. Clearly, Julie didn't have a specific type when it came to her romantic interests.

One evening, Julie and her friend Tanya decided to head out to a local bar, hoping to meet some interesting men and maybe add a new chapter to their love lives. But Julie had no idea that this night would turn into an exciting exploration of diverse connections.

At the bar, Julie found herself chatting with three eligible bachelors, each with a unique personality and charm. First, there was Jake, whose sweetness and shyness were endearing. Then, she met Tony, who had a commanding presence and a strong sense of confidence. Finally, there was Stan, who was a bit unconventional and refreshingly different from the others.

Most people might have been puzzled by the differences among these three men, but not Julie. She left the bar that night with a big smile, feeling like she had a unique array of options before her. Instead of sticking to a strict checklist, Julie embraced the diversity in her romantic encounters.

With an open heart and a "Why not?" attitude, Julie gave all three intriguing men her phone number. She couldn't wait to see who would call and set up a first date. Julie's approach to love showcases her Healthy Diversified nature. For her, the beauty of love lies in its unique and diverse expressions, with each connection adding to her vibrant romantic journey.

The Extreme Diversified

Extreme Diversified: An individual who seeks partner Traits that are very different from their own.

So far we have seen that Healthy Diversified individuals are known for their enthusiasm for diversity, which is driven by a love for novelty and fascination. In contrast, a different motivation urges the "Extreme Diversified" toward partners with opposing Traits. Their pursuit of dissimilarity often originates from unhealthy attractions, leading them, unfortunately, to favor harmful characteristics over positive ones. This distinction points to a deeper, more problematic approach to relationships within the Extreme Diversified group.

For example, someone with harmful tendencies, like a narcissist, might deliberately look for a partner who embodies empathy and emotional health. By doing so, they aim to take advantage of their partner's positive Traits, such as generosity and warmth, for their own gain.

Imagine a highly intelligent man who is only drawn to women he perceives to have lower intelligence. He might look for Traits such as *simple-mindedness* or even *foolishness*. If a woman exhibits these Traits prominently, the Extreme Diversified will find himself attracted to her due to his need to feel superior. Such a dynamic can lead him to adopt dominating behaviors, exert excessive control, and engage in demeaning communication.

Take the case of a highly outgoing person who seeks out partners on the opposite end of the social spectrum—those who are notably introverted. For this individual, having a reserved partner might feel like having an effortless spotlight, enabling them to be the center of attention and dominate social interactions without competition. This behavior often masks deep-seated self-esteem issues. Essentially, they're drawn to partners who, by contrast, elevate their sense of self-importance.

People who display these types of preferences may be dealing with unaddressed emotional injuries that need attention and care. Often, the partner chosen on the basis of these unhealthy Traits might be battling their own issues with self-esteem, which they inadvertently project onto their partner. This situation sets the stage for a relationship filled with toxicity, manipulation, and codependency, where both individuals might struggle to find healthy ways to relate to and support each other.

Being in a relationship with an Extreme Diversified partner can be a complex and challenging experience. Here's what it might look like:

- **Toxic Attractions**: Extreme Diversified individuals are drawn to destructive partnerships rather than beneficial ones. This means they may choose partners with opposing characteristics, setting up the relationship for disaster.

- **Issues with Self-Esteem**: Their preference for partners with Traits that contrast with their own is often rooted in self-esteem issues. These individuals seek validation and self-worth through their partner choices.

- **Imbalanced Relationships**: The pursuit of solely incongruous Traits leads to imbalanced relationships with the Extreme Diversified, which may contribute to a challenging dynamic.

These relationship dynamics can be challenging and harmful to the well-being of both individuals involved. Overcoming them typically requires significant personal growth and healing efforts from both partners to foster a healthier, more balanced connection.

The Extreme Diversified: A Case Study

Michael, known for his ambition and focus on career, found himself attracted to Sarah, whose warmth and compassion stood in stark contrast to his own, more hardened exterior. Throughout his life, he'd consistently been drawn to partners who displayed qualities he found less pronounced in himself—kindness, empathy, and an authentic sense of care.

Michael's interest in Sarah stemmed not from a healthy admiration for their differences but from motivations that were unfortunately harmful. Identifying as an Extreme Diversified, he was compelled to seek out partners he viewed as having "weaker" or "inferior" Traits than his own. He believed that by doing so, he could enhance his own self-esteem and maintain control in the relationship. This approach indicates a deeper issue within Michael that goes beyond mere preference for diversity.

As their relationship unfolded, Michael's desire to feel superior led to increasingly troubling behavior. One evening, Sarah mentioned wanting to spend more quality time together, as she missed the emotional connection they once had. Michael, however, had been consumed by his demanding career and personal goals, and he was in the midst of an important project. Rather than understanding and appreciating Sarah's need for emotional closeness, Michael responded dismissively. He insisted that his career and ambitions took precedence over their relationship and Sarah's emotional needs.

Not only did Michael brush off Sarah's request, but he also went a step further by scolding her for being overly emotional and needy. He told Sarah that her expectations for emotional intimacy were unrealistic and that she needed to be more independent. Michael's tone was condescending and insulting, making Sarah feel inadequate and inferior.

The Alike vs. the Diversified Personality Type Questionnaire

Are you someone who always ends up with partners who share your interests, like outdoor activities, music, or specific hobbies? Or do you feel that the differences in inherent Traits add spice to a relationship? Find out by answering the following questions—are you more of an Alike or a Diversified personality?

Please check the box next to each statement that generally applies to your relationships.	A	B	C	D
I prefer being in yin/yang, complementary relationships.		❒		
I feel unsafe being myself if my partner doesn't have nearly the same Traits as me.				❒
I like being in relationships where my partner's and my Traits balance out.		❒		
Familiarity is important to me.			❒	
My friends and family often comment that they're surprised I am with my partner and say, "It doesn't appear to be a match."	❒			
I prefer a partner with some, but not all, Traits similar to mine.			❒	

	A	B	C	D
I think being in a relationship with someone different from me is healthy.		☐		
I find it easiest to connect with people I have much in common with and just enough differences to make it enjoyable.			☐	
I embrace diversity.		☐		
I am turned off by Traits that aren't exactly like mine.				☐
I strongly believe in "opposites attract," even if my partner's Traits aren't good for me.	☐			
I justify my partner's unhealthy Traits and continue to give them chance after chance.	☐			
I think a relationship won't last if there aren't a lot of common Traits.			☐	
I've been told I'm narrow-minded with the partners I look for.				☐
I am drawn to unhealthy Traits that are opposite to mine because this keeps life exciting.	☐			
I can't and won't connect with partners who have Traits foreign to me. It's too weird. I can't relate to them.				☐

Breaking Down Your Answers

Mostly As

If you checked off mostly As, you are an Extreme Alike. This means you have very specific Traits in mind for a partner, and you're quick to dismiss anyone who doesn't match these Traits precisely. You will immediately shut down and shut out anyone who doesn't have the same characteristics as you. You find yourself drawn to partners who mirror your appearance, your mannerisms, and your overall personality.

Mostly Bs

If you checked off mostly Bs, you are a Healthy Diversified. You're in search of the yin to your yang, believing that the ideal partner is one who balances and complements your Traits. You appreciate the richness of experiencing the best of both worlds within your relationship. The differences between you and your partner are seen as mutually beneficial, adding variety and keeping the relationship dynamic and engaging.

Mostly Cs

If you checked off mostly Cs, you are a Healthy Alike. You yearn for a partner who feels like home, displaying many of the same Traits as you. Familiarity is key for you, and you desire someone with whom you can easily connect, share laughter, and enjoy shared hobbies. Your relationship is the kind where onlookers often comment, "You two look great together!" or "You're such a perfect match!"

An Equal Number of Bs and Cs

If you checked off an equal number of Bs and Cs, you appreciate both similarity and diversity in Partner Traits. You value sharing certain personality or physical characteristics, feeling that similarity can sometimes strengthen a bond. However, you also believe differences can enrich the relationship, bringing excitement and broadening both partners' perspectives. For you, the right mix depends on the individual partner and the unique dynamic you share.

Mostly Ds

If you checked off mostly Ds, you are an Extreme Diversified. You subscribe to the idea that "opposites attract," yet this often leads you down a problematic path. Driven by qualities that stem from underlying self-esteem issues, you may find yourself gravitating toward relationships that are ultimately destructive.

Personality Matrix

As we review the Personality Types, please refer to the table below for a concise summary of each type's distinct characteristics. This resource is designed to help you quickly and effortlessly determine which category best describes you or your partner.

Practical vs. Emotional

Healthy Practical	Healthy Emotional
• Driven by logic and practicality • Enjoys routine and structure • Oriented toward teamwork • Focuses on long-term outcomes • Guided by Values	• Driven by what feels right • Seeks excitement and stimulation • Sexually motivated • Appreciates emotional closeness and connection • Guided by Traits
Extreme Practical	**Extreme Emotional**
• Transactional • Ignores feelings • Lacks passion • Unconcerned about chemistry • Rigid in thinking • Focused on Values	• Lacks long-term thinking • Displays low emotional maturity • Impulsive and reactive • Dreamer and fantasy-lover • Addicted to drama • Focused on Traits

Critic vs Optimist

Healthy Critic	Healthy Optimist
• Sees room for improvement • Maintains high standards • Spots flaws easily • Focused on personal growth • Perfectionistic but gives credit where due	• Sees beauty in everyone • Compassionate and loving • Nonjudgmental • Encourages growth • Accepts people as they are
Extreme Critic • Judgmental • Critical and picky • Highly perfectionistic • Impossible standards • Struggles to enjoy the present moment • Partner walks on eggshells • Difficulty maintaining long-term relationships	**Extreme Optimist** • Over-forgiving of destructive flaws • Enables bad behaviors • Ignores red flags, only sees the good • Jumps into relationships quickly • Stays in relationships too long • Not selective enough

Safety Seeker vs. Risk-Taker

Healthy Safety Seeker	Healthy Risk-Taker
• Seeks same or slightly lower Partner Score • Values peace of mind • Prioritizes emotional safety • Prefers staying within comfort zone • Needs predictability	• Seeks a slightly higher Partner Score • Values getting to the next stage in life • Loves to learn from their partner • Enjoys the challenge of growth • Comfortable with change

Extreme Safety Seeker	**Extreme Risk-Taker**
• Seeks a much lower Partner Score • Settles in relationships • Doesn't experience real love/ attraction • Fears deep love/attraction • Passionless relationships	• Seeks a much higher Partner Score • Normalizes feeling insecure in a relationship • Emotional rollercoaster • Turns down good matches

Alike vs. Diversified

Healthy Alike	**Healthy Diversified**
• Seeks kinship • Seeks familiarity and comfort • Seeks a partner who feels like home • Enjoys when a partner has a similar personality, culture, and station in life	• Prefers a mix of similar and different traits • Open-minded and flexible • No strict Trait preferences • Enjoys complementary compatibility
Extreme Alike	**Extreme Diversified**
• Close-minded • Focused on identical Traits • Repulsed by the unfamiliar • Gives in to cultural or peer pressure • Feels superior to those with different Traits • Can be naive or arrogant	• Seeks only opposite Traits • Forms imbalanced relationships • Attracted to destructive Traits • Often taken advantage of • Vulnerable to abusive or selfish partners

Personality Type Indicator

Are you a Practical-Critic-Risk-Taker-Diversified? Or maybe you are more closely aligned with the Emotional-Optimist-Safety Seeker-Alike. In any case, you are likely to identify with one of the personality groups presented below. The table is intended to provide you with a clear framework for understanding and articulating your own approach to love and relationships. Use it as a practical tool to improve communication and foster a deeper understanding between you and your partner.

Personality Types

PCRD Practical Critic Risk-Taker Diversified	**PCSA** Practical Critic Safety Seeker Alike	**PCRA** Practical Critic Risk-Taker Alike	**PCSD** Practical Critic Safety Seeker Diversified
PORD Practical Optimist Risk-Taker Diversified	**POSA** Practical Optimist Safety Seeker Alike	**POSD** Practical Optimist Safety Seeker Diversified	**PORA** Practical Optimist Risk-Taker Alike
ECRD Emotional Critic Risk-Taker Diversified	**ECRA** Emotional Critic Risk-Taker Alike	**ECSA** Emotional Critic Safety Seeker Alike	**ECSD** Emotional Critic Safety Seeker Diversified
EOSD Emotional Optimist Safety Seeker Diversified	**EORD** Emotional Optimist Risk-Taker Diversified	**EOSA** Emotional Optimist Safety Seeker Alike	**EORA** Emotional Optimist Risk-Taker Alike

Part V

Score Distortions

At this stage in your discovery of the Love Formula, you should have uncovered significant insights into how your relationships function and the underlying motives behind them. Ideally, this process has elevated your self-awareness, clarified what is most important in an intimate relationship, and encouraged you to reflect honestly on the decisions you've made in your romantic life so far.

Having explored different Personality Types, it's important to remember that your personality is just one aspect influencing how you assess your Self Score and Partner Score, and it plays a role in shaping the relationships you build. Additionally, you may encounter what we call "Score Distortions." These can appear at any point in a relationship and may affect how you view yourself and your partner.

So what exactly are Score Distortions? They occur when your ability to make healthy Love Formula calculations becomes dysfunctional, leading to choices that enable unhealthy relationship dynamics. Often, Score Distortions result from underestimating or overestimating an important Value, Trait, Self Score, or Partner Score. This misjudgment can skew your perceptions and decisions, affecting how you navigate your relationships.

Such instances of misrepresentation happen because some internal or external force(s) impair your ability to assess yourself or your partner in a healthy way. It's as if you're viewing your relationship through a distorted lens. If you or your partner succumb to these worries or warped perspectives, your relationship may be in trouble.

The extent of Score Distortions can vary greatly, existing on a spectrum similar to many other human behaviors. These Distortions can range from barely noticeable to glaringly obvious. They can be categorized into two types: Personal and Interpersonal.

- **Personal Distortions**: These are irrational thought patterns linked to individual personalities. For example, someone might struggle with an inferiority complex and overcompensate for it or take on the role of a hero or healer, trying to "rescue" their partner. Others may act as self-sabotagers, undermining relationships that show potential, or experience a "case of the ex," constantly comparing every new partner to someone from their past.

- **Interpersonal Distortions**: These distortions are specific to a particular relationship and often disappear when the relationship changes. For example, there might be a Self-Sacrificer and Self-Focused dynamic, where one partner continually makes sacrifices for the benefit of the other. Another example is the Independent and Dependent dynamic, where one partner always assumes a parental or caretaking role. Additionally, there can be severe Infatuation, where one partner excessively adores the other.

Some Distortions may not fit neatly into the categories of Personal or Interpersonal, and that's perfectly normal. The key is to identify these dynamics and understand your role within them. This awareness allows you to make informed decisions and work on transforming your beliefs and behaviors from the inside out.

Even if these concepts of Score Distortions don't strike a chord with you, recognizing them can still provide valuable insights. If you relate to any of these Distortions, it doesn't mean you're stuck! There is always potential for positive change, both within yourself and in your interactions with your partner.

Now let's look into the various types of Score Distortions and the empowering steps you can take to free yourself from these challenges. By understanding and addressing these Distortions, you can pave the way to healthier, more fulfilling relationships throughout your life.

Chapter 18

The Self-Sacrificer

Self-Sacrificer: An individual who primarily works to improve their Partner Score while making sacrifices to their Self Score (the giver).
Self-Focused: An individual who benefits from the assistance and resources of their partner to build their Self Score (the taker).

"Self-Sacrificers" are those who prioritize their partner's well-being and achievements at the expense of their own needs and personal growth. In this dynamic, they take on the role of the "giver," constantly striving to enhance their partner's Self Score, while often neglecting their aspirations and well-being in the process.

On the other hand, "Self-Focused" partners concentrate mainly on their own progress and development, often overlooking the importance of reciprocating support or aiding their partner's growth. In this relationship dynamic, they act as the "taker," leveraging the support and resources their partner provides to improve their own Self Score, while contributing minimally to their partner's needs.

Self-Sacrificers often struggle with low self-esteem and deep-seated insecurities, which lead them to believe that they do not deserve balanced, reciprocal love. This mindset can cause them to accept less than they deserve in relationships, as they view themselves as less worthy of a high Self Score, while placing their partners on a pedestal with an exceptionally high score. Although their heightened empathy is commendable, it frequently clouds their ability to establish and maintain clear boundaries, making their relationships more challenging.

Unfortunately, individuals who habitually prioritize the needs of others over their own often find themselves in situations where their generosity is exploited and their own needs and perspectives overlooked. In relationships with Self-Focused partners, the lack of reciprocal kindness and gestures can subtly communicate to the Self-Sacrificer that they are unworthy of love. This dynamic reinforces the belief that they have not earned genuine affection and appreciation. The Self-Focused partner may, consciously or subconsciously, believe they deserve a higher Self Score, viewing the Self-Sacrificer primarily as a means to elevate their own status.

To further complicate matters, Self-Sacrificers are often adept at excusing their Self-Focused partner's missteps and shortcomings. They value the relationship so highly that they can overlook selfish, inconsiderate, or even abusive behaviors. This type of Distortion is interpersonal, as it involves a degree of consent from the Self-Sacrificer. As Eleanor Roosevelt famously stated, "No one can make you feel inferior without your consent." This dynamic truly exemplifies a "takes two to tango" situation, underscoring the importance of self-reflection. If you recognize yourself in this pattern, you may find that excessive sacrifices in the name of love have led to burnout and emotional exhaustion.

Intriguingly, it is also common for *both* partners to think they're playing the Self-Sacrificer role and start accusing each other of being too Self-Focused. This paradox often stems from differences in love languages, where each partner may not fully understand how the other expresses love. Take Jan and Rodrigo, for example. Jan, whose love language is *acts of service*, might feel that she gives a lot by cooking and taking care of Rodrigo. If he doesn't reciprocate in the same way, she sees herself as the Self-Sacrificer and Rodrigo as Self-Focused. On the other hand, if Rodrigo prefers *gifts*, he might feel unappreciated if Jan doesn't give him tangible presents.

In a relationship where both partners are stable, independent, and self-sufficient, the give-and-take is not a sacrifice; it's a *compromise*. Compromise is a crucial and positive aspect of any relationship, ensuring that both partners' needs are met. On the other hand, sacrifice can turn into a situation where one person gives significantly more than they receive. This imbalance can take a toll on the well-being and happiness of the person constantly making sacrifices.

At first glance, Self-Sacrificers might appear commendable due to their seemingly endless generosity. However, their behavior stems from more than mere kindness. True goodwill is driven by confidence and a genuine desire to be kind, while self-sacrifice often arises from deep-seated insecurity, an intense craving for affection and validation, and a fear of being replaceable. This can lead to giving excessively until it results in complete emotional (and at times, physical) exhaustion and burnout.

Self-Sacrificers may hesitate to set boundaries out of fear of upsetting their partner. For instance, genuine generosity might involve offering someone a ride to the airport on a day off—an act of kindness that fits within one's own schedule. In contrast, self-sacrifice involves taking a day off work to drive someone to the airport, perhaps spending an additional day to help them pack, or waking up extremely early to provide a ride, even when other convenient options like a taxi are available.

Self-Sacrificers frequently sacrifice their own time—time that could be spent on hobbies, interests, and self-care. Their generosity seems limitless, leading to a situation where their partner might start to expect this extreme level of dedication in every aspect of the relationship, especially as their lives become more intertwined and habits solidify. This constant overextension can set unsustainable expectations and erode personal well-being.

Ironically, the approach taken by Self-Sacrificers often leads to the opposite of what they intend. In their effort to elevate their partner, they end up compromising their own self-worth, resulting in a diminished Self Score. As they persistently boost their partner's standing at their own expense, the disparity between their Scores grows, creating an imbalance in the relationship. Over time, this imbalance can become a precursor to relationship failure, as outlined in the section on Relationship Zones.

You might wonder why anyone would willingly engage in such a draining dynamic. The answer isn't straightforward, as both parties derive some benefits from this pattern. For the Self-Focused individual, the advantages are more obvious—they receive continuous support and attention. However, the Self-Sacrificer also gains a sense of satisfaction. There's a deep-seated fulfillment that comes from being needed and from bringing happiness to others. Much like the joy derived from volunteering or contributing to a cause, being the giver imbues people with a sense of worth and purpose.

Over time, Self-Sacrificers may come to realize the unhealthy nature of their relationship dynamics. However, by the time this recognition dawns, they are often deeply invested in their roles, making it extremely difficult to break the cycle of excessive giving. This entrenched commitment can make it challenging for them to pull back and seek a more balanced interaction.

The Self-Sacrificer/Self-Focused Dynamic: A Case Study

Evelyn's history of heartbreaks contributed to deep-seated feelings of rejection, shaping a distressing narrative in her mind. She constantly thought, "I'm not enough, I'm unlovable, and guys will leave unless I meet their expectations." This mindset led her to become the classic Self-Sacrificer, constantly putting others' needs above her own in a bid to feel valued and loved.

One day, Evelyn met Jason, who had had a difficult childhood that left him with deep-seated self-esteem issues. These challenges affected his ability to keep a job and build lasting friendships. Lacking a strong support network, Jason often found himself struggling alone with various personal issues.

Despite Jason's Partner Values Score not matching her own, Evelyn felt a strong pull toward him. Her attraction went beyond superficial assessments; she saw potential in him that he hadn't realized himself. Motivated by a desire to help him flourish, Evelyn quickly became deeply involved in their relationship, providing Jason with abundant attention, comfort, and steadfast support.

As their relationship progressed, Evelyn's commitment to helping Jason heal and succeed grew stronger. She increasingly sacrificed her own time, financial resources, and energy, dedicating herself almost entirely to his needs. This devotion led her to scale back her social and professional engagements significantly. Despite the unequal effort and the sacrifices she made, Evelyn found happiness in the relationship.

Over time, Evelyn's initial enthusiasm began to wane as she noticed Jason's unresolved anger issues. He frequently vented his frustrations on her and showed little effort in finding stable work. Increasingly, he depended on her for financial support and used her love, energy, and encouragement primarily to bolster his self-esteem, contributing minimally to her well-being or the relationship. In this relationship, Evelyn and Jason display a classic Self-Sacrificer and Self-Focused dynamic.

Four Steps to Rebalance This Distortion

So, what's the solution here? Being trapped in a pattern of Self-Sacrificing or Self-Focused behavior doesn't have to be a dead end. Fortunately, there are effective ways to shift these dynamics without having to end the relationship or isolate yourself. The key lies in finding a balance where you respect your own needs and boundaries while also cultivating a healthy interaction with your partner. This approach involves clear communication, mutual understanding, and a commitment to personal growth and relational health.

By understanding and applying the principles of the Love Formula, individuals can be on their way to achieving a healthy balance in their relationships and personal lives. Here are the suggested steps to address this specific Distortion:

1. Revisit the Love Formula

The Love Formula offers a valuable framework for identifying the dynamics between (suspected) Self-Sacrificers and Self-Focused individuals. It helps assess individual personality traits, relationship patterns, and potential imbalances. By thoroughly analyzing both your Self Score and Partner Score, you can more easily pinpoint where imbalances exist in your relationship, providing a clear path for adjustments and improvements.

It's crucial to revisit the Love Formula regularly, concentrating on the overall patterns in your relationship rather than reacting to isolated good or bad days with your partner. A close alignment between your Self Score and Partner Score suggests that you've successfully restored balance by mitigating this Distortion. This continual assessment helps maintain a healthy equilibrium in your relationship.

2. Gain an Outside Perspective

Your family and friends can offer valuable insights, free from the distortions or biases that might color your own perceptions. If they express concerns such as, "He never seems to do much for you, so why do you go out of your way for him?" or "She doesn't seem to appreciate what a great person you are," it's worth taking notice. Such comments could be indicators that it's time to pause and consider whether you might be engaging in self-sacrificing behavior.

Conversely, if friends and family members familiar with your relationship express concerns like, "I don't understand why she stays with you. You don't seem to do much for her," or "You should really make more effort for your partner," these observations may indicate that you are exhibiting Self-Focused behaviors. Such feedback can be a crucial wake-up call, ideally prompting you to reevaluate how much you contribute to the relationship.

3. Understand Your Issues

It can be difficult to face the reality that, despite your best intentions, your actions may have contributed to unhealthy dynamics in your relationship. Remember, we're all on a journey of personal growth, and it's perfectly normal to take a moment to reflect on your role. Ask yourself critical questions: Is this relationship healthy? Does it make me happy? Do I often feel drained? Am I hesitant to ask for what I truly deserve in a loving relationship? Honest answers to these questions can help guide you toward necessary changes and greater fulfillment.

Once you recognize an unhealthy pattern, it's crucial to engage in deep self-reflection, consult someone you trust, or seek guidance from a supportive therapist. Consider exploring questions like "Why might I feel undeserving of love just as I am?" Or, on the flip side, you might ask, "What led me to believe it's acceptable for others to serve my needs excessively?" In a healthy, balanced relationship, emotionally secure individuals naturally reciprocate affection and care, driven by self-love and mutual respect. Understanding the roots of these dynamics can help you foster healthier interactions moving forward.

4. Establish Improved Boundaries and Goals

Rebalancing this Distortion requires setting clear guidelines for behavior and expectations with your partner. It's crucial to understand and confidently express your needs without fear of abandonment or retaliation. Embrace uncomfortable conversations instead of avoiding them; honesty and constructive feedback are essential. Effective communication and firm boundary-setting are key components of a successful relationship..

Evaluate your abilities and commit to personal development. Share your aspirations with your partner, offer mutual support, and celebrate each other's achievements. A strong partnership thrives when both individuals are each other's cheerleaders and coaches. Engage in a balanced give-and-take, embrace the necessity of compromise, and be open to challenging discussions that lead to meaningful progress.

Chapter 19

The Dependent

Dependent: An individual who thinks they need to rely on their partner to attain a high Self Score.
Independent: An individual who is self-reliant in achieving a Self Score.

The Dependent believes that a high Self Score in certain areas—be it financial stability, social status, or any other Value—is unattainable without their partner's help. This belief typically stems from a self-limiting narrative. Dependent individuals might think, "I'm not good/smart/hard-working enough. I could never achieve success on my own." This mindset highlights a perceived deficiency in themselves.

Feeling like you "need" your partner to maintain a certain lifestyle and healthy self-esteem can be pretty unsettling. While depending on others is normal in childhood, leaning on someone as an adult can affect your mental and emotional well-being.

The counterpart to the Dependent is the Independent. These individuals exhibit confidence and the ability to take proactive steps to enhance their own Self Score, demonstrating strong self-reliance. Typically, Independents possess higher self-esteem, feeling secure and confident in their abilities. They recognize that their success and high Self Score are not contingent upon their partner but are the results of their own efforts and capabilities.

Those who fall into the Dependent category often undervalue their strengths, leading to a distorted perception of their own capabilities and contributions. This skewed self-view can be detrimental, causing them to overlook their intrinsic worth and the positive impact they make in a relationship. Recognizing and acknowledging their own qualities is crucial for overcoming these misconceptions and fostering a healthier self-image and relationship dynamic.

On the other hand, Independents often find themselves bearing the emotional weight of their Dependent partners. It's important to highlight "emotional weight" here because depending on a partner for tangible support isn't inherently problematic—if there's mutual agreement. However, Dependents frequently struggle with an internal critic that erodes their self-esteem by relentlessly focusing on perceived inadequacies. This negative mindset can lead to significant discrepancies in their Scores, resulting in conflict, misalignment, and feelings of disconnectedness within the relationship.

Here's an all-too-common scenario: the stay-at-home mother. Being a mother is not only a full-time job; it's an intensely demanding one, though undoubtedly rewarding. Yet many women in this role often feel like Dependents, especially in relation to the household's primary earner, typically the husband. With enough negative self-talk, the mother will fool herself into thinking her value is less than her husband's because in today's narrative, success and power are often measured by wealth. And so, even though she has one of the most difficult—and important—jobs on Earth, her mind will play tricks on her, leading her to underestimate her own Self Score, overestimate her husband's Partner Score, and assume that she can't do without him. Even so, it's important to note that the Independent partner—in this case the husband—does value her highly despite the skewed self-perception of the Dependent.

The Independent has the mental and emotional capacity to provide significant support and encouragement. However, the Dependent often struggles with reciprocating these efforts and may experience shame and guilt when accepting help from the Independent. If the Dependent remains entrenched in their negative self-perceptions and fails to take proactive steps toward their emotional well-being, the Independent may begin to feel overwhelmed and resentful, viewing the Dependent as an emotional burden. This situation can spiral into a detrimental cycle where the Dependent becomes increasingly needy and clingy, driven by the fear of losing the relationship. This fear prompts them to constantly seek attention and reassurance from the Independent, which can strain the relationship further.

The Dependent/Independent dynamic may resemble the Self-Sacrificer/Self-Focused one, but it has distinct characteristics. Unlike the latter, where there might be a clear giver and taker, often driven by one partner's excessive generosity and the other's opportunism, the Independent/Dependent Distortion is not inherently rooted in bad intentions. In this dynamic, both partners generally strive to contribute equally. However, imbalances arise when one partner, often the Dependent, undervalues their Self Score due to challenging circumstances or internal struggles. This contrasts with the Independent, who typically maintains a higher self-esteem. The disparity in self-perception between the partners—and not necessarily a deliberate over-giving or taking—leads to the imbalance.

Another key distinction lies in the motivations of the Self-Sacrificer/Self-Focused dynamic compared to the Dependent/Independent Distortion. In the Self-Sacrificer/Self-Focused relationship, there is often a tacit agreement where both partners fulfill each other's desires to give and take, making it a mutually desired arrangement. However, in the Dependent/Independent dynamic, neither partner is satisfied with the imbalance. Both the Dependent and the Independent strive for a richer emotional connection and quality in their interactions, which the current dynamic fails to provide. This dissatisfaction stems from their desire for a more balanced and emotionally fulfilling relationship, rather than merely validating each other's roles.

The impact on self-esteem differs significantly between the Self-Focused and the Dependent individuals. The Self-Focused partner generally shows little concern about the emotional toll their actions may take on their partner. In contrast, the Dependent is acutely aware of their reliance on the other, often experiencing guilt and shame for not being more self-sufficient. This emotional burden can lead the Dependent to undervalue themselves, negatively affecting their Self Score and perpetuating feelings of inadequacy within the relationship.

Nevertheless, addressing the dynamics within the Dependent/Independent Distortion is vital for fostering a healthier and more balanced relationship. Open communication is key—both partners must feel comfortable discussing their feelings and needs without judgment. Mutual support is also essential, as each partner should encourage the other's personal growth and self-reliance. By prioritizing these elements, the partners can establish a more harmonious and emotionally fulfilling relationship where both individuals feel valued and supported.

The Dependent/Independent Dynamic: A Case Study

Sean and Ariel's paths crossed in Bali, where they immediately felt a strong connection. As they spent more time together, discovering shared interests and values, their bond deepened. They quickly became inseparable, realizing that they had found something special in each other. It was clear as day—they wanted to be together.

But Ariel and Sean faced the daunting challenge of maintaining a long-distance relationship between England and New York. Compelled by her deep love for Sean, Ariel made the bold decision to move to England to be with him. In preparation, she severed ties with New York: She left her job, said goodbye to her friends, sold her belongings, and relocated. However, the transition was more challenging than anticipated. Previously independent, Ariel found herself heavily reliant on Sean as she adjusted to a new country and struggled to find work. This dependency marked a significant change from her former life, further straining her adjustment process.

The most difficult aspect of Ariel's move was her profound isolation. Without friends, family, or a local support network in England, she felt incredibly alone. This isolation led her into depression, which sapped her motivation and undermined her independence. Sean, while supportive, found himself grappling with the mounting emotional pressures and grew increasingly frustrated with Ariel's waning self-esteem. Despite his feelings, Sean remained silent on the matter, not wanting to diminish Ariel's significant sacrifice by expressing his concerns.

Sean deeply loved Ariel, but it became apparent that her depression was worsening, becoming unmanageable.

He tirelessly attempted to support, help, and reassure her, yet his efforts felt increasingly ineffective. Ariel's self-esteem plummeted, leaving Sean feeling helpless and unsure about how to aid her recovery. This dynamic slowly evolved into a Dependent/Independent Distortion, placing immense strain on their relationship and pushing it to the brink of collapse.

Four Steps to Rebalance This Distortion

Whether you see yourself as an Independent or a Dependent, you have the power to restore balance in your relationship. Essential to this process are open communication, mutual support, and personal growth. These elements are key to building harmony and ensuring that both partners experience emotional fulfillment.

Take proactive steps to redefine and prioritize your Values, and honestly assess both your own needs and those of your partner. Critically examine the underlying reasons for dependency in your relationship. Listed below are essential steps designed to help both you and your partner break free from this Distortion, fostering a healthier, more balanced partnership:

1. Revisit the Love Formula

The Love Formula is an effective tool for identifying specific areas where your self-esteem may be lacking and pinpointing how you might be over-relying on your partner's support. Reflect on the Values for which you've rated your partner significantly higher than yourself. Consider where you experience limitations and in what aspects your partner compensates for what you perceive as your shortcomings. Also, think about those areas where you feel a sense of accomplishment. These insights can help you understand the dynamics of your relationship more clearly and guide you toward achieving a healthier balance.

By comparing your self-evaluations with your list of Values and identifying areas of weakness, you can create a practical roadmap for self-improvement and increased self-care. It's equally important to recognize and celebrate your strengths. Aim to elevate these strengths into becoming your Top 5 Values. Essentially, make sure to give yourself the credit you deserve for the areas where you excel. This balanced approach not only boosts your self-esteem but also motivates continued growth and fulfillment.

2. Explore Activities beyond Your Top 5 Values

Who says your Top 5 Values are set in stone? It's a great time to explore new activities and interests. You might discover skills and passions you weren't aware of before. Engaging in these new pursuits can boost your sense of accomplishment, ultimately strengthening your Self Score. This exploration is not just about diversification—it's about enriching your understanding of yourself and expanding what you value most.

Select one of your passions and initiate a project or achievement related to that interest. For example, if writing captivates you, think about publishing a book or an article. If you're enthusiastic about cooking, try inventing a new recipe and sharing it on a blog, in a culinary magazine, or with friends. Completing such projects can boost your self-esteem significantly and allow you to express your individuality independent of your partner. Such personal accomplishments not only enrich your life but also enhance your sense of self-worth.

3. Cultivate a Robust Support System

If you identify as the Dependent partner, it's crucial to surround yourself with friends and family who recognize and appreciate your value. If you find your circle of close friends lacking, don't be discouraged—it's an excellent opportunity to forge new connections. Although it might seem daunting at first, a great way to start is by joining Meetup groups or community activities, either online or locally. These settings can provide a supportive environment for building new relationships and enhancing your social network.

Also remember: The company you keep can significantly impact how well you align with your top Values. It's important to be mindful of this and actively seek out friendships that boost your self-esteem or motivate you to improve your Self Score. For example, if you're concerned about a low Values Score in *health consciousness*, consider surrounding yourself with individuals who prioritize healthy living. Engaging in activities with these people can help you adopt better eating habits, regular exercise routines, and an overall wellness-oriented lifestyle.

4. Cultivate Independence in Your Relationship

While sharing aligned values is essential in a relationship, it's equally important to preserve your individuality. If you're an Independent and find your partner relying on you too much, working toward a more balanced dynamic is crucial. Gently guide your partner toward emotional independence by encouraging self-sufficiency. Support their journey toward higher self-esteem with positive affirmations and by promoting interests and activities that don't revolve solely around the relationship.

Recognize and acknowledge the inner struggles and contributions of your partner to reinforce their value and foster a sense of equality within the relationship. If the dependency Distortion continues despite these efforts, deeper healing may be necessary. While you can offer support, remember that you cannot "fix" your partner. Self-love and emotional independence are personal journeys. Your role here is to provide a safe and supportive environment, communicate respectfully, lead by example, and encourage their growth without assuming a therapeutic role.

Chapter 20

The Savior

Savior: An individual who possesses a high Value Score in a particular category and seeks to "save" a partner with a low Value Score in that area, often to boost their own ego.

Rescuee: An individual who perceives themselves as lacking in a particular Value category and wishes to be "saved" by a partner with a high Value Score in that category.

When one partner significantly outperforms the other in a particular value category, they might fall into the "Savior Distortion." In this scenario, the higher-scoring partner may be tempted to boost their ego by "rescuing" the lower-scoring partner. To this end, the Savior may even lie and manipulate to persuade their low-scoring partner that being with them will improve their life. They might offer access to a lifestyle previously unattainable for the partner or falsely elevate their benefit through association, presenting themselves as a gatekeeper to improved social standing or personal fulfillment.

In this dynamic, the partner with the lower Value Score assumes the role of the "Rescuee." They enter the relationship with the expectation that they will be "saved," believing that their association with the higher-scoring partner will enhance their own Self Score and overall life quality.

In this dynamic, both partners derive certain benefits. The Savior gains a sense of validation, importance, and superiority by assisting someone they perceive as weak and vulnerable. Meanwhile, the Rescuee benefits from the support, potentially improving their Values Score in specific categories due to the assistance they receive. However, this relationship is often tainted by psychological manipulation. The Savior may foster emotional dependencies with assertions like "You can't leave me. You need me now" and demand constant affirmation of their role. The Rescuee, in turn, is expected to continually recognize and validate the Savior as their rescuer, thereby reinforcing an unhealthy cycle of dependency and control.

Additionally, a Savior often boasts about their role in helping others, displaying little humility regarding their contributions. They constantly seek validation, not only from the partner they've "rescued" but also from friends, family, and colleagues. Lines such as "You wouldn't have achieved this without me" are commonly used to reinforce their self-view as altruists or do-gooders. While it might seem that both parties benefit, this dynamic is considered a Distortion because it often involves coercive control and fosters unhealthy dependency. The benefits are superficial and short-lived, masking underlying issues of manipulation and imbalance. Ultimately, this dynamic prevents both individuals from engaging in a relationship based on genuine equality and mutual growth.

If you (the one being rescued) withhold approval or resist the Savior's control, you might shift from a beneficiary to a victim. If you fail to meet the Savior's expectations or assert your independence, the Savior may react negatively. They might express dissatisfaction or resentment by saying things such as, "I've invested so much in you, and you don't appreciate me enough." This response highlights the conditional nature of their support, based more on their need for validation than genuine concern for your well-being.

To make matters worse, if the Rescuee begins to attain any form of self-reliance—be it emotional, financial, social, or otherwise—the Savior may view this as a form of betrayal. This perceived disloyalty can prompt the Savior to abruptly withdraw their support—either overtly or through passive-aggressive behavior. Such actions are aimed at undermining the Rescuee's newfound self-esteem and reinforcing their dependency on the Savior, thus maintaining control within the relationship.

Take, for instance, the case of Harvey Weinstein, which starkly illustrates the dangers of the Savior Distortion. Using his prominent position as a major movie producer, Weinstein manipulated and abused his power over many women. He held considerable sway over the careers of numerous actors and actresses, effectively controlling their fate in the industry by determining their involvement in major Hollywood films. Aspiring actors often felt that gaining his approval was essential for success. This scenario represents an extreme case of the Savior Distortion, where power and control were abused under the guise of professional advancement.

While both the Savior and the Self-Sacrificer may appear as "givers" in their respective dynamics, key differences define their roles. The Savior is driven by a desire to feel superior, manipulating situations to maintain this status—all without genuine sacrifice. Their actions are not about selflessness but about securing a position of power and control over their partner. Conversely, the Self-Sacrificer genuinely engages in acts that may diminish their own Self Score to boost their partner's, often at a personal cost. This type of giving is rooted in true altruism, though it can lead to personal depletion if the care is not reciprocated.

If a relationship breaks down, the Savior might react vengefully, withdrawing support to punish the Rescuee, thereby highlighting their manipulative tendencies. In contrast, a Self-Sacrificer, though hurt, typically seeks to heal and recover from the emotional investment, rather than retaliating or seeking revenge.

Encountering individuals with Savior tendencies can be highly distressing, as their actions often verge on emotional abuse, leaving you shaken and distraught. Despite their attempts to appear heroic, the underlying message remains consistent: "Because you are no longer compliant with my demands, I will now take away something of great importance to you." Resisting the Savior's attempts to disempower you requires strength. If you find yourself dealing with manipulative individuals, it's crucial to recognize that you do not need their intervention to improve your life. Although they may provide help, the assistance often comes at a high emotional cost that may not justify the benefits received. In such a scenario, it's important to assess the intentions behind the help offered and consider the long-term impact it may have on your emotional well-being. You possess the ability to enhance your own life independently. Relinquishing control to a manipulator is not a viable or healthy option.

The Savior/Rescuee Dynamic: A Case Study

Carli had dreams of becoming a famous writer. When she connected with Richard on a dating app, he intrigued her by mentioning his influential connections in Los Angeles and promising they could help make her writing aspirations a reality. Richard also offered to mentor her, acknowledging the potential of her book idea. However, he made it clear that his interest in her extended beyond professional guidance; he wanted a relationship that was more than just friendship.

Richard was quick to clarify that his offer to help and mentor Carli wasn't contingent on a romantic relationship. "I'm not that type of guy," he reassured her, promising that his support would be purely professional. Comforted by his assurance, Carli felt more at ease with pursuing her dream of becoming a writer and was excited about the doors his connections could open.

As their mentoring sessions continued, Richard was both knowledgeable and helpful, fulfilling his promise to guide Carli in her writing career. Although grateful for his support, Carli started feeling that their romantic connection wasn't as strong as she had hoped. Their conversations, once exciting, now lacked spark, and the differences in their lifestyles became more apparent. Realizing it was important to address these feelings, Carli decided it was time for an honest conversation with Richard about her doubts regarding their romantic future.

Richard was disappointed with Carli's decision and insinuated that she wasn't trying hard enough and was giving up too easily by not giving him a chance. Despite his reaction, Carli stood firm. She calmly explained to Richard that she didn't share the same romantic feelings and made it clear that she was not interested in dating him.

Unhappy with Carli's decision, Richard abruptly ended all contact and withdrew his mentorship. He criticized her ability to make sound decisions, leaving Carli feeling blamed and gaslighted. This response revealed the conditional nature of his support, characterizing Richard as a Savior with clear strings attached. When he didn't receive the validation or the relationship he desired, he not only severed ties but also attempted to undermine Carli's self-esteem through disparaging remarks. This instance of manipulation highlights a classic case of emotional coercion from someone who once promised unconditional support.

Four Steps to Rebalance This Distortion

Being involved with someone who exhibits Savior tendencies can be overwhelmingly distressing and often traumatic. If you find yourself in such a dynamic, it's important to recognize that adjusting the relationship might not be enough. Sometimes, the best course of action is to remove yourself from the situation entirely. Prioritizing your mental health and seeking support from friends, family, or professionals can be crucial steps in breaking free from the manipulative cycle and starting the healing process.

Waiting for a Savior to react negatively to decreased validation can escalate into uncomfortable or even dangerous situations. The first critical step to overcoming this Distortion is recognizing that you are caught in such a dynamic. Once you've acknowledged this, you can begin taking concrete steps to reclaim your independence and ensure your safety. Here are some actionable steps to help you regain your freedom and move toward a healthier emotional state:

1. Identify the Savior

When evaluating someone's character, especially if you suspect they might have Savior tendencies, start by asking yourself several critical questions. First, do they display an unusual level of expertise or superiority in areas where you feel less competent? This might be a sign of their self-proclaimed "abundance" or superiority. Next, consider whether they make exaggerated claims about their ability to help you achieve excellence or success in these areas. Such claims can often be a red flag, indicating a potential Savior complex.

Another important consideration is whether the person demands an excessive amount of your time, energy, and attention. Additionally, trust your instincts: Do you sense that their offer to support you is conditional on your willingness to engage in romantic or sexual activities? Reflecting on these questions can provide valuable insights into the character of the individual and help you understand the nature of their intentions.

2. Don't Fool Yourself

Don't allow yourself to be drawn in by the Savior's illusions. Often, they create the appearance of enhancing your Values Score in certain areas, but their true intent is to manipulate and control you. Recognize these tactics for what they are and decide to break free. Attempting to out-manipulate a manipulator is futile and only prolongs your entanglement in a toxic dynamic. Instead, focus on reclaiming your autonomy and moving forward to healthier, more genuine relationships.

Ultimately, navigating a relationship with a Savior is damaging. Such individuals do not genuinely care for you; their interest is rooted in fulfilling their own needs and conditions. This type of pseudo-relationship cannot be repaired because its foundation is weakened by manipulation. Remember, genuine support and assistance come without hidden agendas.

3. Revisit the Love Formula

When dealing with a Savior, use the Love Formula to closely examine the specific Values category where they claim superiority over your skills. Take a moment to honestly assess your own abilities in this area: Are you truly lacking, or might you be too harsh on yourself, resulting in an unfairly low Self Score? Also, critically evaluate the authenticity of the Savior's success. Is it truly earned, or could it be a facade bolstered by illusion and egotism? Try to verify their achievements objectively, independent of the Savior's own biased assertions.

Engaging in this reflective process is crucial for empowering yourself to see the reality of your abilities and the validity of the Savior's claims. By critically assessing both, you can distinguish fact from fiction and liberate yourself from their deceptive influence. This newfound clarity will enable you to make decisions based on genuine self-awareness and not under the shadow of manipulation.

4. Build Your Own Foundation

Genuine passion is the strongest asset you can have to achieve your dreams. Remember, no Savior can build your dream for you—it's up to you to lay the groundwork. Focus on building a solid foundation for yourself. Take charge of your own destiny by relying on your skills and determination. As you grow, aim to gather a support system around your vision rather than fitting into someone else's agenda.

While professional support, whether paid or free, is undeniably valuable, it's important to remember that you are the main architect of your journey. The power to shape your life and achieve your dreams ultimately resides within you. Don't rely solely on someone else to lift you to higher places. As Glinda, the Good Witch of the North, wisely reminds us, "You've always had the power all along, my dear." Embrace this truth, and use it to fuel your independence and success.

Chapter 21

The Sabotagers

Match Sabotager: An individual who will ruin a perfectly good match by convincing themselves that their Self Score is much higher than the Partner Score.

Self-Sabotager: An individual who ruins their chances of increasing their Self Score.

The "Sabotager Distortion" can manifest in two distinct ways: sabotaging the success of your relationship ("Match Sabotager") or sabotaging your personal growth and success ("Self-Sabotager"). The Match Sabotager finds a partner who checks all their important boxes (i.e., has a Partner Score closely aligned with their Self Score) and then looks for reasons to end the relationship. A Self-Sabotager is someone who hurts their own chances of a higher Self Score, which inevitably hurts their partnership and life.

In either case, a Sabotager is someone who blocks their path to success, ultimately ruining any potential with an otherwise great match. Sabotagers aren't necessarily conscious of their tendencies, and oftentimes they do enter relationships with real hopes of finding a long-term connection. However, they can unwittingly introduce toxicity into their relationships. By undermining their own success or the relationship, they create an environment of instability and emotional turmoil. This can leave their partners feeling perplexed, frustrated, or even manipulated, further exacerbating the challenges within the relationship.

A Match Sabotager often struggles with a deep-seated fear of commitment and vulnerability. Despite their genuine desire for a lasting connection, their past experiences of disappointment and pain lead them to associate commitment with potential suffering. Entering relationships with hope, they paradoxically keep an eye out for any signs that might indicate future failure, viewing this vigilance as a form of self-protection. Once the relationship gains a foothold, the Match Sabotager's fear drives them to meticulously scrutinize their partner for any imperfections, often magnifying minor issues as justification for their apprehensions.

Match Sabotagers, who are sometimes aware of their own tendencies, may preemptively tell potential partners that they aren't looking for anything serious. This is often a defense mechanism to avoid deep emotional connections, keeping partners at a distance. Even as a relationship develops, they might stir up unnecessary conflicts, point out minor faults, or gradually diminish the Partner Score. These actions act as a self-fulfilling prophecy, cementing their belief that the relationship will inevitably fail. Whether in the nascent phases or deep into a partnership, their fear of true commitment can unravel the very bond they desire, leaving both individuals emotionally distressed.

On the other hand, the Self-Sabotager is someone who (often unknowingly) acts against their own best interests—consequently undermining their chances of improving their Self Score. This form of self-sabotage not only hampers their personal growth but also has a detrimental ripple effect on their relationships. As they hold themselves back, it often creates tension and dissatisfaction within the partnership, affecting both parties' emotional well-being and the overall health of the relationship.

The Self-Sabotager often grapples with internal conflicts, limiting beliefs, or unresolved emotional issues that hinder their growth. They might find themselves unwittingly acting against their own best interests, perpetuating a cycle of self-doubt and low self-esteem. One frequent challenge for Self-Sabotagers is a fear of success, which, paradoxically, can be as intimidating as failure. Success often brings change and introduces new variables, which can be overwhelming. These personal conflicts not only affect them but also seep into their relationships, where their partner may frequently see them struggling against their potential for success and happiness. This ongoing battle can create tension and instability within the relationship, making it hard for both partners to find satisfaction.

Furthermore, depression and other mental health challenges can greatly amplify the Self-Sabotager Distortion, making it difficult for individuals to break free from negative cycles. Self-discovery and self-compassion are crucial in this regard. This process involves identifying the underlying causes of their self-sabotaging behaviors, which could stem from past traumas, entrenched limiting beliefs, or ongoing emotional struggles.

Understanding the Sabotager Distortion involves recognizing the unique dynamics that define both Match Sabotagers and Self-Sabotagers. By identifying these patterns, individuals can begin a transformative journey.

The Match Sabotager: A Case Study

Malcolm met Letisha when he was just eighteen, and she quickly became his first love and his first serious relationship. Over the next five years, they experienced life's ups and downs together. However, as they approached their fifth year as a couple, Letisha began to feel that she had outgrown the relationship. Her feelings and aspirations had evolved, and she needed a change. When she decided to end the relationship, Malcolm was left utterly devastated. He had not anticipated this change, and the end of his first significant romantic relationship left him reeling from the loss.

Because of this heartbreak, Malcolm came to a very unfortunate conclusion: "Love sucks. Screw love. It never ends well." This statement reflected his deep disappointment and a newfound cynicism about relationships. Feeling betrayed by his experience, Malcolm began to believe that even when a potential match seems perfect—aligned with what one might call a Love Formula—he should be wary and distrustful.

One day, Malcolm met Rebecca, a girl he was attracted to and who had a high Partner Values Score. For the first time in a long time, he felt sparks and butterflies. But a persistent voice in his head sounded a warning, triggering memories of Letisha. Though he genuinely liked Rebecca, he created a false narrative that she couldn't possibly be as great as she seemed.

As a result, Malcolm's actions began to sabotage the new relationship before it could truly develop. He started to pull back, being slow in responding to her messages and sometimes vanishing for days at a time. Even when they were together, he held back his affection, maintaining a distance that wasn't reflective of his true feelings. This behavior was a protective mechanism, born from his fear of experiencing the same pain he had felt with Letisha.

Malcolm's guarded behavior increasingly pushed Rebecca away. His inconsistent communication and emotional distance left her feeling undervalued and disconnected. As a result, Rebecca began to pull back too, ultimately deciding that the relationship wasn't meeting her needs. When she ended it, Malcolm's worst fears were confirmed, reinforcing his cynical view that love inevitably leads to disappointment. This outcome solidified his self-fulfilling prophecy: All romantic relationships are doomed to end in misery.

The Self-Sabotager: A Case Study

Meet George, who places a high Value on *effective communication* in a relationship but paradoxically resists improving his own communication skills. He recognizes that his communication style has driven away past partners and fully understands he needs to improve to maintain a healthy relationship.

One day, his partner Sarah approached him to express her need for more emotional support, hoping for understanding and compassion. However, George responded not with empathy but with dismissal, telling her, "You're being overly sensitive; I'm not responsible for your emotions." This response, indicative of George's struggle with effective communication, left Sarah feeling unacknowledged and deeply frustrated. His inability to provide the support she sought only exacerbated the tension in their relationship.

Despite Sarah's clear attempts to explain her emotional needs, George continued to respond dismissively. Interestingly, George was aware of how poorly he was handling the situation; he could see his harsh reactions but felt stuck in his patterns. This self-awareness, however, didn't lead to change. As time passed, the relationship began to suffer significantly. Sarah felt increasingly neglected and misunderstood, which only deepened her frustration and sadness. On the other hand, George experienced a familiar sense of failure as he watched another relationship crumble due to his inability to communicate effectively and empathetically.

Despite understanding the damage his blunt communication caused, George found himself unable to change. At the root of his struggles lay a deep-seated fear of vulnerability and possibly even a fear of what success in his relationships might bring. These fears had hardened into deeply ingrained beliefs that made genuine openness and change daunting for him.

George is a typical Self-Sabotager. His resistance to change, rooted in deep-set fears and insecurities, has gradually eroded the quality of his most significant relationships, affecting not only his personal connections with friends and family but also his professional interactions. And despite seeing the clear negative consequences of his actions, George remains stuck.

Four Steps to Rebalance This Distortion

Breaking free from the patterns of either the Match Sabotager or the Self-Sabotager requires a significant amount of dedication and a deep level of self-awareness. If you find yourself repeatedly "ruining things" in your relationships, even when you seem to have found a potentially perfect match according to the Love Formula, it's time to reflect deeply on your actions and motivations. This recurring theme is a signal that underlying issues need to be addressed.

If you find yourself trapped in the cycle of being a Match Sabotager or a Self-Sabotager, consider these vital steps. They are designed to empower you to restore balance in your relationships and permanently escape the destructive patterns of this Distortion. Subsequently, you can build more fulfilling and stable connections that are free from the turmoil of past patterns.

1. Revisit the Love Formula

Healing begins with recognizing your own contributions to the problems at hand. Apply the Love Formula to assess a relationship you're concerned about. Take a close look at how well your actions match your intentions. If you find yourself pulling away, ending things prematurely, avoiding difficult conversations, or stirring up conflict without cause, it's possible you're getting in your own way without even realizing it.

Take a moment to think about whether you've set the bar too high for your partner, focusing too much on small issues, or if you've been holding back on important aspects such as intimacy, touch, attention, or affection. It's also worth considering whether you've been avoiding important personal growth steps that could help you improve as an individual, regardless of your relationship status.

Furthermore, if you find yourself self-sabotaging, take a look at whether your Self Score has been dropping or staying the same across different aspects of your life. Think about how your choices are influencing your chances of improving this score. What improvements can you make? More critically, consider whether there are deep-seated fears holding you back from living your ideal life and reaching your full potential.

2. Communicate Honestly with Yourself and Your Partner

Honesty is imperative. If you've just ended a relationship with someone who had a similar Partner Score, remember that finding a truly compatible match isn't easy, especially in the complex world of modern dating. Take some time for a genuine self-assessment to figure out why you walked away from what seemed like a promising connection. And remember, communication is key!

Pause for a moment and consider these questions: Did you end the relationship over something minor? Did you disappear without explanation or keep your messages short and uninterested? Were you often rescheduling, always late, or missing dates? Are you afraid of getting too emotionally involved? Do you have deep-rooted fears of getting hurt or unresolved issues from previous relationships? After thinking these through and maybe realizing you didn't give the relationship your all, talk to your partner. Express your willingness to work on improving things together.

3. Challenge Negative Thoughts

Often Match Sabotagers and Self-Sabotagers make decisions based on negative narratives in their minds. If you don't consciously decide to deeply heal from your past traumas and prepare yourself to date seriously, then there's no point in reconciling with your partner or even looking for someone new.

Instead, it's time to recognize frequent negative thoughts that loop around in your mind, especially those related to relationships, self-worth, or vulnerability. Challenge the validity of these negative thoughts. Ask yourself if they are based on past experiences, unfounded fears, or self-limiting beliefs. Take time to heal by engaging in activities that promote self-care, self-reflection, and emotional well-being. This may involve practices such as mindfulness, journaling, or pursuing hobbies that bring joy.

4. Seek Professional Help

Seeking professional help can be a game changer for those who tend to sabotage their relationships, especially if it's due to a fear of commitment or feelings of low self-worth. Working with a therapist or counselor can help you explore the deep-seated reasons behind these feelings. This process usually includes examining your past experiences, understanding your attachment style, and addressing any unresolved issues that might be driving your self-sabotaging behaviors.

In all this, the Love Formula highlights the crucial role of compatibility and shared values in relationships. Professional guidance can be instrumental in aligning your actions with your genuine desires and fostering more authentic connections in the future. It also helps in understanding the elements that affect your Self Score and how commitment plays into that dynamic.

Chapter 22

The Black Hole

Black Hole: An individual who continuously and consistently lowers your hard-earned Self Score.

"Black Holes" are people who, whether they mean to or not, can undermine your self-esteem, leading you to assign yourself a lower Self Score. They suck the confidence right out of you. These Black Holes can affect you in two ways: 1) by actually reducing the Self Score you've worked hard to build or 2) by skewing your perception of your Self Score. This can happen because they make you question the good opinion you have of yourself.

Black Holes can severely disrupt your peace of mind. Being around them may lead you to doubt your inherent worth and accomplishments, which can lower your Self Score and self-esteem. As we know, these doubts can profoundly affect how you give and receive love.

As your self-esteem dips, the effects ripple out, especially in how you interact with others. When you're unsure of your own value, it becomes harder to accept love and kindness from others. You might start questioning why someone would care about you or appreciate you, which can make you withdraw from relationships or react defensively. On the flip side, these doubts can make you overly dependent on receiving validation to feel good about yourself, which can strain even the healthiest of relationships.

The impact on how you give love is just as profound. When you're feeling low about yourself, your capacity to extend empathy, patience, and understanding to others diminishes. You might find yourself less generous or quicker to anger as you're operating from a place of hurt and insecurity. This can create a vicious cycle: Your relationships suffer, which in turn, can make you feel even worse about yourself.

What's tricky is how Black Holes do their work. They might use guilt trips, harsh criticism, manipulative tactics, lies, passive aggressiveness, or even bullying. Little by little, they chip away at how you see yourself, and they do this through creating constant drama, picking fights, spreading rumors, talking down to you, or acting like they're the smartest in the room. Getting dragged into their negative outlook can really lower your own self-esteem, especially if this turns into emotional abuse.

The Black Hole Distortion happens when someone starts dumping their insecurities onto you. Maybe they're feeling unsure about their own life, so they start picking at yours. For instance, if they're not happy with where their career is going, they might make snide remarks about your job or belittle your achievements. It's like they're trying to offload their insecurities onto you because it's easier than dealing with them on their own.

At the beginning of a relationship, Black Holes can actually appear to be very charming. They often zero in on what's great about you—your humor, intelligence, kindness—and make you feel really seen and appreciated. But soon enough, they flip the switch and start using tactics such as gaslighting and mind games to make you doubt yourself. In the worst cases, they might even convince you that no one else would want you, which is absolutely not true.

Make sure not to mix up Black Holes with other Distortions. While Self-Focused individuals might use their partner to actively boost their own Self Score, Black Holes aren't looking to become better people at all. Instead, they focus on knocking down your Self Score—to feel better about themselves. This is why it's crucial to recognize when you're dealing with a Black Hole. Understanding their behavior helps you protect your own self-esteem and keep your mental health in check. Handling these interactions wisely can save you a lot of emotional turmoil and help keep your life balanced and healthy.

While the picture I've painted of Black Holes might seem a bit one-sided, it's crucial to remember the role you play in this dynamic. Everyone who feels affected by a Black Hole has one thing in common: They're adults who have allowed these personalities to influence their lives to some extent. It's on you to decide whether or not this continues any further.

Setting and enforcing healthy boundaries isn't just possible in this scenario; it's necessary. Reflect on this: How much of your peace are you willing to sacrifice? It can be tough to pull away from people, especially if they're close to you. But ultimately, whether you keep them in your life or cut them loose is a decision only you can make.

The Black Hole: A Case Study

Jack and Emma, a couple deeply committed to each other, faced the challenges of college life together. Realizing that he needed to boost his *health consciousness* Values Score, Jack set a New Year's resolution. Starting with a self-assessment that placed him at a modest 10/20, he was determined to make significant improvements.

In the first two weeks, Jack threw himself into his new routine. He exercised up to four times a week, switched to a diet rich in fresh fruits and vegetables, and cut out alcohol. These positive changes not only improved his health but also boosted his self-esteem, raising his Value Score in this category to 16/20.

But Jack's new lifestyle choices were starting to impact Emma. They used to enjoy socializing over drinks, but now Emma found herself missing her usual companion. She also couldn't help but notice Jack's improved appearance, which triggered feelings of jealousy and insecurity. A month into Jack's health-focused changes, Emma was feeling nostalgic about their old routines. In an effort to reclaim some of that past, she urged Jack to join her for a night out, appealing to him with, "You're my boyfriend, don't leave me to go out alone!"

Jack agreed, albeit reluctantly, and once out, Emma encouraged him to keep the drinks coming. They didn't get back home until around four in the morning, their night capped off with fast food that broke Jack's diet rules. The next morning, Jack woke up with a hangover, missed his gym session, and found himself slipping back into his old habits.

Here Emma played the role of a Black Hole by tempting Jack to stray from his health-focused path. Now Jack was at a crossroads. He could either fall back into his old habits, let frustration get the better of him, and allow Emma's influence to derail his progress, or he could take a moment to regroup, set clear boundaries with Emma, and look for ways in which they could both enjoy healthier activities together.

Four Steps to Rebalance This Distortion

If you have a Black Hole in your life, it's important to create positive boundaries to protect your well-being. Recognize how they drain your energy and happiness. Once you see this, develop a clear plan to minimize their negative impact while finding ways to bring more joy and positivity into the relationship.

If you notice Black Hole tendencies in yourself, it's a signal to start a journey of self-awareness and personal growth. Use the following steps as a guide to help you work through these behaviors, with the Love Formula serving as the foundation for your improvement:

1. Revisit the Love Formula

Take another look at your Love Formula and ask yourself these questions: Have you seen a significant drop in your Self Score since you started spending time with your partner? Are your Values starting to mirror your partner's more than your own true beliefs?

For instance, if you're spending a lot of time with someone who values superficial things and material wealth, you might find yourself starting to prioritize these in your own Top 5 Values. It's important to recognize if your Self Score has noticeably dropped because of these relationship dynamics. A significant decline could be a strong sign that you are interacting with a Black Hole.

2. Establish Positive Boundaries

Recognizing your own tendencies is crucial when navigating relationships, particularly with Black Holes who create emotional turmoil. It's essential to set clear boundaries and avoid getting pulled into needless drama. Effective communication is key in handling relationships with these individuals. Make sure to avoid reinforcing negative behavior and be open about your personal needs, particularly when discussions become tense or uncomfortable.

By prioritizing honesty and mutual understanding, you can respect each other's differing viewpoints without letting them infringe on your personal boundaries. This is key to keeping the relationship healthy and balanced.

3. Minimize Negative Conversations

When dealing with Black Holes in relationships, it's important to act deliberately. Cut down on negative interactions by steering clear of conversations that typically spiral into criticism. By distancing yourself from these draining exchanges, you foster a healthier, more positive atmosphere, which can boost your Self Score.

Recognizing triggers that lead to negative exchanges can empower you to preemptively address or avoid them. For instance, if certain subjects consistently lead to conflict, it might be wise to discuss them only in a structured setting or with a mediator present.

4. Self-Reflection and Growth

If you think you might be acting like a Black Hole in your partner's life, it's time to take a long hard look at yourself. Reflect on how your actions might be affecting their self-esteem and overall happiness. Commit to personal improvement and aim to be a supportive, uplifting presence in your relationship instead of a negative one.

Understand that being a Black Hole often triggers feelings of guilt, shame, or blame. It's okay to acknowledge your mistakes— take a moment to consider whether your actions uplift or discourage others. To really get to the heart of the problem, have the courage to ask, "Have the people around me been Black Holes, normalizing this kind of behavior?" Remember, growth is a continuous, lifelong process for everyone, even those who have shown Black Hole tendencies.

Chapter 23

The Deceiver

Deceiver: An individual who will manipulate or lie to their partner to artificially inflate how they measure up to their partner's Values.
Low-Level Deceiver: An individual who will conceal certain aspects of their life.
Mid-Level Deceiver: An individual who will provide only partial truths about their life.
High-Level Deceiver: An individual who resorts to extreme manipulation and outright lies about their life.

The "Deceiver Distortion" happens when someone manipulates their partner to appear more compatible and boost their image, presenting themselves as a better Love Formula match than they truly are. This behavior can vary widely—some may be only slightly misleading, while others are fully aware and intentional in their deceit. Essentially, these individuals are trying to convince everyone, including their partners, that they should be perceived in a certain way.

Can you manipulate someone's attraction to you? Yes, but it won't last; these tactics are usually just a temporary fix. If you try to mold perceptions by concealing your true self, you'll eventually hit a wall, and your real personality will come through. The Deceiver Distortion manifests in three degrees: low, mid, and high. These levels indicate the depth and intensity of the deception.

It's important to note that people can engage in deception at any stage of a relationship. Some might be dishonest right from the early days of dating, while others may begin behaving deceptively after some time in more established, long-term relationships. The timing and manner in which they choose to reveal the truth depend on their reasons for the deception and their circumstances. Let's look at each level of deceit in more detail:

A Low-Level Deceiver conceals aspects of their Love Formula Score without outright lying. Instead, they might influence their partner's assumptions through their behavior or appearance. Let's take Lina, for example, a Low-Level Deceiver who is in the early stages of dating Alex. Her top Values are *financial stability* and *success*, but she's recently hit a rough patch in her career that has temporarily affected her finances.

Rather than sharing her career and financial struggles with Alex, Lina chooses to keep these issues hidden as they're just getting to know each other. She uses behavior and appearance, like dining at upscale restaurants and planning weekend getaways, to maintain an image of financial stability. Lina carefully avoids bringing up her work problems or recent financial difficulties, instead directing their conversations to the more positive areas of her life.

Lina also keeps up a polished and well-maintained appearance to fit her partner's idea of success. She cleverly avoids situations that might expose her current financial strain. For instance, she steers clear of conversations about costly hobbies and dodges events where she'd be expected to make a financial contribution.

In this scenario, Lina isn't lying about her finances, but she *is* shaping Alex's perceptions through her actions and appearance. Her goal is to create a favorable impression and sustain a certain image while they're still in the early stages of their relationship. However, as things progress, Lina could encounter difficulties if she decides to come clean about her financial situation, especially since Alex might have already developed certain expectations based on her earlier, misleading signs.

Next, we have Mid-Level Deceivers. These individuals share half-truths, usually delivered in a vague or convoluted way. They hint at the reality of their situation but always frame it positively, much like the adept "spin doctors" you might find in political circles.

Consider Laura, a Mid-Level Deceiver, who has been seeing Mark for a few months. She highly values her independence and is financially secure. However, she has temporarily moved back in with her parents to save money for a personal creative project. Rather than being upfront about her living situation, Laura chooses to share only partial truths, always casting her choices in a positive light.

For instance, when Mark asks about her living situation, Laura mentions spending more time with her family lately and enjoying the company. She also avoids explicitly stating that she has moved back in with her parents to save money, instead framing the increased time spent at home as a way of strengthening family bonds.

In doing so, Laura focuses on the positive aspects of her decision, emphasizing the supportive family environment and the chance to concentrate on personal growth. She minimizes the financial reasons for her move, portraying it instead as a deliberate and beneficial lifestyle choice.

While Laura never directly lies, she carefully crafts her narrative to present her living situation in the best possible light. This kind of deception may lead to complications as the relationship develops, particularly if Mark learns the complete truth and realizes that Laura's initial descriptions were specifically designed to project a more favorable image.

Finally, there are High-Level Deceivers who engage in outright lies and extreme manipulation, preventing their partners from making informed choices about their suitability. Take the case of Kayla, a High-Level Deceiver, who is starting a romantic relationship with Jamie. Jamie values *communication* and *financial stability* highly, and he often jokes disparagingly about his brother's personal blog, calling it a "waste of time." Influenced by this, Kayla presents herself as a financially secure businesswoman.

She exaggerates details about her work routine, claiming she spends many hours each day at the office, involved in intense business decisions and company affairs. She fabricates achievements, overstates her investment returns, and distorts her personal expenses, all in an effort to earn Jamie's respect.

In truth, Kayla works as a part-time receptionist and spends the rest of her time pursuing her passion for photography and managing a personal blog focused on travel and lifestyle experiences.

Kayla takes significant steps to maintain the false image she's created. For instance, when invited to a company holiday party, she tells her coworkers she'll be out of town, while simultaneously telling Jamie that the party isn't worth attending. By doing this, she prevents both herself and Jamie from experiencing a more authentic version of her life.

This type of deception involves consistently giving false information and using complex strategies to uphold a facade. High-Level Deceivers risk damaging the trust in their relationship, as they prevent their partner from having a true understanding of their shared interests and lifestyle compatibility.

From Deception to Transparency: A Case Study

Education ranked highly among Simon's Values, and although he had a bachelor's degree, he felt somewhat intimidated as he prepared for a date with Lisette, who had a PhD. He perceived her advanced degree as a mark of her being more impressive.

For months, Simon had embellished his educational qualifications on his dating profile, claiming to have a higher degree than he actually did. Aware that Lisette might have seen this misleading information, he wondered if her interest was based solely on his supposed level of education. As he got ready for the date, a growing unease prompted a moment of self-reflection.

Upon reflection, Simon thought, "What's the harm in letting her get to know me first? I can be honest later." With this in mind, he didn't clarify his actual education level during their first date. The evening unfolded naturally, with plenty of laughter and an undeniable connection, all of it hinting at the potential for something more despite the omission.

As the second date approached, Simon felt the weight of his secret increasing. The truth about his educational background hung over him, and he worried it might ruin everything. What if he hadn't fully won her affection yet, and she left him for this "small" detail? Overwhelmed by fear, Simon stuck to his lie. This time, however, Lisette asked more probing questions about his academic program, the duration of his studies, and his graduation year. With each question, Simon sunk deeper into the deception.

By the time their third date rolled around, Simon felt the pressing need to come clean. When the conversation naturally drifted toward education, his demeanor shifted to a more earnest tone. With a deep breath, he chose vulnerability over pretense, fully aware that he risked embarrassment and a difficult conversation. He admitted that his admiration for her had driven him to misrepresent his education; he feared appearing inadequate. Lisette's reaction was mixed: She felt empathy for his insecurity but also a sense of betrayal. Why had he felt the need to deceive her?

She decided to continue seeing Simon, deciding that his initial lies hadn't caused irreparable harm. However, the incident left a lasting impression; she couldn't shake off the feeling that Simon was capable of outright lying if it benefited him. As a result, her trust in him was diminished, perpetually tinged with the memory of his deceit.

Unfortunately, Simon's insecurities led him to misrepresent himself, damaging his chance at a genuine connection. It wasn't his educational background that bothered Lisette; she was unfazed by that detail. Instead, what hurt the relationship was his choice to deceive her.

Four Steps to Rebalance This Distortion

If you think your partner might be deceptive, open and honest communication is essential to rebuild trust and maintain a healthy relationship. If you notice that you're exhibiting traits of a Deceiver, it could be a sign of underlying issues such as low self-esteem or fear of abandonment.

Remember, personal growth is an ongoing journey, and a truly supportive partner will be there for you when you're honest and show your real self. A great partner will back your efforts toward self-improvement in any area of life, starting with complete transparency. Embrace who you truly are—that's the key! Now let's look at the steps you can take to address and correct this type of Distortion:

1. Self-Reflection

The first step is self-reflection: Determine if you exhibit behaviors of a Deceiver—and whether at a low, mid, or high level. There's no reason to feel ashamed about recognizing this in yourself. At some point, many of us have felt the urge to hide our true selves from fear of judgment or abandonment. Acknowledging this is vital if you aim to build a relationship that thrives on compassion, authenticity, and love.

Also, take some time to consider if your partner might be showing signs of deceptive behavior. Closely observe how they behave and communicate to better understand the dynamics of your relationship. Being aware of these patterns is vital for fostering mutual understanding and creating a strong foundation of trust and openness in your partnership.

2. Revisit the Love Formula

Taking time to evaluate your Values is crucial to understanding the authenticity of your self-representation. Ask yourself if the Values you profess to hold are truly manifested in your daily actions and decisions. Is there a noticeable discrepancy between what you say is important to you and how you actually live your life? Such inconsistencies can be revealing and warrant deeper introspection.

Next delve into the differences in Scores between you and your partner. This can help identify specific areas where your Values, expectations, or lifestyles may not be perfectly aligned. Understanding these differences is key to addressing potential conflicts and enhancing mutual respect and understanding in your relationship.

3. Build Healthy Self-Esteem and Self-Worth

Being loved for who you truly are is possible without having to pretend to be someone else. To build healthy self-esteem, start by speaking kindly to yourself, acknowledging your achievements, and setting achievable goals. Regularly remind yourself of your strengths and celebrate even the smallest successes. When tackling big goals, break them down into smaller, manageable steps so you can feel a sense of progress along the way. And remember to be kind to yourself—mistakes are a natural part of being human and learning.

Build a circle of supportive friends and family, and don't hesitate to seek professional help if you need it. Committing to ongoing learning and personal development can significantly boost your confidence and help you grow. Keep in mind that developing healthy self-esteem is a continuous process. It takes patience and dedication to appreciate and embrace what makes you unique.

4. Foster Open Communication

Foster a relationship based on open and honest communication, whether you've been deceptive or are dealing with deception from your partner. To mend trust, fully acknowledge any dishonesty and openly discuss your reasons without making excuses. Establish a safe, judgment-free environment that encourages your partner to openly express their feelings and concerns.

Clear communication is crucial for rebuilding trust, encouraging honest discussions, and understanding how deception has affected your relationship. Embrace the vulnerability accompanying these conversations. It's this openness that can lead to mutual growth and a deeper connection.

Chapter 24

The Overcompensator

Overcompensator: An individual with a low Self Score in one or more Values categories who overcompensates by either 1) seeking a partner with a high Value Score in that area or 2) diligently working to elevate their overall Self Score by focusing on improvement in another Values category.

Meet the "Overcompensator"—someone who tends to underestimate their own abilities in one or more of their Top 5 Values, leading them to try and compensate for what they see as deficiencies. This compensation can manifest in two ways. First, they might look for a partner who excels in areas in which they feel inadequate, thinking, "I'm not strong in this area, so I'll find someone who is." Alternatively, they might overemphasize another Value, attempting to cover up their perceived weaknesses by excelling elsewhere, as if to say, "I might not be good at *this*, so I'll become exceptional at *that*." These insecurities can significantly skew their Love Formula, impacting their choice of partners in relationships.

In the first scenario, the Overcompensator seeks partners who can offset their perceived shortcomings, motivated by the desire to boost their own Self Score. For example, someone who highly values social status but feels insecure about their own standing in society might look for a partner who is well-liked and respected. This approach is often seen as a way to enhance their own reputation through association.

Consider a person who feels deeply insecure about their educational background, especially having grown up in a family of physicians. Matching their family's educational and professional achievements is a daunting task and not one that everyone desires or is equal to accomplishing. Feeling as though they haven't lived up to these family expectations, they might feel diminished in worth. To counteract this, they may be drawn to a partner who possesses the qualities they believe they lack, such as a doctor with a successful career. This behavior is typical of an Overcompensator who seeks a partner to "make up" for their perceived deficiencies, hoping to gain external approval. Within the framework of the Love Formula, they might rate themselves low in a specific Self Value area, and naturally, they are attracted to someone with a high Partner Values Score in that same area.

In the second scenario of the Overcompensator Distortion, an individual amplifies a particular Value to cover up a perceived personal shortcoming elsewhere. Imagine someone who feels inadequate in reaching their career goals compared to their peers. To counter this, they might throw themselves into another area, like adopting a health-conscious lifestyle. While aiming to live healthily is beneficial on its own, they might take it to an extreme, striving to be the fittest or the most knowledgeable about health trends. This intense focus can lead them to be seen as an Overcompensator. According to the Love Formula, this behavior is a way to offset a low Self Value Score in one area by overachieving in another, more controllable aspect.

Self-improvement is a positive goal, but problems arise when an Overcompensator's insecurities deepen into an inferiority complex. Intriguingly, these can also evolve into a superiority complex, where the individual starts to believe that they are better than others. This shift often happens as they devote excessive time and energy to another area of their lives to compensate for perceived shortcomings. For example, someone might immerse themselves in becoming a fitness enthusiast—engaging in daily intense workouts, perfecting their abs, and strictly managing their diet. As they achieve these fitness goals, they might begin to look down on those who are less active or fit.

Furthermore, Overcompensators might project their own self-esteem issues onto their partner, often being overly critical. This behavior can strain the relationship, as emotionally healthy partners might start feeling that they deserve a less critical and more supportive environment.

Consider Oliver and Amanda, who enjoyed a healthy and happy relationship for a year, treating each other with love and respect—perfectly in line with their Love Formulas. However, the dynamic shifted when Oliver landed his dream job. During his first week, the competitive nature of his new workplace made him struggle with impostor syndrome and dissatisfaction with his professional environment. Constant criticism from his colleagues made him question his capabilities and self-worth, which not only affected his performance at work but also led to a decline in his Self Score.

Even when he was returning home each day feeling exhausted, distressed, and drained of self-confidence, Oliver kept his struggles hidden from Amanda, fearing she might view him as a failure. He thought that he couldn't cope emotionally if she also started seeing him in a negative light. Despite his attempts to conceal his troubles, Amanda noticed a shift in his behavior: He suddenly developed a new shopping habit and became overly focused on his appearance. Confused by these changes, she wondered if he was trying to impress his colleagues at work, speculating that he felt the need to upgrade his wardrobe, cologne, and accessories to fit into his new corporate environment.

Oliver became obsessed with his image, significantly elevating his Value Score in this aspect. Remarkably, this shift in his self-perception led him to be overly critical of Amanda, unfairly lowering her Partner Values Score based on her appearance. This was a projection of his own feelings of inadequacy; by focusing on her supposed shortcomings, he diverted attention from his own insecurities, unintentionally eroding her self-esteem. The result was a strained relationship, with Amanda shouldering the burden of Oliver's projected insecurities, which took a toll on her emotional health.

Individuals who have a strong sense of self-worth and maintain healthy boundaries typically won't put up with negative behavior from their partner for long. In such scenarios, the relationship might end, which could further aggravate the self-esteem issues and distorted perceptions of the Overcompensator.

Dealing with an Overcompensator in a relationship involves recognizing the subtleties of their behavior and getting to the heart of their insecurities. Promoting open communication and creating a supportive environment can help. These actions encourage the

Overcompensator to start recognizing their true self-worth more authentically.

The Overcompensator: A Case Study

Consider Jill's situation. Throughout her childhood and adolescence, she and her close friends often found themselves competing in various areas of life, which sometimes led to tensions. As they grew older, her friends achieved notable success, frequently highlighting their accomplishments on social media. This constant exposure made Jill feel inadequate and overshadowed, leading to an inferiority complex despite her own significant achievements.

Soon Jill's dating life became increasingly influenced by her friends' opinions. Driven by a desire to keep up with their perceived success, Jill often rated herself poorly on her Self Score, convinced that she fell short in comparison to others in almost every area. Enter Sam, a confident twenty-three-year-old with an unconventional path.

Despite a promising start on their first date, Jill felt her insecurities flare up during their second outing when she discovered Sam's modest lifestyle. He had dropped out before earning his high school diploma and now worked a low-paying job while pursuing his passion for art. Moreover, Sam held a dismissive view of social media's importance and maintained a small circle of friends.

Sam's unconventional choices, which defied societal norms, triggered Jill's fear of judgment from her friends. Her low self-esteem and the desire to maintain a certain image led her to end the relationship, prioritizing public perception over genuine compatibility. This decision, driven by her need to be seen with someone of higher status and popularity, highlights how an Overcompensator's distorted perceptions can adversely affect their romantic relationships. Jill's developing inferiority complex also illustrates how unresolved feelings of inadequacy can fuel the rejection of potential matches.

Four Steps to Rebalance This Distortion

Addressing the Overcompensator Distortion and overcoming an inferiority complex involves a strategic approach: repairing distorted views in interpersonal relationships and recognizing the influence of external factors. By addressing excessive criticism, setting healthy boundaries, and reaching out for support, we can develop self-awareness and move beyond the relentless pursuit of external validation.

Additionally, it's important to critically examine your motives for seeking social validation. Embracing humility and recognizing your own worth are key to forming genuine connections and growing as a person. Consider reducing your screen time, setting limits on social media use, and taking regular breaks to foster a healthier balance. Following these steps can positively impact your well-being and lead you toward a more fulfilling and authentic life.

1. Confront and Set Boundaries

Identify and address excessive criticism from friends, family, peers, or acquaintances who may act like Black Holes. Create strong boundaries by trusting your instincts and assertively using "I" messages to express your feelings.

If you find the pressure to constantly showcase achievements overwhelming, it might be helpful to seek support. Consider options such as counseling, mediation, or discussing the situation with a supervisor. These resources can provide guidance and help you manage the stress associated with such expectations.

2. Disconnect and Prioritize Quality

Create a plan to reduce social media use and limit screen time by scheduling specific times for checking apps. Consider taking an entire day off from all screens, spending time outside, and strengthening face-to-face relationships. Unfollow content creators who trigger negative feelings and focus on surrounding yourself with positive influences.

Focus on quality rather than quantity by curating a social media feed that is uplifting and motivating. Rethink the idea that social media is a stress reliever, as excessive use can actually be harmful. Set limits for your ideal time spent on social media, and try a week-long break from it to potentially see a positive change in your well-being.

3. Revisit the Love Formula

Use the Love Formula as a self-evaluation tool. Examine your Values Scores to pinpoint areas where you might be overcompensating, pouring too much energy into specific Values to cover perceived weaknesses. This reflective exercise can offer deep insights into your behaviors, laying a strong groundwork for personal growth and more accurate self-assessment.

By recognizing areas where you might be overemphasizing certain Values to compensate for others, you can start cultivating a more balanced and authentic self. The Love Formula serves as a guiding compass, helping you navigate the complexities of your emotions and behaviors. This fosters greater self-awareness and supports positive transformations in your relationships and personal growth.

4. Build Healthy Self-Esteem

Focus on building your self-confidence and self-acceptance. Embrace who you truly are by recognizing your strengths and celebrating your achievements without relying on external validation or comparing yourself to others. Remember that your value is intrinsically connected to your unique qualities and personal experiences, not just what society expects of you or how successful others around you are.

Develop a strong sense of self-appreciation and resilience to grow your self-esteem authentically. For someone who tends to overcompensate, this step is especially important. Shift your focus from seeking external validation to recognizing and appreciating your inherent merits. This approach will help you cultivate a more authentic and satisfying sense of self-worth.

Chapter 25

The Infatuated

Infatuated: An individual who boosts their Partner Score to the point of worship.

The "Infatuated" Distortion describes an individual who sees their partner through a lens shaped by fantasy. They experience feelings of profound admiration, leading them to think, "He/she is just so perfect!" In terms of the Love Formula, this feeling can be expressed as, "Your Score is exceptionally high, way higher than mine!"

As we know, it's normal for partners to have slightly different Scores. But what if one person views their Partner Score as much higher and feels no need to balance things out? This leads to infatuation. When you overly elevate your Partner Score, it can trigger intense and sometimes overwhelming emotions. This might even turn into a kind of worship, where you're convinced that this person is incredibly special, making you think, "I'll be damned if I let them out of my sight!"

With every conversation, shared laugh, and gentle touch, your brain releases chemicals that make you feel elated, almost as if it's shouting, "This is amazing!" However, it's important to stay aware, as these feelings can sometimes deepen into intense preoccupations. Obsession, which can be highly destructive in a relationship, involves placing someone at the very center of your world and neglecting other important relationships. When someone becomes obsessed, their attention can significantly shift away from family, friends, and work. They may become consumed with doing whatever it takes to "win over" or "keep" the person they are fixated on.

These measures might involve adopting unhealthy dieting practices, spending excessively on appearance-related items such as outfits, perfume, makeup, or hairstyling, and even engaging in risky sexual behaviors or other activities to please the partner. The tendency to obsessively replay past interactions and imagine future ones can resemble the exhilarating high of an addictive drug. Additionally, one may also be caught up in a constant countdown, with days and minutes meticulously tracked until the next meeting with the partner.

When someone is deeply infatuated with their partner, it can often irritate their friends and family. This usually occurs because the infatuated person might talk about their partner excessively, making it the dominant subject of every conversation. This unrelenting focus can make others feel overlooked or as though every discussion with the individual inevitably swings back to their romantic relationship. Over time, this pattern can understandably become frustrating for those around them.

Make no mistake: Being blinded by love is a real phenomenon. When you're deeply enchanted, it's easy to overlook your partner's flaws. This might mean not noticing when they treat you selfishly, if they behave irresponsibly (like being flaky or unreliable), or when they face challenges in maintaining healthy relationships. These challenges could include poor communication skills, troubled interactions with family, or a lack of enduring friendships.

Furthermore, infatuation often leads to an imbalance where your needs might go unnoticed, making a healthy relationship difficult. In cases where both partners are equally infatuated, often seen during the honeymoon phase, the relationship can feel like blissful perfection. It's a wonderful feeling, and there's something to be celebrated there! However, as time passes and emotions stabilize, this intense phase usually subsides. Brain chemistry adjusts, and you begin to see your partner more realistically, recognizing that they, like everyone, have flaws.

While the ecstasy of infatuation during the honeymoon phase is exhilarating, it's important to recognize that it can lead to a Distortion if prolonged and left unchecked. This intense focus can lead you to neglect other important aspects of your life, such as your career, family, and friendships, causing your Self Score to decline without you even noticing. It's easy to become so consumed by your emotions that you overlook these priorities, spending too much time and energy on your relationship.

In some cases, one person may move past the infatuated honeymoon phase while the other remains deeply immersed in it. This creates a significant imbalance in the relationship. The person who has transitioned beyond the initial intense feelings may struggle to match their partner's level of affection, which can lead to feelings of guilt. This mismatch can make navigating the relationship quite challenging for both partners.

When one person remains deeply infatuated, they may also become a Self-Sacrificer. This role is characterized by excessive generosity, a tendency to forgive too easily, and a constant quest for their partner's attention and approval. Such individuals often overlook their own needs, struggling to assert themselves or communicate what they truly need from the relationship. This overwhelming desire to please can lead to a power imbalance, making it difficult for them to stand up for their own well-being.

The Infatuated: A Case Study

Meet Alex and Taylor, a couple who once reveled in the thrill of mutual infatuation. In their honeymoon phase, each believed they had found their ideal partner. Their interactions were like scenes pulled straight from a romantic film, filled with heightened emotions and a sense of perfect harmony.

As time went on, Alex's feelings of infatuation began to wane, but Taylor's deep admiration continued unabated. Alex still cared deeply for Taylor, but he noticed a shift in his emotions. He started to see Taylor's flaws more clearly and realized the importance of adopting a more balanced and realistic perspective of their relationship. The once-mutual enchantment now gave way to a clear imbalance.

Taylor's obsession continued, straining their relationship. She frequently went to great lengths for Alex, organizing elaborate surprises, sending lavish gifts, and demanding near-constant attention. In contrast, Alex, overwhelmed by these expectations, struggled to return the same intensity of affection. Although he genuinely cared for Taylor, her boundless enthusiasm became overwhelming. This created a dynamic where Taylor's displays of affection felt more suffocating than fulfilling for Alex.

The relationship grew increasingly imbalanced as Taylor compromised her own well-being in an effort to maintain the initial enchantment. This sacrifice created tension, making it challenging for them to openly discuss how their feelings and needs were evolving. Caught between his genuine affection for Taylor and his struggle to meet her lofty expectations, Alex was left feeling overwhelmed and smothered—and guilty for it.

Four Steps to Rebalance This Distortion

To overcome the Infatuated Distortion, it's essential to actively work toward mental balance. This includes recognizing and dealing with personal insecurities, avoiding manipulative behaviors, and cultivating genuine connections rooted in mutual respect. The Love Formula highlights the significance of striving for a balanced approach in relationships, ensuring that both partners' needs and feelings are equally valued.

This approach encourages individuals to prioritize their own well-being, interests, and social connections and to understand that a healthy relationship flourishes when it involves two emotionally sound people blending their lives together. By adopting the Love Formula principles, individuals can mitigate the risks associated with the Infatuated Distortion. This fosters stable, mutually enriching relationships that are deeply connected and genuinely supportive.

1. Identify the Signs

If you find yourself constantly preoccupied with thoughts of your partner and longing for their presence, it's important to pause and recognize the signs of infatuation. Ask yourself: Are you willing to go to great lengths for them and are fascinated by every detail of their existence? Acknowledging these signs is the first step toward gaining a healthier perspective on your relationship.

Additionally, pay attention to your partner's behavior—if they display signs of excessive neediness, constant giving, or an overwhelming desire for your attention and validation, these may be indicators of deep infatuation. Trusted friends or family members can also provide an external perspective, helping both of you navigate the intense emotions associated with infatuation more effectively.

2. Discover Your Personality Type

The next step to moving beyond infatuation involves a deep dive into your own personality tendencies. By filling out the questionnaire in Part IV, you can discern whether you lean more toward Values or Traits (Practical vs. Emotional). This self-reflection is vital as it helps you recognize recurring patterns in your behavior, understand your inherent tendencies, and identify areas where you might be susceptible to Distortion. If you find yourself categorized as an Extreme, it suggests a vulnerability to this kind of Distortion and signals a potential imbalance in your relationship.

The Love Formula is about understanding not just your partner but also yourself and how your personality affects your perception of and approach to relationships. This step can help you cultivate healthier connections that are rooted in authenticity and mutual understanding.

3. Revisit the Love Formula

Examine the Love Formula closely to identify the specific Traits or Values that make you feel infatuated. Are these feelings tied to Traits, Values, or perhaps a combination of both? Completing the Love Formula questionnaire will help you better understand which areas you perceive your partner to excel in. This insight is crucial for recognizing where your perceptions may be heightened, helping you address any potential biases in how you view your relationship.

The process of developing self-awareness can offer valuable insights into your own expectations and desires. If you find yourself assigning a low Self Score, it might suggest that you need to practice more self-compassion and respect. Use this opportunity to cultivate a more balanced and realistic view of both yourself and your partner.

4. Reconnect with Your Life

Recall the days before you met that extraordinary person—the family and friends you used to regularly spend time with, text, and talk to. They miss you, and chances are, you miss them too. It's important to remember that no relationship should cost you other meaningful connections, including the one with yourself. Take some time to reflect on your life and pinpoint any areas that you might have been neglecting of late. Have your work, studies, exercise, sleep, or hobbies been pushed aside?

Remind yourself that you are more than just someone's partner. A healthy relationship is formed between two emotionally sound individuals who maintain their own interests and social networks, incorporating their partner into their life to an extent that feels right for both. It's important to understand that smothering isn't appealing. Learn to distinguish between codependent, independent, and interdependent relationships, and strive for a balance that supports personal growth and mutual respect.

Chapter 26

The Nostalgic

Nostalgic: An individual who measures their current Partner Values Score and Partner Traits Score against those of a former significant other.

Meet the "Nostalgic"—someone who often evaluates their current partner's Values, Traits, and Partner Score against those of an ex. This Distortion is driven by unresolved feelings for a former partner. When you remain tied to past relationships, your perception of a new partner is skewed, preventing a clear and fair assessment of the present relationship.

It's common to feel a longing for a past lover after a breakup. In these moments, some individuals may seek out a new partner who reminds them of their ex. This search for a "replacement" can be driven by feelings of rejection or unresolved issues from previous relationships. Consequently, a Nostalgic person might find themselves with a partner whose Love Formula alignment isn't that optimal, which can impede the growth of a healthy and fulfilling relationship.

It's natural to appreciate the same positive qualities in future partners that you valued in past relationships. After all, relationships serve as learning experiences, helping you identify which Traits work well for you and which don't. For instance, you might have appreciated your previous partner's communication skills or their sense of adventure and spontaneity. However, it's important to differentiate between drawing lessons from past relationships and trying to find an exact duplicate of a former partner. This behavior becomes a Distortion when you start seeking a carbon copy, which might lead you to miss out on wonderful potential partners simply because they don't fit a predetermined mold.

Your attraction to a past partner can influence you, either consciously or subconsciously, to seek someone whose Values and Traits Scores are similar to theirs. For example, you might have cherished your ex's ability to keep a spotless house, maintain a well-stocked pantry, and present delicious meals. If you catch yourself specifically looking for a partner who can match your ex's pasta-making skills, grocery shopping habits, or flair for holiday decorating, this indicates a significant Distortion in your Love Formula. This level of specificity can prevent you from seeing the unique qualities other partners might bring to the table.

You may rank *education* among your Top 5 Values, but what education means to you may be wildly different from what it means to someone else. You might prioritize finding a partner with a similar educational background, while someone else might value practical, hands-on experience from the "School of Life." Generally, these different interpretations of the same Value don't hinder a successful relationship. However, if you are experiencing the Nostalgic Distortion, such as a fixation on finding a partner with a PhD because your ex had one, it could significantly narrow your openness to other potential matches who could also be a great fit.

When you find yourself yearning for an ex, it's natural to subconsciously seek out familiar Values and Traits in new partners. This desire for familiarity often stems from our comfort with past relationships. However, it's crucial to approach new connections with an open mind, allowing them to reveal their unique qualities instead of simply trying to recreate what was lost. The latter tendency can often indicate an "unhealed wound." Recognizing this pattern is important, and it's vital to resist the urge to replicate past relationships.

If you observe that your partner often compares you to their ex or expresses disappointment when you do not match specific characteristics, then they are exhibiting Nostalgic tendencies. This behavior can be a red flag, indicating that they have not fully moved on from their past relationship.

The Nostalgic: A Case Study

Consider Monica, who remained deeply attached to the memory of her ex, Mike, a skilled musician known for his laid-back, carefree demeanor, which Monica found irresistibly attractive. As Monica began to date again, she unknowingly carried this Nostalgic Distortion into her new relationships. She found herself searching for characteristics that were reminiscent of Mike, influencing her perception and expectations of new partners.

Despite encountering several intriguing potential partners, Monica repeatedly found herself dismissing them if they lacked Mike's musical talent and easygoing nature. Unconsciously, she had come to believe that a shared passion for music and a carefree personality were essential for any successful relationship. This belief led her to overlook other qualities that could have contributed to a fulfilling partnership.

Monica's narrow focus led her to overlook potential partners such as Alex, a kind and ambitious professional with a passion for outdoor activities. Although Alex wasn't musically inclined—unable to tell a trombone from a ukulele—and maintained a more structured lifestyle, he had unique qualities that could have enriched Monica's life and brought balance to their relationship.

In this story, Monica's strict adherence to a specific mold based on her past relationship prevented her from recognizing potential connections in others. This Nostalgic Distortion narrowed her dating prospects and hindered her ability to develop meaningful connections with individuals who could have enriched her life in different, yet equally fulfilling, ways.

Four Steps to Rebalance This Distortion

To overcome the Nostalgic Distortion, it's crucial to break free from the hold of past relationships and open yourself up—heart and mind—to new connections. Taking time for self-reflection, reassessing your Love Formula, and consciously choosing to date individuals with diverse characteristics can help you embark on a more authentic and fulfilling romantic journey.

Remember, your past does not define your future. To this end, the Love Formula acts as your guide, directing you toward partners whose compatibility matches your evolved self. Seize the opportunity for growth, appreciate the uniqueness of others, and foster relationships that truly reflect who you are today. By doing this, you open yourself to a love that moves beyond past influences, thrives in the present, and holds promise for a brighter future. Below are actionable steps to help you address and overcome the Nostalgic Distortion:

1. Embrace Self-Reflection

If you find yourself identifying with this Distortion, acknowledge that you are in the process of healing, yet you might be seeking your ex's qualities in new relationships. This isn't fair to your current partner or to yourself. It's important to move forward and seek happiness, trusting that there are many wonderful Traits and people out there who may align with you even more deeply than your ex did.

Embrace the growth and evolution you've experienced since your past relationship. You are not the same person you were when you first met your ex, and this change opens the door to potential partners who could be an even better match for the person you've *become*. Stay open to these possibilities and allow yourself to explore relationships that could enrich your life in new and exciting ways.

2. Revisit the Love Formula

Set aside time to deeply engage with the Love Formula, particularly focusing on reassessing your ex's Partner Scores. Reflect on the categories that strongly appealed to you, and consider why you find yourself consistently looking for these Traits in someone new. Understanding these preferences can help you identify what truly matters to you in a partner and guide you in finding a relationship that aligns with your current needs.

This powerful self-awareness tool helps guide you toward a more open-minded and nuanced approach to new connections. Identifying specific Traits and Values that are important to you sets the stage for the possibility of forming healthier, more fulfilling relationships in the future. This understanding allows you to approach potential partners with clarity and a fresh perspective, increasing the likelihood of a successful and satisfying relationship.

3. Explore New Horizons

Embark on a journey of meeting and dating individuals who are different from your ex. Allow yourself the space and time to adjust; while you may not feel an instant attraction, maintaining an open mind and heart can help you discover and appreciate diverse qualities in others. This approach can broaden your perspectives and lead you to more fulfilling relationships that align with the person you are now.

Exploring relationships with people who have different characteristics from your ex can be both liberating and refreshing, adding a sense of novelty and enjoyment to your dating life. Recognize the personal growth you've experienced since your past relationship, which highlights the importance of continually updating the Love Formula to reflect your current Values, Traits, and aspirations for future partnerships. This process opens up new possibilities and enhances your potential for building more enriching and meaningful connections.

4. Cultivate Individual Growth

Concentrate on your own personal development and growth. Dedicate time to activities that bring you joy, improve your skills, and contribute to your overall well-being. By focusing on your own growth, you can break free from the pattern of seeking a partner based on past experiences. This shift allows you to approach new relationships with a fresh perspective and a stronger sense of self.

As you grow and evolve, your preferences and priorities are likely to change. This personal evolution enables you to move beyond the confines of past relationships and opens the door to diverse, fulfilling connections that resonate with who you are now. Moreover, being secure in your individuality enhances your ability to contribute positively to a partnership. This strong foundation promotes mutual respect and appreciation, fostering relationships that are rooted in the present and not overshadowed by the past.

Chapter 27

The Competitor

Competitor: An individual who is hyper-aware of their Partner Score and constantly tries to compete with them in their shared list of Values.

The "Competitor" is characterized by a heightened sensitivity to their Partner Score, frequently engaging in competition, particularly in the realm of shared Values. While a bit of friendly rivalry can be harmless, when this competitive spirit infiltrates the romantic relationship, it prompts important considerations. Is occasional competition acceptable, or does its consistent presence raise concerns? Does it contribute positively to the relationship, or does it often lead to issues?

It's important to think about whether your partner often ends up on the losing side. While teasing each other playfully once in a while can be enjoyable, constantly poking fun at them when you win might quickly get old. What seemed funny at first could become a regular annoyance, leading to more nights spent apart. Too much competition could create a tricky situation.

Competitive partners turn relationships into an ongoing struggle to outdo each other. It's a constant race to come out on top with respect to their Top 5 Values. Even in case of occasional disagreements, if you accidentally hurt them, their competitive side might push them to get back at you. So, it's wise to be careful about how much competition is going on.

Usually, relationships with competitive partners don't start off on a distorted note. The Distortion tends to sneak in gradually. Initially, both partners appreciate each other's success and motivation, giving them an extra reason to stick together. They genuinely support and cheer each other on for the most part. Why? Because they see their partners as motivated winners, leading them to consciously shower their significant other with praise just for being awesome. Many would also consider them a power couple.

So, when does the shift happen?

The trouble begins when one person notices the other's progress surpassing theirs. While these competitive individuals initially celebrate each other's victories, jealousy starts to subtly seep in over time. The game of comparison repeatedly kicks off in their minds, reflecting in their actions and conversations. Their lives are built around a competitive framework, and their partners are viewed not as allies but as rivals in a race. Instead of walking side by side, they see their partners as competitors striving to reach the finish line first.

This scenario often unfolds within the realm of Type A personalities—individuals who are outgoing, driven to achieve, and exhibit strong planning skills. Fueled by a penchant for competition and a focus on societal status, these personalities prioritize upholding their name and prestige in all situations. Consequently, the constant drive to excel and showcase their worth becomes a significant factor in their relationships.

Consider a Type A personality grappling with insecurities about their achievements. While not all Type A individuals feel threatened by their partner's success, those who are inherently competitive and harbor unresolved insecurities may subconsciously see their partner as competition. This slippery slope often transforms every aspect of their relationship into a competition—be it debates, games, cooking skills, humor, social interactions, or even karaoke performances.

For people who don't view their partners as rivals, these ongoing challenges can be draining. Competitors, fueled by the desire to win, often fail to recognize the potential risks to their relationship. At the very least, this dynamic exhausts one or both partners; at its worst, it can become toxic, leaving the noncompetitive partner feeling isolated and unsupported.

The Competitor's relentless pursuit of superiority frequently leads to frustration and resentment, particularly when feeling threatened by their partner's success. In some cases, the noncompetitive partner might find themselves downplaying their accomplishments, fostering a sense of guilt and stifling their joy. They aim to sidestep potential drama that could arise if, for instance, they were invited to an exciting party, achieved an A on a test, or received a down payment on a mortgage from their parents. In the presence of a partner exhibiting this type of Distortion, noncompetitive individuals tend to stay quiet and express additional humility to maintain harmony in the relationship. In a healthy relationship, partners celebrate each other's successes, but the Competitor's constant need to win can disrupt this dynamic.

When a Competitor encounters a setback, they might react by starting arguments, withdrawing emotionally, making passive-aggressive comments, or exhibiting controlling behaviors. These reactions can leave their noncompetitive partner feeling confused and perpetually cautious, always feeling like they need to tread carefully. Worse yet if the Competitor belittles their partner in social settings, it not only damages the relationship but also chips away at the confidence of the partner on the receiving end.

In relationships where both partners are constantly competing, celebrating each other's successes can become difficult. Every achievement might be met with comparison, criticism, and a toxic dynamic that fosters feelings of inadequacy and jealousy. This continuous competitive atmosphere erodes intimacy, strains the relationship, and prevents both partners from genuinely enjoying each other's accomplishments.

The Competitor Distortion can deeply undermine a healthy relationship. A constant drive to outdo each other wears down trust, support, and respect over time. Recognizing this pattern is the first essential step. Once you're aware of it, you can start working toward a more balanced and supportive relationship where both partners feel valued rather than compared.

To overcome the Competitor Distortion, it's important to prioritize empathy, kindness, and genuine support for each other's achievements. Recognizing the importance of validation and consistently affirming your partner's worth can help create a positive atmosphere conducive to mutual growth. This supportive environment allows both partners to thrive and celebrate each other's successes without the shadow of competition.

The Competitor: A Case Study

Anjali and Kurt had enjoyed three years of what seemed like a perfect relationship, filled with mutual love and admiration. They were the quintessential power couple: attractive, career focused, and seemingly in sync. However, beneath the surface of their enviable connection, a subtle undercurrent of competition began to emerge. Anjali found herself increasingly comparing her own support network to Kurt's seemingly more stable and supportive family life, which slowly began to color her feelings and strain their relationship.

Over time, Anjali's feelings of jealousy and competitiveness intensified. She increasingly felt the need to outshine Kurt in social settings, a change that made her act out of character. She tried to capture attention with jokes and startling comments, but this behavior gradually turned her into someone her friends and Kurt hardly recognized. Unfortunately, this strategy backfired, leading to her becoming alienated from Kurt and their mutual friends and resulting in her social circle shrinking significantly.

As Anjali saw her social popularity slip, her frustration and anger deepened. She grew resentful of Kurt's ability to effortlessly attract respect and support from those around him. This resentment led to increasingly toxic behavior, with Anjali often belittling Kurt in front of their friends and repeatedly questioning his judgment. The situation reached a breaking point when she began to openly resent the time Kurt spent socializing with friends, further straining their relationship.

In the end, Anjali's competitive drive, combined with her resentment and relentless desire to outshine Kurt in social settings, eroded the very foundation of their once-promising relationship. This need to "win" in social interactions ultimately led to the relationship's downfall, as the mutual respect and support that once defined their partnership faded away.

Four Steps to Rebalance This Distortion

Partners should function as a cohesive unit, building a strong friendship rooted in mutual support across all circumstances. An ideal partnership is characterized by attentiveness to each other's needs, an understanding of subtle cues, and a commitment to a shared journey. Rather than competing against each other, partners should work toward inclusivity and collaboration, fostering an environment where both can thrive together.

A harmonious partnership prioritizes unity and shared experiences. In real-life relationships, competitiveness and pettiness offer no rewards and can even drive away a potential soulmate. It's essential to recognize that you and your partner are on the same life journey, and celebrating each other's successes benefits the collective "us." If you find yourself stuck in a competitive mindset, it's important to shift your perspective. Your partner's achievements don't detract from yours; they enrich your shared journey. For those who identify with the Competitor Distortion, consider taking the following steps to bring balance back into your relationship:

1. Revisit the Love Formula

Utilize the Love Formula to evaluate your Self Score and Partner Score. By gaining a deeper understanding of the unique qualities each of you brings to the relationship, you can better appreciate the collaborative effort required for a successful partnership. Recognizing these contributions helps both partners thrive.

Remember, a strong partnership isn't built on constant competition but on a mutual commitment to each other's well-being and fulfillment. Embracing this mindset allows you to see how you complement each other, dispelling any feelings of inadequacy. Recognize that differences—for instance, in skills such as tennis or cooking—enrich your shared life, adding variety and enjoyment. Rather than striving for dominance, comparisons should be used to celebrate a harmonious blend of each partner's strengths and interests.

2. Build Your Empathy

Your partner chose you because they appreciate and love you for who you are. When you prioritize competitive instincts over your partner's emotional needs, it can damage the long-term health of the relationship. Neglecting your partner's emotional well-being in favor of competition can diminish trust, support, and mutual respect—all crucial elements of a thriving partnership.

Whether your partner excels or struggles in certain areas, it's crucial to prioritize kindness. Before making any competitive remarks, take a moment to consider how your words might affect the other person's feelings. Cultivating a habit of speaking kindly and supportively contributes to a positive environment, enhancing emotional safety and intimacy. By softening the competitive edge, both partners can more fully appreciate each other's significance in their lives.

3. Promote Mutual Support

When your partner consistently tries to outdo you, it may be a sign of underlying insecurities and a struggle with self-confidence. Offering sincere compliments and genuinely expressing pride in each other's achievements can be an effective way to counteract this. Such positive reinforcement can help boost confidence and reinforce mutual support within the relationship.

Providing support during times of mental and emotional struggle is a shared responsibility that greatly benefits the relationship. When both partners engage in offering this support, it helps alleviate the internal pressures each may feel, facilitating a shift from a focus on proving themselves to nurturing a healthier and more connected relationship.

4. Highlight Their Role in Your Success

Recognition and appreciation are crucial components of a healthy relationship. Partners feel fulfilled when their contributions are acknowledged as meaningful. Whether it's celebrating a promotion, maintaining good health, or cultivating friendships, it's important to express gratitude to your partner for their support in your happiness and success. Simple gestures, such as thanking them for preparing a healthy meal or acknowledging their kindness toward friends, play a significant role in making them feel valued and appreciated.

Remember, it's the small, consistent acts that truly fortify a relationship. Regularly reassure your partner of their importance, emphasizing that your achievements are the result of teamwork. Thriving together is key to achieving shared success for a stronger, more unified bond.

Chapter 28

The Cheater

We started the book with my personal (heart-wrenching) story of being cheated on. We haven't yet talked about cheating in detail and what causes it, mainly because it's such a nuanced phenomenon that it would be impossible to attribute it to a single Personality Type, Relationship Zone, or Score Distortion. Cheating draws from all these dynamics, and understanding it requires us to examine it through multiple lenses.

For clarity, let's define cheating in two distinct ways: *emotional* and *physical*. Both forms can happen at any stage of a relationship and, unfortunately, they share the same consequence—a deep betrayal that can shatter trust and damage self-esteem. Emotional cheating often begins subtly—a lingering glance, a shared emotional connection that wasn't deliberate or intentional. Physical cheating is more overt but just as painful.

So, what causes someone to cheat? At its core, cheating often stems from dissatisfaction. Whether driven by boredom, resentment, or an unfulfilled emotional need, this dissatisfaction can fester when it's left unaddressed. Dissatisfaction, coupled with an inability to communicate, lack of empathy, and impulsivity, can increase the likelihood of emotional or physical cheating if the opportunity presents itself.

Let's explore how the concepts from this book help us better understand this painful Distortion.

Cheating Across the Relationship Zones

Cheating can happen in any of the Relationship Zones we've discussed. In the Red Zone, partners who struggle with low self-esteem may also lack respect for each other. When conflict arises, loyalty can crumble. In some cases, the resentment is so deep that cheating is almost weaponized—one partner may even want the other to find out as a way to cause hurt or assert dominance, sending the message, "I can do better."

In the Yellow Zone, cheating is also common, but for different reasons. The High Scorer in the relationship may feel bored or restless, knowing they have the upper hand. They're less afraid to lose their partner, which can lead them to devalue the relationship, making them more susceptible to seeking excitement elsewhere. On the flip side, the Low Scorer might cheat to seek validation. They may feel insecure or unappreciated and seek attention elsewhere to feel better about themselves, knowing they are in a less powerful position.

Even in the Green Zone, where stability usually reigns, cheating can occur. Here, predictability can turn into boredom. Without addressing this creatively, partners may find themselves drifting emotionally or physically. The innocent flirtation at work—those simple questions like, "How was your weekend?"—can slowly evolve into something more. The subtle nature of this type of cheating makes it all the more dangerous, as it often falls into grey areas, leaving emotional boundaries blurred.

Cheating and Extreme Personality Types

Cheating is also influenced by Extreme Personality Types, which are characterized by a lack of balance and a higher likelihood of dissatisfaction in relationships. For instance, an Extreme Emotional might act on impulse when deeply hurt, seeking solace in someone else's arms as a way to self-soothe. For them, cheating isn't necessarily premeditated—it's a reaction to intense emotions.

On the other hand, an Extreme Practical may stay loyal to their partner only as long as they perceive the relationship as valuable in helping them achieve their goals. When their partner is no longer seen as supportive, the Extreme Practical may begin to lose interest and entertain the idea of seeking alternatives. This can manifest as them going on dates or exploring new possibilities while still in a committed relationship, as they search for someone they perceive as a better match.

Extreme Safety Seekers often find themselves in relationships that offer security more than stimulation. In the process, they tend to suppress their more emotional side to avoid developing deep feelings, prioritizing safety over emotional connection. So, what happens when someone like the charming barista at the coffee shop offers a flirtatious smile? It might stir up long-suppressed butterflies, sparking a desire for more of those feelings. "Wow, that felt good," the Extreme Safety Seeker may think. "Maybe I'll swing by tomorrow just to say hi—keeping it safe, of course." This temptation to seek emotional excitement can introduce a complex layer of feelings in someone who usually avoids them.

Meanwhile, the Extreme Risk-Taker is more prone to cheating when they believe they've "settled" for a partner who doesn't meet their high standards. The moment a more appealing or higher-scoring individual shows interest, the Extreme Risk-Taker may stray.

The Extreme Critic, who believes no one is ever good enough, may cheat out of chronic dissatisfaction, always seeking the elusive "perfect" partner. No one ever seems good enough, and as a result, they may continuously look for an ideal partner that doesn't exist. This restless pursuit of perfection leaves them vulnerable to infidelity, constantly chasing a fantasy that can never be fulfilled.

Cheating and Relationship Distortions

Both emotional and physical cheating can stem from any type of Distortion. Let's take a closer look at how these forms of infidelity might manifest in a relationship.

In the dynamic between the Self-Sacrificer and the Self-Focused, the latter may be prone to emotional or physical cheating simply because they prioritize their own needs above all else and fail to value their partner appropriately. Meanwhile, the dynamic between the Dependent and the Independent often falls within the Yellow Zone, which, as previously discussed, can breed dissatisfaction for both parties. This dissatisfaction can create an environment where cheating becomes more likely.

In the Savior vs. Rescuee dynamic, the potential for infidelity exists for both partners. The Rescuee, often fitting into the Extreme

Practical category, may not be fully emotionally committed to the relationship, making them more susceptible to cheating. On the other hand, the Savior likely grapples with self-esteem issues and may seek affirmation elsewhere. If their need for validation is not met within the relationship, they might be tempted to look for it outside.

When it comes to the Sabotager Distortion, the connection to cheating is pretty obvious—it is the ultimate act of sabotaging a relationship. Individuals with this Distortion lack empathy and wisdom, and their infidelity is often motivated by a desire to create chaos within their relationships. They may cheat to undermine their partner's self-esteem or provoke a dramatic confrontation. Such actions are often driven by a deep-seated need to create turmoil within their own relationships.

The Black Hole may use cheating as a tool to undermine their partner's self-esteem and make them question their worth. Even if they don't directly admit to cheating, they might subtly drop hints to evoke jealousy and insecurity. Remarks such as "Oh, Brittany brought a homemade shepherd's pie to work, and WOW, that girl has skills!" or "I guess Josh is big on fitness now, huh? Did you see his bulging arms? Damn, any girl with him would be so lucky to have THAT" are designed to provoke and manipulate their partner's emotions.

Both Deceivers and Overcompensators are characterized by their highly sensitive egos, which, when challenged or threatened, might lead them to seek validation outside their current relationship. This quest for external affirmation often stems from their own insecurities and a focus on self-interest rather than the well-being of their partners.

In a relationship between the Infatuated and their partner, the mismatch is often so significant that dissatisfaction is inevitable and can arise on both sides as time progresses. This type of dynamic typically falls within the Yellow Zone, where the imbalance and resulting discontent continue to grow, further destabilizing the relationship.

In the unfortunate scenario where a person with the Nostalgic Distortion receives a random text from an ex, the consequences can be predictable. Given their strong attachment to the past, they might feel an overwhelming sense of excitement about reconnecting. This emotional response can easily lead them to waver in their current commitment, as the pull of past feelings begins to overshadow their present relationship.

The Competitor often struggles with low self-esteem and a sensitive ego, a potentially toxic combination in relationships. They frequently experience dissatisfaction, resentment, and anger toward their partner, emotions that might drive them to seek solace elsewhere. The underlying motive in such cases is typically a deep-seated need for validation, as they look for external affirmation to bolster their fragile sense of self-worth.

As we have just explored, cheating can occur in virtually any scenario. Now, let's turn our attention to practical steps that we can take to address and correct this Distortion, aiming to improve relationship dynamics and prevent such issues in the future.

Four Steps to Rebalance This Distortion

Most cheaters don't wake up thinking, "How can I screw over my partner today?" We're human, and we make mistakes. Sometimes we act selfishly; sometimes we're driven by anger, and at other times, we're simply unaware. In today's world, the opportunities for cheating are more accessible than ever, and temptations are everywhere. Sometimes we actively seek them out, and at other times we let it happen if the chance arises. The truth is that cheating causes significant damage that can linger in your current relationship and even affect future ones.

Let's review some practical steps to rebalance this Distortion and mitigate its impact.

1. Deepen Your Understanding of the Topics Discussed in This Book

Grasping the complex reasons behind acts of betrayal is crucial. This knowledge will aid not only in healing from past hurts caused by infidelity but also in recognizing potential warning signs in relationships. Avoiding cheating involves cultivating self-respect, discipline, and empathy—qualities that all stem from wisdom. This book aims to equip you with the wisdom necessary to navigate these challenges in both current and future relationships more effectively. By understanding the underlying dynamics and motivations discussed here, you can build stronger, more resilient bonds based on trust and mutual respect.

Furthermore, this book provides insights into how personal vulnerabilities and relationship dynamics converge to create scenarios where cheating might occur. By closely examining these elements, you can develop a more proactive approach to managing your relationships. This involves not just identifying and addressing issues as they arise but also fostering a deeper connection with your partner through honest communication and shared Values.

2. Calculate Your Love Formula

It's essential to identify whether you fall into any of the described Zones or Personality Types discussed here and to understand your vulnerability to cheating, whether as the victim or the perpetrator. Both you and your partner should undertake this assessment together, which will help you see how infidelity has impacted your relationship Scores. Cheating often arises from either short-term frustrations or deep-seated dissatisfaction. If your partner has cheated, it's crucial to delve into the sources of their dissatisfaction. This doesn't excuse the act, but understanding the underlying reasons is important if you choose to stay together and rebuild the trust. If you were the one who cheated, the Love Formula can help you understand why you rationalized such behavior. This insight is vital for personal growth and preventing future incidents, leading into our next discussion point.

3. Have An Honest Conversation with Yourself

Selfishness has no place in a healthy, lasting relationship. Reflect on any tendencies you might have toward cheating and dig deep to understand the origins of these impulses. It's crucial to stop perpetuating pain. If you're hurting, it's important to identify where that hurt is coming from and consider whether your partners truly deserve such betrayal. If you've been cheated on, remember that you are not obligated to either stay or leave—everyone responds differently, and there is no right or wrong way to handle such situations. However, if you find yourself repeatedly victimized, either by multiple partners or by a partner who shows no signs of changing, you need to seriously consider what you want and deserve. Cheating is a profound disrespect, and while people can make mistakes, it's essential to cultivate strong self-love and distance yourself from those who cause you pain.

4. Communicate!

Communication is undoubtedly the foundation of any healthy relationship. If mistakes have occurred in the past, remember that it's never too late to address them. Open, honest dialogue is key to understanding each other's perspectives and feelings. It's crucial to not only apologize sincerely but also discuss why the mistake happened and how both partners can work together to prevent similar issues in the future. Effective communication involves listening as much as speaking and requires both partners to be genuinely engaged and committed to improving the relationship. By taking these steps, you pave the way for a relationship that is not just about surviving challenges but thriving through them, building trust, and deepening your connection.

Part VI

Building Healthy Relationships

To develop healthy relationships, it's important to move past old grievances and practice forgiveness—toward both yourself and your partner. Let go of any guilt, shame, or regrets. In this section, we'll explore how to begin forging a healthier connection with your partner and, importantly, with yourself as well.

Moving forward requires letting go of the past, as it signals a commitment to personal growth. Naturally, we often cling to what's familiar, even when it no longer benefits us. There is a lot of anxiety associated with facing the unknown and overcoming our deeply ingrained attachments to the past—which requires a high level of self-awareness and genuine courage. While challenging, this process is crucial for growth and opens the door to new opportunities.

For those aiming to improve their relationship, this section provides tips on how to use the communication tools discussed in this book. It's important to identify sources of dissatisfaction and address them in a fair and reasonable manner. Relationships are always changing, and it's important to keep up with these shifts. If you're currently in a relationship, embrace the idea that love evolves over time. By adapting your Love Formula to new situations, your relationship will not only survive but *thrive*.

For those who are single and looking, this section provides useful insights. Use this period for self-reflection, to understand what you want from love, and to learn from your past relationships. Set clear intentions for future relationships and learn how to recognize compatibility early. We'll also discuss the merits of being single and how they can contribute to your personal growth, helping you prepare for a great relationship when the time is right.

Whether you're single or in a relationship, this final section acts as a guide for fulfillment and self-confidence. Happiness is the goal here.

Chapter 29

Why It's Hard to Let Go

Moving on can be a challenging endeavor. There are numerous, complex reasons why we remain bound to our past. The difficulties in letting go may include misconceptions about potential partners, excessive reliance on others' approval, the comfort of familiarity, or entrenched Values and Traits that no longer serve us. In this chapter, you'll gain insights on how to gracefully handle farewells and boldly move forward.

1. We are Delusional

A common challenge in letting go is the potential for delusion. This occurs when your perceptions deceive you, leading you to see situations differently from what they are in reality.

When you're feeling lonely, your brain might paint a rosier picture of a past relationship than was actually the case. It's a natural response—when you're hurting or feeling empty, your mind looks for quick fixes to ease the discomfort. You might find yourself wishing to go back, remembering only the good times with your ex. Meanwhile, the arguments and bad moments get tucked away and are only remembered through conscious effort.

Months or even years after a breakup, it's common to slip into nostalgia. You might find yourself reminiscing about the good times—laughing together, cuddling, and sharing intimate moments. You long for the comfort of their touch and the support they offered. In these moments, it's easy to forget why the relationship ended. The arguments, the mismatches, and the dissatisfaction that once felt so overwhelming can seem less significant. This is because our minds tend to glorify the past, painting an idealized picture of our ex as the perfect partner.

Essentially, you're missing a certain lifestyle and overlooking the concrete reasons—like your Love Formula Scores—that clearly showed why the relationship wasn't right for you.

Now you find yourself missing them and might even start to rearrange your Values—thinking, "Well, even though he wasn't great at communication, he was a social butterfly, and that is really important to me now!" It's common for your mind to highlight the good parts and minimize the bad, leading to an inflated view of how suitable they were as a partner.

The reality is that the breakup, whether initiated by you or your partner, happened due to a mismatch—perhaps due to issues such as poor communication, domestic responsibilities, or financial management. There might have been some Distortions in how you both viewed each other's qualities, or perhaps clashing Personality Types led to a toxic situation. The reasons can vary widely, but fundamentally, your Scores were different enough to make the relationship unsustainable.

So why do the regrets start to kick in *after* the breakup?

Our memories aren't perfect. They don't act like precise recordings of what happened; rather, they reconstruct past events, influenced by our current emotions, beliefs, and even what other people suggest. Over time, these memories can change, leading us to remember things not as they truly occurred—and our feelings about those memories can shift as well.

Our emotions play a big role in shaping our perception of the world. This is clear in "emotional reasoning," where we interpret our experiences through the lens of our feelings instead of basing them on objective facts.

Our expectations and the emotions they stir up often lead us to see things not as they are but as we hope or expect them to be. This tendency is known as "expectation bias," a common cognitive Distortion.

Expectation bias and hope both have a powerful influence on how we perceive reality. When hope is strong, it can shape our expectation bias. For example, if you're hopeful about getting back together with an ex, this optimism can color your expectations and actions, leading you to see the relationship's potential in an overly romantic light. Simply put, we often indulge in wishful thinking and overlook or minimize facts that don't match our desires, resulting in a distorted view of reality.

We need to identify, question, and modify our biases and delusions by engaging in introspection, increasing our self-awareness, and continuing to learn. In some cases, seeking professional help can be beneficial. These steps will help us gain a more balanced and realistic view of ourselves and the world.

The Challenge of Letting Go: A Case Study

After three years together, Jennifer and Tom noticed their once-strong connection weakening. Tom became distant, making even simple conversations difficult. Laughter was rare, and their romantic life had dwindled. Despite her strong feelings for him, Jennifer found it hard to see a future together, a sentiment Tom shared as he too felt the increasing gap between them. Their Love Formula Scores reflected this growing divide, leading them both to agree that parting ways was the best decision.

In the initial weeks after the breakup, Jennifer felt a sense of relief that the hardest part was over, and she was eager to start anew. She began socializing more, enjoying her newfound freedom. She reveled in these experiences, surprised by how much she had been missing out on while she was with Tom.

About five weeks after the breakup, Jennifer started dating again. She enjoyed nights out, filled with dancing and flirting, but it soon began to wear on her. Even with her newfound independence, she missed the comfort of having someone close, someone to come home to and share special moments with. Memories of Tom started to resurface—trips they had taken together, his humor, and their intimate times. As her longing increased, Jennifer reached out to reconnect with Tom, but he was no longer interested.

The truth was that Jennifer had been unhappy in the relationship and had fallen out of love. Her Love Formula's Values and Traits assessment confirmed this dissatisfaction. Yet in her loneliness, her mind painted a misleading picture of happiness, comfort, and fulfillment, causing her to remember their time together differently.

Let's explore other reasons it's difficult to let go and do the inner work needed to prepare ourselves for the love we desire.

2. We Lean on Our Partner for a High Self Score

Have you ever gone through a breakup and thought, "My life would have been so much better if we had stayed together"? Believing that a partner boosted your Self Score and sense of self-worth is another reason moving on can be so tough.

It's natural to view our partners as adding practical or emotional value to our lives; we often enter relationships expecting to find peace, intimacy, or support. So when someone we relied on is no longer there, we might feel a void. However, many people are capable of fulfilling these roles, not just your ex. You might be so focused on the benefits they brought that you're depending on them to boost your sense of self-worth.

However, thinking you need someone else to boost your confidence can actually prevent you from becoming confident on your own. Waiting for someone to return not only holds you back but also stops you from finding a true match and experiencing a fulfilling Green Zone relationship.

Anything another person adds to your life, you can provide for yourself. Consider what your partner was enhancing in your life— was it status, security, family connections, or something else? You don't need to rely on their achievements; you have the potential to reach those milestones on your own. Even if your goals seem out of reach, you can find the confidence to be happy with who you are now, knowing that you're continually growing.

It's important to realize that breakups can usher in new opportunities. This change can be a catalyst for personal growth and self-discovery. Although we might initially see only the downsides to being single, it gives us a chance to discover our strengths, develop self-reliance, and gain a better understanding of our own needs and desires.

Viewing these moments as opportunities can help us manage changes in our relationships more effectively. While it's normal to feel lonely, deep regret may signal that you're viewing the situation unfairly and that your sense of self is still too connected to theirs. In other words, you might think your self-worth is heavily reliant on your relationship with them.

Release the belief that you need them. You don't require your ex-partner's social circle, family connections, prestige, or financial resources to feel confident about yourself. If you have a low Self Score, it's a sign that you need to focus on building your self-respect and self-love, especially if you feel like you're not living up to your own standards.

When your self-worth is low, you're more likely to end up in unhealthy, toxic, and fleeting relationships. This lack of self-esteem can lead to self-sabotage and a reduced sense of your own importance, which might cause you to withdraw and stay isolated for longer than is good for you. The key to attracting the right partner is to first be confident in yourself. This doesn't mean you need to show off excessively. Instead, it's about understanding who you are, being true to yourself, recognizing your Values and worth, and being proud of what you bring to the table. The right person will acknowledge and cherish those qualities.

When we respect and love ourselves, we establish clear expectations for how we want to be treated. This self-respect enhances our capacity to form healthy and satisfying relationships. Self-love is crucial for understanding our own needs and desires, which in turn fosters more open and honest communication with our partners. It's an ongoing journey, but it's vital for both our personal development and the well-being of our relationships.

So how do you improve your Self Score? Start by recognizing that you have full control over how you view your own value and that of others. You determine your own worth, and you assess that of your partners.

When you're confident, you tend to give yourself a high Self Score and keep a realistic view of your Partner Score, avoiding skewed perceptions. It's important to take responsibility for how you see yourself. Although it's normal to be affected by what others think, ultimately, we have control over our self-image and can also influence how others see us to some extent.

As psychologists such as Roger Birkman have pointed out, our perceptions influence everything we do. When we gain more perspective on our perceptions, many other things fall into place. The key to confidence isn't just your Self Score, it's consistently improving it with an upward trend. Suppose you start at 50%. That might seem low, but what if you make small, consistent efforts to increase that number to 60%? Seeing this progress can boost your confidence. And if you can improve to 60%, why not set your sights on 70%, 80%, or even 90%?

An upward trend in your Self Score can foster optimism, making higher achievements feel within reach and helping you see yourself as capable of reaching 90%. Even if you're currently at 70%, the important thing is that you're improving. Being satisfied with your progress is key.

Taking small steps to improve your confidence by boosting your Self Score in just one or two areas at a time can set you on an upward trajectory. Remember, there's a big difference between genuine self-assurance and merely putting on a show of confidence.

True confidence stems from an inner belief in your own abilities, regardless of external opinions or circumstances. It is built on self-acceptance, recognizing both your strengths and weaknesses, which fosters resilience and the courage to tackle new challenges.

On the flip side, false confidence is just a facade, usually put on to mask insecurities and self-doubt. It's fragile because it relies on external validation and can quickly fall apart under criticism or adversity. Cultivating genuine self-assurance, on the other hand, enhances mental well-being, improves decision-making, and leads to more fulfilling relationships. It's an investment that benefits all areas of your life.

Note that authentic confidence comes from a deep-seated belief in your own abilities, independent of external validation. In contrast, false confidence is about appearing competent to others, even if internal doubts persist. When using the Love Formula, it's essential to be brutally honest with yourself about your Self Score in each category. True confidence emerges when you take pride in who you are and choose to see the beauty in everything, including yourself.

Leaning on a Partner for a High Self Score: A Case Study

Throughout their two-year relationship, Nicki cherished her role as Jose's girlfriend. Jose, a well-known celebrity photographer in their community, boosted her visibility. Nicki took pleasure in the recognition that came from being associated with him.

Over time Nicki's pride began to dominate her conversations with friends. At their gatherings, she often highlighted Jose's latest Instagram photos and the impressive number of likes they received, reveling in the quasi-celebrity status it gave her.

However, behind closed doors, their relationship was intensely toxic, filled with Red Zone dynamics. Ultimately, the challenges proved too overwhelming, leading to their breakup.

Devastated by the separation, Nicki's self-confidence suffered greatly. In the weeks that followed, she noticed Jose removing all their photos from Instagram, and her number of followers began to dwindle. Her phone rang less often, and she felt her popularity waning. This loss of status became her primary concern, driving her to long for not only her former popularity but also Jose's return.

3. We Crave Comfort and Familiarity

We naturally seek comfort in our relationships, often gravitating toward what's familiar. Letting go can be difficult when you've grown accustomed to specific Values and Traits in your ex-partner, which can make it hard to be open to new possibilities.

But consider this: Could it be that you're giving your partner an overly high rating simply because you're familiar with them and their ways, and you haven't explored other options? This sense of comfort and familiarity might be holding you back from moving on and could lead you to dismiss potential partners who differ from your ex.

If you're drawn to comfort and familiarity in Values, it means you've grown accustomed to a certain lifestyle and routine with your partner. This might include a certain spending level, fitness standards, amount of downtime, or social life quality.

Sometimes, the lifestyle you shared with a former partner can deeply influence your expectations for future relationships. You might find yourself automatically comparing every new person or situation to your past experiences. When something doesn't fit the familiar mold, it can create obstacles in moving forward and embracing new opportunities. This mindset may prevent you from seeing the unique qualities of new partners or experiences, causing you to miss out on the joys of exploring different aspects of life and love. Therefore, it's important to recognize that each relationship has its own unique dynamics, challenges, and joys.

Rather than using past relationships as benchmarks, try to view each new encounter as a distinct journey. Moving beyond comparative judgments can enhance your enjoyment of the present and lead to deeper, more authentic connections. It's like entering a new world—one unburdened by past limitations and open to fresh experiences. If you fixate on finding someone who matches your ex's Partner Score in your Top 5 Values, you risk becoming overly selective and narrow-minded about potential matches, closing yourself off from a myriad of opportunities.

This narrow-mindedness can extend to Trait preferences as well. This involves seeking strong connections, emotional closeness, and high attraction. When laughter is easy, conversation flows, and the vibe feels effortless, it usually indicates that a partner aligns with our Trait preferences, making us feel deeply connected. Often, we get stuck in the past because we long for the "soulmate" connection we had with an ex, believing that such a connection can only be replicated with a specific set of Traits. We grow so accustomed to certain physical or personality characteristics that we start to think they are the only match for us.

If you're seeking immediate comfort and familiarity, your approach to potential relationships may be too black-and-white, resembling a light switch that's either on or off. This leaves no space for a gradual connection to develop. Without instant closeness, you might dismiss potential matches too quickly, driven by a desire for immediate intimacy. Often, this restrictive mindset is the underlying issue.

For many, achieving comfort and familiarity with Traits takes time and involves building a foundation—a slow and steady burn. If this is your approach to love, closeness is a process, and people "grow on you." Quirks that once seemed strange become endearing, unusual hobbies begin to intrigue you, and unique physical features turn into charming attributes that you grow to love.

Regardless of whether we favor instant or gradual connections, our innate desire for comfort and familiarity, coupled with a hesitation to open up to others, can make it challenging to move forward.

The saying "The best way to get over someone is to get under someone else" might seem lighthearted, but there is some truth in it. In terms of The Love Formula, the best strategy for reducing your attachment to an ex is by establishing a connection with someone who better matches who you are now.

Give yourself permission to meet new people and be open to building intimacy with someone different. As you start to appreciate and value the Traits of someone new—someone who isn't like your ex—you might find that, both consciously and subconsciously, you begin to lower your ex's Partner Score in your mind.

Jumping into a new relationship right away might not be the best move for you, but it's also important to stop moping and dwelling on the past. Stretch beyond your comfort zone, give other potential partners a chance, and allow time for their Partner Score to develop. It's crucial to give these new prospects enough time to establish their place in your life—this is a process that shouldn't be rushed.

By giving potential partners a chance, you allow them to positively impact your life and lay the groundwork for closeness and connection

As your relationship progresses and you face life's challenges, comfort and familiarity will naturally develop and strengthen. On allowing the relationship to grow organically, you might find that these new connections are as rewarding—or even more so—than those from your past. Embracing change and being open to new beginnings, even when faced with uncertainties, is crucial. It's not about replacing the past; it's about learning, growing, and adapting to write new chapters in your life story.

The Struggle with Detachment: A Case Study

Alissa and Jonas enjoyed a loving two-year relationship before they decided to go their separate ways due to different life goals. Alissa wanted to travel the world and live adventurously, while Jonas preferred to stay in one place, finish his studies, and pursue a stable career. Recognizing this fundamental mismatch, they mutually agreed to end their relationship.

As Jonas moved on and thrived, Alissa found herself missing the comfort of someone she had grown so close to. She held on to the memories of their time together, especially their laughter. For Alissa, laughter had become synonymous with love. The joy she shared with Jonas became a significant emotional anchor. Now any potential partner had to match or exceed the happiness and comfort that Jonas's sense of humor had brought her.

As the years passed, Alissa dated various partners, but none of the relationships worked out. She was so focused on Jonas and the unique way he had made her laugh that she overlooked how long it had taken to develop that level of closeness with him. She expected to find an immediate connection similar to the one that had taken years to build with Jonas. This unrealistic expectation became a major barrier in her search for new love.

Unfortunately, Alissa's attachment to Jonas and the comfort he provided became a roadblock to new relationships. Her yearning for that familiar closeness prevented her from fully opening her heart to the possibility of finding love with someone else.

4. We Have Unhealthy Values and Traits Preferences

Have you ever noticed that you keep falling into the same types of toxic relationships? It might feel like the same problems keep occurring—just with different people. Whether you realize it or not, this pattern likely stems from a fixation on certain unhealthy Traits and/or Values. While it's natural to have preferences, if your relationships consistently end badly, it might be time to reevaluate the Traits and Values of the people you've been choosing.

Adopting unhealthy Values can result from focusing too much on superficial aspects and neglecting the importance of Values that contribute to emotional well-being. For example, prioritizing *social status* over effective *communication* and *good manners* might not lay the groundwork for a healthy relationship. Similarly, valuing *career success* over *family* could lead to mismatches with those who prioritize family life, potentially creating a pattern where you consistently choose partners who are more focused on their work.

You have the power to choose your Top 5 Values and arrange their importance as you see fit. The way you prioritize these Values and the importance you give to each one is completely up to you. Remember, you're not limited to just a Top 5 list; you can expand your list to include Top 10 or even Top 20 Values if that suits your needs better.

At the same time, it's important to understand that even though your ex-partner may have excelled in the Top 5 Values you prioritized during your relationship, these aren't the only Values that can enrich your life. Other Values can be just as impactful, if not more so, depending on your current circumstances and goals.

- What if you were to replace *social status* with *communication and manners*?

- How about if you replaced *health and fitness* with *pursuing a greater purpose*?

- Can you imagine how your love life could have shifted if you replaced *popularity* with *honesty*?

Generally speaking, adjusting your Values can lead to personal growth and might increase your chances of meeting compatible partners.

Now let's discuss unhealthy Traits. If you consistently find yourself attracted to Traits such as *dominance* or *self-absorption*, this could stem from unresolved issues or negative influences from important figures in your life, such as parents.

Changing your Trait preferences can be more difficult than adjusting your Values. How do you control the physical and personality Traits you find attractive? The process is challenging because it involves delving deep into your subconscious and essentially reprogramming it. Expecting different results from the same actions, as Rita Mae Brown pointed out (though the quote is often misattributed to Albert Einstein), is like a form of insanity.

Reprogramming yourself to be attracted to partners who don't fit the type you've always liked or the Values you've always held isn't easy. However, it's worthwhile to examine whether your rigid preferences are holding back your love life. This self-reflection is crucial for understanding how your personal biases or fixed expectations might be limiting your chances of securing meaningful connections. This introspective process could lead to personal growth and a more flexible approach in your relationships, ultimately enriching your love life in surprising and fulfilling ways.

So far, we've discussed why letting go can be challenging. Remember, you are the one who determines the Self Score and Partner Score; these are based on your own Values and decisions. It's completely normal to feel down after a breakup, but it can also be an opportunity for personal growth. However, if you're struggling to move on for an extended period, it might be because you've placed too much importance on your ex's Partner Score and undervalued your own.

To restore balance, it's a good idea to revisit the Love Formula. Assess your current Values and Traits honestly—the positives and the negatives. After a breakup, you might find yourself giving your ex too much credit or you might need to reevaluate your own Values and Traits.

Ultimately, keep in mind that everyone has worth. While breakups can be painful, they don't diminish your worth. Recognizing your own value, especially during tough times, is essential. Now let's explore how unconscious habits, such as being attracted to "Bad Boys" or "Fixer-Uppers," influence your choices and what can happen when you break free from these patterns.

Revisiting Preferences: A Case Study

Sally, a woman in her mid-thirties, recently went through a painful breakup. Despite finding it hard to move on, she acknowledged her part in the relationship's outcome and realized she had ignored early warning signs: The man she was dating had shown signs of unreliability and other potentially harmful traits.

After spending a few months healing, Sally decided it was time for a change. She committed to making healthier choices in her relationships, refusing to ignore any red flags that could threaten her mental or physical well-being. While she was still figuring out exactly what "healthier" meant, she was determined not to settle for anything less than she deserved.

Four months after her breakup, Sally met Eddie, a kind and reserved man who wasn't her usual type. Although she felt only a moderate attraction at first, she recognized that Eddie had the Values and Traits that were good for her. Deciding to explore this new connection, Sally chose to give it a chance and see where it might lead.

Surprisingly, Sally's attraction to Eddie grew stronger over three months of dating. She not only grew to adore him but also found herself getting turned off by the Traits she had once sought in partners. Through deliberate effort and this new relationship, Sally realized she had previously mistaken emotional unavailability and arrogance for desirable Traits, overlooking the importance of openness and reliability. Now her relationship with Eddie showed great potential, and she couldn't have been happier.

Healing and Moving Forward: Navigating Life after a Breakup

Healing after a breakup isn't something that happens overnight, even with the help of the Love Formula. It's important to acknowledge the pain that comes with ending a relationship. Depending on how long and intense the relationship was, giving yourself enough time to go through the various stages of a breakup is essential for your well-being and recovery.

The Love Formula can be particularly helpful when you find yourself stuck on your ex for an unreasonably long period or when you're having trouble attracting a compatible partner.

As you begin to apply the Love Formula to your current or past relationships, be prepared for unexpected emotions to surface. This is often influenced by the dynamics of the relationship or how it ended. If you find that you're still harboring feelings for your ex, this process of reflection can reveal why you're finding it difficult to move on.

After a breakup, it's common for your self-esteem to suffer, resulting in a Self Score that might be lower than it should be and possibly lower than your Partner Score. At this juncture, it's important not to judge yourself from your ex's perspective. This book aims to boost your self-esteem, not diminish it. Becoming aware of the factors that influence how you see yourself and your ex is the first step toward rebalancing the Love Formula and improving your self-assessment.

The focus is *not* on scoring highly in your partner's Top 5 Values and Traits; instead, it should always be on positively changing how *you* perceive your own Top 5 Values and Self Score. This shift is key to enhancing your self-respect and self-love.

Using your partner's Love Formula to rate yourself is not an effective way to win back an ex. The key to rekindling a past relationship or attracting a new partner is to have confidence in your own high Self Score and let that self-assurance be evident.

Additionally, it's important to recognize that you have limited control over how your partner evaluates you and perceives your Personality Type. Changing their perceptions is not within your control; any change must originate from them, based on their own experiences, just as your perceptions of them are shaped by yours.

Although various factors such as past experiences, Personality Type, and potential Distortions can influence your Self Score; it's important to remember that these factors are not completely out of your control. While changing your identity can be difficult, you do have control over how you perceive yourself. And this self-perception not only affects your choice of partners but also influences the kind of partner you are and how you collaborate in building a relationship.

Improving how you see yourself can make you a more considerate and understanding partner, leading to healthier and more rewarding relationships. It also sets the stage for building a relationship based on mutual respect, understanding, and shared Values, which are key to overcoming life's challenges and supporting the growth and happiness of both partners. Essentially, changing your self-perception can fundamentally shift the course of your relationships, guiding them toward more satisfying outcomes.

Chapter 30

The Love Formula for Self-Help

The Love Formula isn't just about romantic relationships—it can serve as a valuable tool for fostering personal growth and nurturing the relationship you have with yourself. You can do this by assessing your self-esteem through your Self Score.

Don't brush off the impact of small actions—they can be game changers. Even if these actions seem tiny at first, their collective effect over time is pretty powerful. You might not notice a big change right away, but as these small steps pile up, they gradually reshape how you see yourself. Keep taking these little strides toward self-improvement or self-love, and you'll start noticing a significant boost in how you view yourself.

So what's the result? *Your Self Score goes up.* Consistently adding up these positive actions builds a pattern that lifts your overall self-esteem and satisfaction. And the best part? This positive shift spills over into your whole life, making it happier and more fulfilling, no matter your relationship status.

To kickstart your journey toward positive self-perception and an upward trajectory, check out the next steps. They follow the same logic that powers the Love Formula.

The first step is to complete Table 1 provided below where you can indicate your Top Values (remember that you can have more than five and you can adjust their weightage according to their importance to you). Then give yourself a Values Score for each one to calculate your Total Values Score.

Table 1 (sample): *Total Values Score*

Values	Importance (%)	Evaluation
Education	20	18
Health Consciousness	20	19
Income	20	15
Sociable	20	15
Family	20	16
Total Values Score	= 100%	**= 83**

Table 1: *Total Values Score*

Values	Importance (%)	Evaluation
Total Values Score	= 100%	

The next step is to develop Sub-values. You'll generate a new table outlining Sub-values corresponding to the Values that you aim to improve. These Sub-values represent finer aspects of a Value, and focusing on them contributes to elevating your Sub-values Score for each, consequently enhancing your overall Values Score.

Table 2 (sample 1) illustrates this example so you can better understand their function. For instance, let's consider the *education* category. Each Sub-value within this category encapsulates your specific definition of "education."

Table 2 (sample 1): *Sub-values Score (Education)*

Education Sub-values	Importance (%)	Evaluation
Traditional Schooling/ Degree	30	25
Political Awareness	25	15
Intellectual Conversation	20	15
Understanding of World Events	15	10
Knowledge of History	10	5
Sub-values Score	= 100%	**= 70**

Let's look at a second example below with Sub-values for *health consciousness.*

Table 2 (sample 2): *Sub-values Score (Health Consciousness)*

Health Consciousness Sub-values	Importance (%)	Evaluation
Physical Exercise	30	25
Healthy Nutrition	25	20
Daily Supplements	20	15
Nature Walks	15	15
Fit Appearance	10	8
Sub-values Score	= 100%	**= 83**

Now it's your turn to decide which Value you'd like to work on first. Then list five Sub-values and score yourself for each one.

Table 2: *Sub-values Score*

Sub-values	Importance (%)	Evaluation
	30	
	25	
	20	
	15	
	10	
Sub-values Score	= 100%	

The third step is to Create Your Action Plan. Our initial example identified *education* as a Value to focus on. It's time to develop specific Action Plans for each of the Sub-values. Here's an example of what that may look like:

Table 3 (sample 1): *Action Plan for Education*

Sub-value 1	Traditional Schooling	• Enroll for certification, diploma, or degree
Sub-value 2	Political Awareness	• Watch more news channels • Read more world news • Listen to podcasts • Read research papers
Sub-value 3	Ability to Engage in Intellectual Conversation	• Listen to podcasts • Surround myself with people interested in intellectual topics • Read more books on a variety of topics (culture, art, etc.)
Sub-value 4	Awareness of World Events	• Read more books • Watch documentaries • Listen to audiobooks
Sub-value 5	History	• Read history books • Watch documentaries • Join social media groups of history buffs and experts

Table 3 (sample 2): *Action Plan for Health Consciousness*

Sub-value 1	Physical Exercise	• Gym three or four times weekly • Stretch ten minutes per day • Run twice per week for three miles or more • Walk thirty minutes per day
Sub-value 2	Healthy Nutrition	• Intermittent fasting twice per week • Healthy fats and carbs/no junk food • 1,600 calories daily
Sub-value 3	Daily Supplements	• Daily multi-vitamins • Daily probiotics • Reassess quarterly
Sub-value 4	Nature Walks	• Hike twice per week • Beach walk once a week • Line up a hiking buddy
Sub-value 5	Fit Appearance	• Strength training • Do chest stretches for posture

Now it's your turn!

Table 3: *Action Plan for* _________________

Sub-value 1		
Sub-value 2		
Sub-value 3		
Sub-value 4		
Sub-value 5		

The Love Formula's adaptability to various life aspects makes it a versatile tool for personal development. While emphasizing small, consistent actions, it highlights the cumulative power of incremental steps that result in a significant positive shift over time. Identifying your Values, assigning Sub-value Scores, and creating Action Plans enable a journey of self-discovery and improvement.

Beyond individual growth, the Love Formula can pave the way to finding great love. As you invest in understanding and improving yourself, you cultivate qualities that enhance your relationship with yourself and make you a more attractive and fulfilled individual, laying the foundation for meaningful and lasting connections with others!

Chapter 31

A Guide for Couples

The Love Formula serves as a valuable tool for gaining clarity on personal needs, understanding relationship essentials, and evaluating both current and past relationships. Committed couples can leverage the Love Formula to

- Enhance communication

- Deepen emotional intimacy

- Navigate challenges more effectively

- Foster personal growth while supporting each other in the process.

With any relationship, doubts can arise, prompting questions about compatibility and the potential for a better match elsewhere. According to the Love Formula, the most fulfilling relationships occur when both partners assign similar—*or closely aligned*—Scores. Substantial discrepancies in Scores may lead to misalignments, increased toxicity, conflict, and disappointment, risking a decline in overall relationship satisfaction. Therefore, evaluating and aligning Scores is fundamental for cultivating a healthier, more fulfilling partnership.

While we extensively covered the concept of the Green Zone in Part III, it's essential to acknowledge that even the most robust relationships encounter challenges. If uncertainty about your relationship ever arises, the Love Formula serves as a valuable tool for both partners, offering a structured approach to gaining clarity and dispelling worries, enabling you to determine whether you're with your ideal match.

Complete the Love Formula with your partner, either guided by a couples therapist or in the privacy of your own home. If you see matching *high* Scores (because, don't forget, comparing *low* Scores can lead to Red Zone dynamics), you know you're exactly where you should be: in the Green Zone. Be sure to consider not only individual Scores but also the comparative Scores between you and your partner for a holistic understanding of the relationship dynamics.

It's also crucial to consider the Scores from both individuals' perspectives. What might seem like a manageable difference to one person might be a more significant concern for the other. Highlight the potential for mismatched expectations. For example, if one person sees a small point difference positively, while the other sees it as a substantial gap, it could lead to misunderstandings.

The Love Formula's effectiveness extends beyond individual Scores, emphasizing the shared understanding and alignment of Values between partners. Building a strong and harmonious relationship requires regular communication and mutual respect for each other's perspectives.

The next step involves sharing your answers—and this requires vulnerability, openness, compassion, and self-love. Discussing Values and evaluating how both partners measure up can be a challenging yet enlightening and joyous conversation. This is crucial for truly understanding each other and appreciating the nuances that make your relationship unique.

Sharing your answers may also illuminate the level of appreciation you both have for each other. It's common to overlook our partner's positive attributes and focus on minor flaws, leading to feelings of being undervalued. Expressing gratitude for the good in your partner is vital, as this balances the tendency to criticize or fixate on imperfections.

For Green Zone couples, the Love Formula encourages acknowledging and celebrating each other's greatness, enhancing an already good relationship. However, if you notice Score discrepancies, especially in Red or Yellow Zone relationships, addressing these issues is essential. This requires increased openness and vulnerability, acknowledging that the path to resolution may be challenging.

The willingness to undertake the Love Formula together signals a mutual commitment to fighting for the relationship. Calculating Scores and sharing results are initial steps toward finding stability and common ground worth preserving.

If both partners identify themselves in the Red or Yellow Zone after applying the Love Formula to their relationship, revisiting those chapters and strategizing a journey into the Green Zone is recommended. Remember, you've got this! Seeking the assistance of a relationship counselor or couples' therapist can expedite the process of moving into a better Zone.

Understanding each other's Personality Type is also very important in relationship discussions, as this provides a deeper insight into the partners' thought processes and motivations, fostering better empathy, communication, and overall harmony.

Next, you'll find a series of steps and questions to guide you through your relationship journey.

1. Initiating the Love Formula Journey

- Complete the Personality Questionnaires and share your answers with each other.
- Complete the Love Formula and openly discuss your answers.

2. Understanding Each Other's Values and Expectations

- Do you and your partner have mostly shared Values?
- What is most surprising about your partner's Love Formula?
- Are you meeting each other's standards? Are there areas where expectations aren't aligned?
- Do you meet your own standards as well as you meet your partner's?

3. Self-Evaluation and Mutual Understanding

- How would you rate your self-esteem based on your Self Score?
- Do you think you've assessed yourself and your partner fairly? Are you being too harsh or too lenient with your evaluations?

4. Assessing Relationship Dynamics

- Which Zone does your relationship currently fit into (Red, Yellow, or Green)?
- In areas where you fall short of your partner's standards, are you willing to make improvements?
- Have you identified any of the Distortions in your relationship dynamics?
- Which Personality Type do you each fall under? Do you identify with one or more Extremes?

5. Working toward a Healthier Relationship

- If applicable, what changes or compromises can you both make to reach the Green Zone?
- How can you foster better communication to understand and respect each other's needs and differences?
- What steps can you take to enhance emotional intimacy and mutual support in your relationship?
- How can you both contribute to creating a more fulfilling and harmonious relationship dynamic?

As you journey through this guide, remember that forging a fulfilling relationship is a continuous process of learning, understanding, and growing together.

Embrace the challenges as opportunities to strengthen your bond, and celebrate the successes as positive milestones in your shared journey. Remember, the strength of your relationship lies not just in the joy of perfect moments but in the resilience and love you exhibit during the imperfect ones. Let the Love Formula be your guide to navigating the complexities of love with grace, empathy, and a deeper appreciation for each other.

Chapter 32

A Guide for Singles

Embracing singlehood is a unique and often transformative experience. While some find solace and freedom in being alone, others may struggle with the challenges it brings. It's a time for personal growth and focusing on one's career, home, family, and friends—a healthy choice for many. However, prolonged singlehood might sometimes mask deeper issues that need attention. In such cases, the Love Formula can be an insightful tool for introspection and personal growth.

When singlehood extends for a considerable duration, it's essential to introspect whether this is a choice driven by contentment or an unconscious result of past hurts and fears. Distortions, as we have discussed, are mental barriers that can prevent us from moving forward in our romantic lives. They are often remnants of past experiences, signaling the need for caution but also potentially hindering future relationships. Applying the Love Formula for self-analysis allows you to confront these barriers, eventually finding a way to move forward with an open heart.

Using the Love Formula to evaluate self-love and confidence is a vital step in this journey. If your Scores reveal areas that need improvement, don't be discouraged. Instead, view it as an opportunity for growth. Addressing these Distortions can clear the path for new relationships filled with love and happiness. Remember, nurturing self-love and confidence is key to overcoming fears or past experiences that might cloud future opportunities for fulfilling relationships.

For those in the pursuit of love, the Love Formula is a blueprint. It augments intuition in relationship decision-making, providing clarity on the dynamics with potential partners. High matching Scores with someone signify a promising start, while significant differences might call for careful consideration and reflection. Thus, the Love Formula becomes a compass, guiding you toward more harmonious connections and a more balanced perspective in relationships.

It's also important to regularly apply these principles, not just in challenging times but also in celebrating your achievements and those of your potential partner. In this context, recognizing the signs of singlehood veering into areas of concern is crucial. Symptoms such as depression, loneliness, lowered self-esteem, or an unhealthy fixation on past relationships can indicate underlying issues. Human connection, especially in a romantic context, is often fulfilling. The key is in choosing the right type of relationship and acting appropriately within it, along with striving to attract a healthy partner while committing to behaviors and attitudes that foster a Green Zone relationship.

Understanding your Love Formula Score and aligning your Top 5 Values and Traits with those conducive to healthy relationships is an integral part of this journey. Identifying any Distortions within yourself and being open to making changes to address them are vital steps toward personal and relational growth. Committing to becoming emotionally healthier and enhancing self-confidence is not just about preparing for a future relationship but also about improving your overall quality of life.

To this end, reflective self-questioning can be enlightening for singles. Here are a few themes and questions for you to consider:

1. Understanding Past Relationships and Their Impact

- Have you experienced relationship traumas in the past that are being carried to current relationships?
- Did your past relationships leave you feeling unfulfilled, sad, or drained and longing for something better?
- How do you characterize your previous relationships—are they mostly in the Red, Yellow, or Green Zone?
- Are you carrying unresolved emotional baggage that affects your current relationship dynamics?

2. Reflecting on Current Singlehood and Relationship Patterns

- Have you been single for an unusually long time?
- Do you want to be single because that's your spirit's calling, or do you long for a long-term and stable connection?
- Do you harbor fears of dating or becoming too involved?
- Do you consistently fall for a certain type of person, and is this pattern healthy?
- Do you fall hard and quickly in relationships?
- Are you frequently finding yourself in relationships that don't fulfill you (kissing one too many frogs)?

3. Evaluating Personal Standards and Expectations

- Are your relationship standards realistic, or are they hindering your chances of finding a partner?
- Do you set expectations in relationships based on past experiences or societal pressures?
- Are you focusing on the right qualities?
- To what extent do your standards reflect what you genuinely need and want in a relationship, as opposed to what you think you should want?

4. Assessing Self-Perception and Willingness to Grow

- How do you view yourself and your relationships, and are you willing to make necessary changes for emotional health and self-confidence enhancement?
- Have you identified any Distortions in yourself?
- Are you willing to make changes in how you view yourself and your relationships?
- Can you commit to becoming emotionally healthier and enhancing your self-confidence?

5. Looking at Compatibility and Future Relationship Potential

- Do you have a healthy Love Formula Self Score?
- Are your Top 5 Values and Traits conducive to healthy relationships?
- How do your relationship expectations align with your personal growth and development plans?
- Are you ready to embrace the vulnerabilities and challenges that come with a committed relationship?

For singles, the Love Formula presents a pathway to understanding and transforming how you view relationships and yourself. Whether you choose to embrace singlehood or seek a partner, your journey is unique, and the Love Formula is here to help you every step of the way.

Conclusion

Love is complex—multifaceted, elusive, yet undeniably beautiful. Throughout this book, we've explored it from every angle: the psychological, the sociological, and the mathematical. But after all the theories and formulas, what stands out most is this: the foundation of love lies in truly knowing yourself. Only through self-awareness can you create a relationship that's healthy, fulfilling, and built to last.

We've unraveled the myths woven by movies and grand romantic gestures, and what we've uncovered is far more profound. Love, at its core, is about vulnerability, the bravery to show up as your true self, and the strength to build something authentic with another person. It's not about perfection—it's about connection, growth, and understanding.

Yes, this book has been a journey, but it's so much more than that. It's a living guide to help you not just find love but to thrive in it. With the tools and insights you now hold, you're better prepared to recognize what you need, and just as importantly, how your partner fits into the intricate dance of a shared life.

I want you to feel that "Love Can, In Fact, Be Calculated" isn't just something you've read—it's a companion on your path, evolving with you. Whether you're single, in a relationship, or simply seeking clarity about who you are, let this book be your steady guide, reminding you to honor your own needs and desires, while also embracing the delicate art of understanding those of your partner.

As we conclude, remember: This is not the end—it's the start of something far more meaningful. Armed with this knowledge, you have the power to cultivate not just connections with others but a deeper connection with yourself. And that's the foundation of extraordinary love.

Keep this book close, return to it when you need wisdom or comfort, and let it remind you that you are worthy of a love as remarkable as you are. You've got this—and love, in all its forms, is within reach.

Epilogue

My Personal Love Formula Journey

Throughout this book, the spotlight has been on you and how the Love Formula can uplift your self-esteem, provide lessons from the past, and enrich your relationships. I've also shared stories of how real people have changed and grown by using the Love Formula and applying these principles. Now it's time to unveil my own history, peel back my layers, and show you my vulnerabilities.

I want to take you through my personal journey to demonstrate the profound impact of consistent, small steps leading to positive momentum. This is the key to recovering from heartbreak, boosting self-confidence, and rediscovering a love deeper and more meaningful than ever before. My hope is that through my story, you'll see that no matter the challenges, there's always a path to love that's better and stronger than ever.

Let me take you back to a time when I was dating Austin. I really admired him as he aligned with my Values of *education*, *financial stability*, and a respected *social image*.

He also fit my Trait preferences almost perfectly; he was older, humorous, sweet, loving, and from the same cultural background. However, my infatuation blinded me to all of the red flags, and I tolerated unkind behavior from Austin.

Over time, his treatment of me deteriorated—he became lazy, arrogant, and condescending, disappearing for days as a form of punishment after arguments. Despite the clear signs of a bleak future, my Extreme Emotional tendencies led me to believe things would improve.

Unsurprisingly, Austin left me in the most painful way possible. I was left completely shattered.

The confusion, hurt, and longing were overwhelming. And yet it was the perfect moment to put the Love Formula to the test.

Days after our breakup, I assessed him at a 90% Partner Score, while I gave myself a Self Score of 74%. There was a significant 16% difference. It became clear that I was experiencing an Infatuated Distortion. I viewed him through rose-colored glasses, was in denial about the breakup, and was desperately trying to win him back.

However, Austin had moved on.

And, though it seemed *impossible* at the time, I moved on too. Not only did I journal regularly, but I also revisited the Love Formula several times during the healing process. Now I share with you my vulnerable journey with highlights from my journal. Let's begin by understanding my mindset *two weeks* after our breakup.

Journal Entry: 2/24/2021, *Two Weeks Post-Breakup*

My current emotions are resentment, betrayal, and anger. I am experiencing severe work and money-related stresses. I have anxiety about my future. My self-esteem is low. I have poor health and nutrition.

Table 1: *Self Score Two Weeks Post-Breakup*

Values	Importance (%)	Evaluation
Honest/Reliable	30	27
Occupation	25	20
Purpose	20	18
Financial Choices	15	3
Education	10	8
Self Score	= 100	**= 76**

Table 2: *Partner Values Score for Austin Two Weeks Post-Breakup*

Values	Importance (%)	Partner Evaluation
Honest/Reliable	30	**20**
Occupation	25	**24**
Purpose	20	**15**
Financial Choices	15	**14**
Education	10	**10**
Partner Values Score	= 100	**= 83**

Table 3: *Partner Traits Score for Austin Two Weeks Post-Breakup*

Traits	Importance (%)	Evaluation
Cultural Background	30	30
Humor	25	20
Physique	20	15
Generous	15	10
Alpha	10	9
Partner Traits Score	= 100	**= 84**

Table 4: *Priority Allocation*

Values	30
Traits	70
Total	**= 100**

Table 5: *Partner Score for Austin Two Weeks Post-Breakup*

Partner Values Score	24.9
Partner Traits Score	58.8
Partner Score	**= 84** (rounded from 83.7)

Table 6: *Love Formula Score Two Weeks Post-Breakup*

Self Score	76
Partner Score	84
Love Formula Score	**= -8%**

Two weeks after our initial breakup, I had given Austin an 8% rating above my Self Score. This caused me to take a moment and self-reflect on our relationship dynamics. *Did I always think he was above me?* Most likely, yes. Throughout our time together, the fear of losing him had weighed on me, and I questioned whether I could ever find someone on his perceived level.

It appeared as if we were a perfect match in many aspects, but I always felt that I fell significantly short when it came to *finances*. The truth is, during our relationship, I was not financially stable. As a student at UC Irvine, and after graduating, being employed at a startup with shaky leadership, my income was modest. In stark contrast, Austin flourished in a successful business. This led me to undervalue my financial standing and overestimate his worth in this area.

What else can be gleaned from my journal entry? Well, I awarded him an incredible twenty out of thirty for *honesty* and *reliability*. To jog your memory, he frequently punished me during our relationship by disappearing for days after arguments, and suspicions of infidelity lingered in my mind. *How did I assess him in this way, given these glaring issues?* The heartbreak and diminished self-esteem definitely clouded my judgment, resulting in an inaccurately high Partner Score, granting him more credit than he warranted.

I was so distraught by the breakup and had no closure. So I decided to assume *his* Love Formula calculations! In other words, I tried to get in Austin's head and make speculations on how he may have rated me. Looking back, I wouldn't advise doing this. I now understand that my actions were driven by a desperate need to seek his approval.

Despite the heartbreak, I knew it was time to move on, guided by logic and a sense of pride. I started picking up new hobbies, building friendships, and making bold career moves—things I hadn't felt motivated to do while I was with Austin. It became clear that a change was needed, so over the next five weeks, I switched up my routine, hung out with different people, explored new interests, and even got a dog for company.

More importantly, my yearning for Austin turned into resentment. I felt frustrated about putting in effort only to be disrespected and undervalued. Once I regained my peace, I could see the chaos his presence had caused in my life. His toxic ways had messed with my mental stability, and it was only after taking care of myself that things started making sense.

Let's see how I slowly but steadily climbed out of that emotional pit, with The Love Formula playing the roles of cheerleader, therapist, and mirror all at once.

Journal Entry: 4/15/2021, *Two Months Post-Breakup*

I got my new dog, Marlon, about two weeks ago, and it's been helping me snap out of my depression. I've been more mindful of my nutrition and self-care. I also got back on Hinge and had a fun conversation! About Austin, it was a tough couple of months, but I'm finally feeling better about the situation. I really think I dodged a bullet.

Table 1: *Self Score Two Months Post-Breakup*

Values	Importance (%)	Evaluation
Dependable	30	29
Occupation	25	20
Purpose	20	18
Financial Choices	15	6
Education	10	8
Self Score	= 100	**= 79**

Table 2: *Partner Values Score for Austin Two Months Post-Breakup*

Values	Importance (%)	Partner Evaluation
Dependable	30	15
Occupation	25	25
Purpose	20	17
Financial Choices	15	15
Education	10	10
Partner Values Score	= 100	**= 82**

Table 3: *Partner Traits Score for Austin Two Months Post-Breakup*

Traits	Importance (%)	Evaluation
Humor	30	25
Physique	25	18
Cultural Background	20	20
Alpha	15	10
Generous	10	7
Partner Traits Score	= 100	**= 80**

Table 4: *Priority Allocation*

Values	40
Traits	60
Total	**= 100**

Table 5: *Partner Score for Austin Two Months Post-Breakup*

Partner Values Score	32.8
Partner Traits Score	48.0
Partner Score	**= 81** (rounded from 80.8)

Table 6: *Love Formula Score Two Months Post-Breakup*

Self Score	= 79%
Partner Score	= 81%
Love Formula Score	**= -2%**

So two months post-breakup, I rated myself at 79% and him at 81%! Only a 2% gap this time—way healthier than the previous month. How did that happen? Well, I figured out I'd been overrating him in the crucial category of *dependability*. Turns out, he wasn't trustworthy at all.

I also bumped up my Self Score in *occupation* and *financial choices* because why not? Just because I was finishing school and being underpaid at my last job didn't mean I wasn't professional and smart with money. My self-esteem received a much-needed boost.

Another important shift was the Priority Allocation of Values and Traits. The latest Love Formula showed a better balance than the previous one, hinting at a move toward a Healthy Emotional rather than an Extreme Emotional Personality Type. So not only did his overall Partner Score drop, but also my Self Score also went up because I realized I'd been too hard on myself. The outcome? Just a 2% difference, signaling a triumph over my Infatuation Distortion.

Journal Entry: 4/29/2021, *Ten Weeks Post-Breakup*

Fast forward two more weeks. At this point, I was becoming very comfortable with my new life routine, my new friends, my new pup—it was as though I had created a new identity for myself. I regained my confidence, something I hadn't felt the entire time I was with Austin. Here's my entry from that time:

My social life has been very fulfilling, especially when I hang out with Guillermo and Jake. I always feel so much better around them. My friends make me feel very loved and respected. I'm super grateful for them. Things are still unstable at work, but I've been applying for jobs and feeling confident I will get somewhere soon. I also shut down most of my social media, which has increased my overall productivity. I've been noticing a shift in Values too. I've now included health consciousness in my Top 5 Values.

Table 1: *Self Score Ten Weeks Post-Breakup*

Values	Importance (%)	Evaluation
Dependability	30	28
Financial Choices	25	22
Occupation	20	7
Purpose	15	14
Health Consciousness	10	8
Self Score	**= 100**	**= 79**

Table 2: *Partner Values Score for* Austin Ten Weeks Post-Breakup

Values	Importance (%)	Partner Evaluation
Dependability	30	20
Financial Choices	25	24
Occupation	20	18
Purpose	15	5
Health Consciousness	10	7
Partner Values Score	= 100	**= 74**

Table 3: *Partner Traits Score for Austin Ten Weeks Post-Breakup*

Traits	Importance (%)	Evaluation
Comfort/Familiarity	30	28
Cultural background	25	25
Humor	20	15
Generous	15	7
Alpha	10	8
Partner Traits Score	= 100	**= 83**

Table 4: *Priority Allocation*

Values	40
Traits	60
Total	= 100

Table 5: *Partner Score for Austin Ten Weeks Post-Breakup*

Partner Values Score	29.6
Partner Traits Score	49.8
Partner Score	**= 80** (rounded from 79.4)

Table 6: *Love Formula Score Ten Weeks Post-Breakup*

Self Score	= 79%
Partner Score	= 80%
Love Formula Score	**= -1%**

Seeing those Scores brought a wave of relief and made me acknowledge the progress I'd achieved. It dawned on me that I, and only I, determine my value. Ten weeks after the post-breakup, I had officially overcome the mindset that Austin was superior to me. I finally viewed him as someone "on my level," so to speak. His worth no longer eclipsed mine, signaling a significant improvement in my self-esteem and how I perceived our dynamics.

Journal Entry: 5/6/2021, Eleven Weeks Post-Breakup

The following excerpt illustrates the importance of keeping positive people around you and avoiding the Black Holes described in Chapter 22. Below is an entry from my journal detailing a disagreement with a Black Hole friend. I vividly recall the incident. Even after we had ended the conversation, my entire body was shaking with anxiety. And, to my utter annoyance, Austin had once again resurfaced in my thoughts.

I was doing pretty well, but then I got into a fight with a friend who fits the description of a Black Hole, and my mind started the relentless chattering. I feel so broken right now. I don't know what I'll do for work. I'm honestly feeling hopeless again. And, as for Austin, I know I'm not back to square one, but I feel like I am. My stomach and heart hurt again. Today I cried for the first time in weeks.

Table 1: *Self Score Eleven Weeks Post-Breakup*

Values	Importance (%)	Evaluation
Purpose	30	27
Occupation	25	20
Financial Choices	20	5
Dependable	15	15
Health Consciousness	10	9
Self Score	= 100	= 76

Table 2: *Partner Values Score for Austin Eleven Weeks Post-Breakup*

Values	Importance (%)	Partner Evaluation
Purpose	30	25
Occupation	25	24
Financial Choices	20	19
Dependable	15	5
Health Consciousness	10	4
Partner Values Score	= 100	= 77

Table 3: *Partner Traits Score for Austin Eleven Weeks Post-Breakup*

Traits	Importance (%)	Evaluation
Comfort/Familiarity	30	30
Cultural Background	25	25
Humor	20	13
Generous	15	10
Alpha	10	10
Partner Traits Score	**= 100**	**= 88**

Table 4: *Priority Allocation*

Values	40
Traits	60
Total	**= 100**

Table 5: *Partner Score for Austin Eleven Weeks Post-Breakup*

Partner Values Score	30.8
Partner Traits Score	52.8
Partner Score	**= 84** (rounded from 83.6)

Table 6: *Love Formula Score Eleven Weeks Post-Breakup*

Self Score	76%
Partner Score	84%
Love Formula Score	**= -8%**

This regression was an emotional reaction. Why did I feel so awful all of a sudden? Engaging in an argument with a Black Hole can shake your confidence, and if you're in the process of healing, it's all too easy to revert to old thought patterns. The crucial lesson from this journal entry is clear: Be cautious of the Black Holes. Also, difficult situations can lead you to idealize an ex, boosting their Partner Score as you lose confidence in yourself. Some people arouse anxiety and a sense of inadequacy. Maintain a safe distance from them; otherwise, you might slide backward into a negative cycle. You've made significant progress, and you certainly don't want your peace disrupted. You've come too far for that.

Journal Entry: 5/11/2021, *Twelve Weeks Post-Breakup*

Perhaps the most illuminating entry in my journal shows that I reconnected with an old friend who "gets" me, and I started working! These two factors led to a shift in both my self-esteem and Self Score.

I've reconnected with Courtney—she's such a good soul, and I'm so grateful for her kindness and wisdom. Also, I am finally working! I am getting a lot of positive feedback for a new direction. I'm thinking about Austin less. My emotions are a lot less charged. I think I'm bouncing back from last week's slip.

Table 1: *Self Score Twelve Weeks Post-Breakup*

Values	Importance (%)	Evaluation
Purpose	30	28
Dependable	25	24
Financial Choices	20	9
Sociability	15	14
Occupation	10	8
Self Score	= 100	**= 83**

Table 2: *Partner Values Score for Austin Twelve Weeks Post-Breakup*

Values	Importance (%)	Evaluation
Purpose	30	23
Dependable	25	13
Financial Choices	20	18
Sociability	15	5
Occupation	10	9
Partner Values Score	= 100	**= 68**

Table 3: *Partner Traits Score for Austin Twelve Weeks Post-Breakup*

Traits	Importance (%)	Evaluation
Humor	30	23
Cultural Background	25	25
Kind / Good Person	20	7
Physique	15	10
Alpha	10	10
Partner Traits Score	= 100	**= 79**

Table 4: *Priority Allocation*

Values	40
Traits	60
Total	**= 100**

Table 5: *Partner Score for Austin Twelve Weeks Post-Breakup*

Partner Values Score	27.2
Partner Traits Score	47.4
Partner Score	**= 75** (rounded from 74.6)

Table 6: *Love Formula Score Twelve Weeks Post-Breakup*

Self Score	83%
Partner Score	75%
Love Formula Score	**= +8%**

BOOM!! These Scores make perfect sense. My focus is solely on myself and on pursuing my dreams, and it feels great. I'm genuinely over Austin, and he seems like a distant memory.

Witnessing my Self Score soar significantly higher than his brought a sense of satisfaction. I saw my growth as I wrote my journal entry twelve weeks post-breakup. I cared less, my priorities had shifted, and, most crucially, I recognized the importance of including "Kind/Good Person" in my list of preferred Traits, thereby significantly lowering Austin's Partner Score.

I finally found some peace with the breakup because I realized I would never take him back, even if he tried to return. My mindset transformed from "Am I good enough for him?" to "Is he good enough for me?" The resounding answer? *Hell, no.*

My Three Key Takeaways

First, breakups are tough. Post-breakup blues can create illusions about your ex's Partner Score (overvaluing them) and your own (undervaluing yourself). I explained the same in the section titled "We are Delusional" in Chapter 29.

Give yourself some time: weeks or even *months*. Don't buy into the emotional *"woe-is-me-I'll-never-have-it-this-good-again"* story. It's not reality.

If you undertake inner work using the Love Formula and other uplifting resources, you'll wake up one day and realize the following truth: "I can do better!"

Second, it's crucial to stop moping, hiding, binge-watching Netflix, and indulging in comfort foods while obsessing over your ex or lamenting, *"Is there any hope for us*?" or *"How can I get them back? Whaaaaaa!"* Get out. Leave the house and that mindset. It might seem like a safe cocoon, but I'm telling you, it's actually a prison.

Socialize. Get fresh air. Go dancing. Maybe even get laid (if you can do so without getting emotionally involved), or at least get a massage and some hugs. Have some laughs with kindred spirits. Be with people who get YOU and value YOU. This will help you appreciate yourself again, raise your Self Score, and feel much better.

Engaging in activities and social circles different from your ex's will help you experience novelty (good for your brain chemistry, remember?), feel a sense of belonging, and expand your horizons. And have something to look forward to on Saturday night!

Third, COMPLETE THE LOVE FORMULA.

And analyze it thoroughly!

Let it sit for a week or a month, and then redo it. And analyze it thoroughly again. Because this one tool, which is far more than just one thing, can serve as your mirror for much greater self-understanding, self-compassion, and self-empowerment.

As I healed from my breakup, my Values shifted, both quantitatively and qualitatively. Similarly, your Trait preferences may also change because as you alter your mindset, the Traits you're attracted to will also change. Keep an open mind. You are not the person you were when you first got together with Mr. or Ms.

No-Longer-Right-for-Me. You can, and you will, find your way back to yourself again. And onward and outward to more love than ever.

Journal Entry: 10/25/2021, Austin Who? Celebrating a New Love

After a five-month break from testing the Love Formula, this upcoming journal entry reflects the positive transformations I underwent. I found myself in the relationship of my dreams, a testament to my improvements. The inner work with the Love Formula played a crucial role in elevating my awareness and standards for a partner, simultaneously boosting my self-esteem.

Three and a half months ago, I met Kevin. He didn't have the "typical" Traits I've been drawn to in the past, but something about him told me, "Just see where it goes." Thankfully, my instincts to keep him close were strong, and now I am grateful to say I am in a healthy, committed, respectful, and loving relationship.

Spoiler alert: Kevin is now my husband! Here's what my Love Formula looks like for our relationship:

Table 1: *Self Score*

Values	Importance (%)	Evaluation
Dependability	30	28
Career	25	22
Family	20	18
Health Consciousness	15	13
Purpose	10	9
Self Score	= 100	**= 90**

Table 2: *Partner Values Score for Kevin*

Values	Importance (%)	Evaluation
Dependability	30	28
Career	25	24
Family	20	19
Health Consciousness	15	14
Purpose	10	7
Partner Values Score	= 100	**= 92**

Table 3: *Partner Traits Score for Kevin*

Traits	Importance (%)	Evaluation
Humor	30	27
Vibe/Presence	25	22
Physical Appearance	20	19
Generous/Thoughtful/Empathetic	15	13
Outgoing/Extroverted	10	5
Partner Traits Score	= 100	**= 86**

Table 4: *Priority Allocation*

Values	50
Traits	50
Total	**= 100**

Table 5: *Partner Score for Kevin*

Partner Values Score	46
Partner Traits Score	43
Partner Score	**= 89**

Table 6: *Love Formula Score*

Self Score	90%
Partner Score	89%
Love Formula Score	**= +1%**

Here the Priority Allocation for Values and Traits stands at fifty–fifty. So Kevin's total Partner Score is 89%, and mine is 90%. This aligns perfectly with a balanced, healthy, and trust-filled relationship.

How did I manifest this? It's not about luck but rather a conscious decision to no longer engage in toxic relationships. Working actively on shifting my Values and preferred Traits has also been pivotal in reaching this point. Granted, even in this relationship, a part of me occasionally harbored a slight fear of losing him, which at times impacted my confidence. The key takeaway is that the Green Zone requires ongoing effort, especially for those who have experienced traumatic situations. It's easy to slip into negative self-talk, so keeping that in check is vital.

Every person and every relationship is a work in progress. Despite not always feeling "perfect" or "100% healed," I find myself in the best relationship of my life. I feel ready to be in the moment and appreciate what I have, fully embracing my journey.

Acknowledgments

Where do I even begin? This book is the culmination of the twists and turns life has thrown my way—each "failure" reshaping my journey and expanding my perspective. Every obstacle deepened my understanding of human nature and the intricacies of love. To those who walked beside me during those challenging times, and even those who contributed to the difficulties, I extend my gratitude. Without you, this work would not have found its true inspiration.

To my friends, family, past partners, and my current partner: Your stories and insights into relationships have been invaluable. You allowed me to see your journeys, and from them, I wove much of what's found in these pages. Thank you for trusting me with your experiences.

I've known love, loss, and the beauty of love again. I am grateful for all of it—the sweet and the bitter. Writing this book, and sharing my vision of what makes a successful relationship, fills me with hope. I sincerely wish that my insights help others who have walked a similar path, guiding them to discover a love that brings them peace.

And to you, dear reader: Know that you are worthy of love that is rooted in compatibility, growth, and harmony. Thank you for allowing me to share this labor of love with you. It is my deepest hope that my exploration of love offers you the tools to find healing, peace, empowerment, and, ultimately, happiness.

Finally, a heartfelt thank you to Kevin, my husband and my rock. I am immensely grateful for you, and I love you with all my heart.

References

Brown, Anna. "Nearly Half of U.S. Adults Say Dating Has Gotten Harder for Most People in the Last 10 Years." *Pew Research Center*, August 20, 2020. https://www.pewresearch.org/social-trends/2020/08/20/nearly-half-of-u-s-adults-say-dating-has-gotten-harder-for-most-people-in-the-last-10-years.

Chamie, Josephine. "Dating in a Changing America." *The Hill*, August 17, 2021. https://thehill.com/opinion/finance/568146-dating-in-a-changing-america.

Firestone, Lisa. "How Your Attachment Style Impacts Your Relationship." *Psychology Today*, July 30, 2013. https://www.psychologytoday.com/blog/compassion-matters/201307/how-your-attachment-style-impacts-your-relationship.

Hatoum, Ida Jodette, and Deborah Belle. "Mags and Abs: Media Consumption and Bodily Concerns in Men." *Sex Roles* 51 (2004): 397–407.

Heming, G., et al. 2006.

Homans, George C. "Social Behavior as Exchange." *American Journal of Sociology* 63, no. 6 (1958): 597–606.

Lee, Kyung Mi. "Settling Down: Romance in the Era of Gen Z." *Yale News*, February 14, 2020. https://yaledailynews.com/blog/2020/02/14/settling-down-romance-in-the-era-of-gen-z.

Nye, F. Ivan. "Is Choice and Exchange Theory the Key?" *Journal of Marriage and Family* 40, no. 2 (1978): 219–233.

Parker, Kim, Juliana Menasce Horowitz, and Renee Stepler. "Americans See Different Expectations for Men and Women." *Pew Research Center*, December 5, 2017. https://www.pewresearch.org/social-trends/2017/12/05/americans-see-different-expectations-for-men-and-women.

Raypole, C. 2020. 12 Ways to Boost Oxytocin. *Health (May)*.

Raz, Guy. "What Happens to Our Brain When We're in Love?" Ted Radio Hour, interview with Helen Fisher, April 25, 2014. https://www.npr.org/transcripts/301824760.

Righetti, Francesca, Ruddy Faure, Giulia Zoppolat, Andrea Meltzer, and James McNulty. "Factors That Contribute to the

Maintenance or Decline of Relationship Satisfaction." *Nature Reviews Psychology* 1, no. 3 (2022): 1–13.

Russello, Salenna. "The Impact of Media Exposure on Self-Esteem and Body Satisfaction in Men and Women." *Journal of Interdisciplinary Undergraduate Research* 1 (2009): Article 4.

Ryan, Michael. "Sexual Selection and Mate Choice." In *Behavioural Ecology: An Evolutionary Approach*, edited by John R. Krebs and Nicolas B. Davies. Blackwell Publishing, 1978.Tashiro, Ty. "The Science of Happily Ever after: How Millennials Are Beating the Odds to Find Love." *TIME*, April 28, 2014. https://time.com/72678/the-science-of-happily-ever-after-how-millennials-are-beating-the-odds-to-find-love.

Tugend, Alina. "Too Many Choices: A Problem That Can Paralyze." *The New York Times*, February 26, 2010. https://www.nytimes.com/2010/02/27/your-money/27shortcuts.html.

Walker, Leonore E. *The Battered Woman*. Harper, 1979.

Waynforth, David, and R. I. M Dunbar. "Conditional Mate Choice Strategies in Humans: Evidence from 'Lonely Hearts' Advertisements." *Behaviour* 132, no. 9–10 (1995): 755–79.

Wu, Katherine. "Love, Actually: The Science behind Lust, Attraction, and Companionship." *Science in the News*, February 14, 2017. https://sitn.hms.harvard.edu/flash/2017/love-actually-science-behind-lust-attraction-companionship.

About the Author

Zoey Charif, born in Afghanistan and raised in Vancouver, Canada, is a Criminology graduate from Simon Fraser University. Her academic journey didn't stop there; she furthered her education in Data Analytics at the University of California, Irvine, allowing her to combine her keen interest in human behavior with incisive analytical skills.

Since 2008, Zoey has been dedicated to a personal project close to her heart—developing a theory and valuable tips and techniques that help people enhance their self-esteem and overcome life's lows. Her commitment to this work over the last fifteen years stems from her own experiences and a strong desire to make a positive impact in the lives of others.

In her debut book, Zoey brings together her unique perspective, academic background, and a deep understanding of human emotions. Her aim is to guide readers through their own journeys of self-discovery and enhanced interpersonal relationships by offering practical and actionable insights.